The Collected Yaps of the
WEE GINGER DUG

Volume 2

by

Paul Kavanagh

WEE GINGER DUG BOOKS

D1342442

Published in 2015 by Wee Ginger Dug Publishing

ISBN Paperback: 978-0-9934057-1-6
ISBN eBook: 978-0-9934057-3-0

A CIP catalogue copy of this book can be found in the
British Library and the National Library of Scotland.

Published with the help of Indie Authors World

Cover by Maurice Rapallini

Dedication

For Andy, and for all those who believed in Scotland
but are no longer with us. We will carry them in our
hearts and memories forever.

Introduction

I started this blog because I was trapped indoors caring for Andy, my partner of 25 years. He suffered from vascular dementia and could not be left unattended. His illness meant that he slowly lost all those parts of himself that had made me fall in love with him all those years ago. I never stopped loving him, but our relationship changed, I ceased to be his partner, and became his carer.

Eventually his illness took him, and he passed away just a few days before the Scottish independence referendum. One of his last acts was to sign his postal ballot paper, and he voted yes for Scottish independence. Andy wasn't Scottish, he was born and brought up in London, the son of an Irish immigrant. He spent his life in England and Spain, I brought him to Scotland in his final years as I knew I would need support to look after him as his illness progressed. In Scotland Andy found love, acceptance, compassion and care.

Dementia is a cruel illness. As I watched Andy slowly lose his personhood, his gifts and skills, and grieved for him while he still lived, I came to realise that I was losing myself too. Carers give everything, they give of themselves until there's nothing left. So I started the Wee Ginger Dug blog, named after our dog Ginger, a rescued Spanish mutt. Walking the dog was the only time I ever got to myself.

Writing gave me a wee island where I could be myself, and I'd sit on the sofa and type on the laptop while Andy sat beside me. Typing for my sanity, typing for myself, typing for a Scotland that lived only in dreams and hopes. What I never realised, lost as I was in the concern of a carer, and then lost in the grief of loss, was that this blog touches others.

One year on and Andy's loss still hurts, but the raw and bleeding edges of the hole in my heart have scarred and hardened. I miss him, I miss who I used to be be when we were together. But the loss has become a part of me, and I'm learning to live with it. As I wept during the days after his death, dazed and devastated, uncomprehending in the magnitude of grief, I slowly came to realise that there could still be hope, and that's what kept me going. I can live and love again. I can hope, and I can still dream.

And I have the readers of the blog to thank for that, the kind strangers who showed me that there was still a reason to hope, to fight, to go on. They gave me a reason to get up in the mornings, they gave me a purpose. They showed me that a country is a community, a community of care and compassion. With people like them in it, Scotland's future is assured.

And here we are, a year on, a referendum lost but a country gained. We're still here, still fighting, still persuading, still arguing, still being. With every word, with every day, we show that another Scotland is possible.

We don't all agree. After a year it's clear that the independence movement was always broad coalition of diverse views, distinct voices, and different opinions. We have disagreements, but that's a good and healthy thing. We are a nation not a political party, but we remain united in the belief that power rests with the people of Scotland, that the best people to decide on the future of this land are those who live here and love here. We remained united in the knowledge that our country's many problems and issues can only be tackled successfully when we as a nation take collective responsiblity into our own hands and we stand before the world as an equal.

The referendum was not the end, it was only the beginning. But one thing is clearer now than it ever was, our day is coming, the confidence of a people grows, the realisation is made in more and more minds that Scotland unleashed and unchained can only grow and flourish.

Scotland is no longer submerged, we've come to the surface and we're breathing the fresh clean air again.

We do this for Andy, we do this for Margo MacDonald, we do for all those who believed in Scotland but are no longer here. We carry them in our memories and we will never forget. We'll carry them to the independent Scotland that they believed in and fought for. And we do this for our children, we do this for ourselves. It's happening. We are not afraid any more.

I'd like to thank Maurice Rapallini for the cover design of this book, and Sinclair and Kim Macleod of Indieauthorsworld.com for all their help and assistance in making this book a reality. And most of all I'd like to thank my mother Martha, my brother Tony, my nephew Steven and my good friends Frances and John for all the love and support they gave during the most difficult and painful period in my life.

Paul Kavanagh

May 2014

1 May 2014
Last orders in a nation of drunks

Shee that fuckn Alicshammin. Shee whit he'sh fuckn cawin ush noo? Fuckn nation a fuckn drunksh sho we ur. At'sh whit he sayed aye, sayed sho in the Shcotshman. Mush be true. He'sh been at the voddie wi his pal Vlad... Naaaw shtraightup. You cawin me a liar pal?

Whit you laffin fur? Dae you no know who ah mur? Dae ye? Right. A'm a fuckn MP so fuckn shutit.

Haw Jim, Jim ... shee'sh ush wan o thae boatles err. Naawww, the super stremf cider ya clown. Nane a that fuckn Newton Merrns wine wank.

Right, noo, fuckn shutit, where wis ah ...

Cannae haud his wine that Alicsammin. Caws hissel Scottish. Cannae haud his wine. Fuckn hate im. He'll no fuckn tell me ah've hud enough. Nation a drunks ma erse. Fuckn Alicshammin.

Gie's another wan ae thae boatles err.

He waants tae make us pey mair fur wur swally. Fuckn baaaaaastert.

See that Alicshammin, pure dead embarrassment so he is. Pure showin up he gie's ye. No lik me. Ah kin haud ma swally. So ah kin. Naedbie fae Labour's ever gied a showin up like that. Nivver. The Hoose a Commons committee sayed it was aw jist a wee misunderstaunnin. Disnae count. Ah peyed it back. Ah've goat the receipts an a note fae ma maw.

Nation a drunks. Ah'm pure affrontit. You should be affrontit too. See whit he sayed? Fuckn Alicsammin. He sayed

"... there is something deep about Scotland's relationship with alcohol that is about self-image - lack of confidence, maybe, as a nation - and we have to do something about it."

He's jist sayed your maw's an alkie. So he huz. Is that no some cheek. You should be angry. Ah'm tellin ye tae be beelin, that's how you should be angry. Fuckn Alicsammin.

Fuckn self image. Ah look in the mirror an ah hink ah look pure great. So ah dae. An it's no cheap this self image. You should see ma dry cleanin bills. Ah huv tae dae aw that fur youse. You owe me. So's Ah look good on the telly. Kiz Ah'm a fuckn Labour MP.

No lik him. Ah hate him. He's jist vain. No lik me. Fuckn Alicsammin.

Whit dae ye mean, see wursels as ithers sees us. Ah kin see you're bein a wide-o, ya wee bastert. Ah'm a Labour MP. You'll respeck me. Kiz Ah'm a fuckn Labour MP. Ah'm the peepil's party me.

Who're you cawin a sell out? Wi yer wee hoose and yer wee life. Ah fuckn made sumhin ae masel. Ah peyed ma dues, done ma time. Ah done whit the party waantit. So youse fuckn owe me. It's jist ferr. Ah huv tae go and deal wi aw these important people and pretend lik Ah gie a shit. No lik youse. Fuckn no marks tellin me whit tae dae. That wull be right. Don't youse talk tae me aboot self image. Fuckn Alicsammin.

Haw err a polis, moan huv a wee dance. Mooaaan... ya humourless bastert. Wur jist huvin a wee laff.

Whit's it aw fur anyway? We've goat nae language, we jist talk shite insteid. We've goat nae culture, jist look at me. Ah'm a fuckn Labour MP.

Ah love Scotland. Ah really love it. Ah love it so much ah've goat four hooses. That's four times mair than you. Ah love Scotland four times mair than you. Ah'm proud. Ah'm dead proud. Whit huv you goat tae be proud ae but me? You owe me. Ah'm a fuckn Labour MP.

Fuckn Alicshammin. Disnae waant tae talk aboot isshsooosh. No lik me. Pleys the fuckn man no the baw. So he diz. No lik me. Fuckn hate im.

Don't gie me that pish. Don't gie me that. Sayin yer no votin fur Alicsammin, ye're votin fur independence. Well yese urnae. Ah'm the politician. Ah'm the expert. Ah'll tell youse whit yese ur votin fur. At's the wey it works.

Whit dae yese waant tae chynge it fur? Jist gaunnie no? Fuckn Alicsammin.

Gie's anither boatle err.

That was a party political broadcast on behalf of the Scottish Labour Party.

2 May 2014
Project Fear gets chibbed by chi

There won't be much in the way of updates over the weekend. I've got to do exciting things like cleaning the toilet and de-minging the oven. All those joyous wee jobs that you keep putting off in the vain hope that perhaps a magic pixie will come in the middle of the night and do them for you. But the magic pixies are all fully occupied creating a grassroots movement out of plastic offcuts for Better Together, courtesy of a Tory donating millionaire and a London PR company that specialises in rebranding through the medium of New Age woo, as discovered by Douglas Daniel, writing on Wings Over Scotland.

Millionaire Tory donor and city financier Malcolm Offord got together with London based branding and marketing company Acanchi and the right wing think tank the Centre for Social Justice and spontaneously started a mass movement. The clever little things. And they even managed to attract more attention from the UK media in just one day than pretty much the entirety of the vast and truly grassroots movement forming the diverse yes campaign has grown over the past two years - a grassroots movement that now dwarfs the official yes campaign in size.

Offord is an advisor to the Centre for Social Justice which claims to seek "effective solutions to the poverty that blights parts of Britain". It's a right wing outfit set up by Iain Duncan Smith in 2004, in the wake of his Epiphany in Easterhoose when he realised a more effective solution to the problem of getting re-elected was to sell benefits cuts to Tory voters by dressing them up in a glossy package of hangwringing.

The Centre for Social Justice was described by Tim Montgomery of the Tory website Conservative Home as a part of the Conservative movement. Offord was formerly the director of the organisation's North Britain branch, Social Justice Scotland. The Scottish branch seems to be defunct, or at least its website is no longer online. Not much grassroots movement there then.

Acanchi wants to rebalance Project Fear's chi to reposition it in the Scottish voting market, or somesuch. There's very little difference between PR woo and New Age woo - which most often consists of shallow misunderstandings of ancient, complex and deep philosophies. Chi is the energy that runs through the universe in Taoist belief.

It's sort of the Chinese version of the Mediaeval European belief in the four humours that were supposed to regulate the health and well being of the body. If they got out of balance you got sick. Project Fear has obviously got far too much bile and melancholy. Come to think of it, that's pretty much all they've got. Good luck with rebalancing that then.

Acanchi was founded by Fiona Gilmour, who describes herself as a "thought leader" and a "leading expert on country positioning strategy". People pay a lot of money for fancy sounding words with ambiguous meanings. That's what kept ancient Greek readers of the entrails of oxen in business. Same principle as chi, but you get sausages at the end of it. Better Together should have tried that instead. We might not get a positive case for the Union but a piece and square slice is always welcome. They missed a trick there.

The company was responsible for a new slogan for the Tourism Board of the island of Mauritius. For a reported £625,000 they came up with "Mauritius, c'est un plaisir" a slogan which was immediately subject to widespread ridicule for its blandness and for costing almost £50,000 per letter.

Acanchi accepted a contract from the Israeli government in 2008, in an effort to boost the image of Israel in the UK. According to the pro-Palestinian website Intifada-palestine.com, Fiona Gilmour, claimed Acanchi aimed to "unlock the magic that can be used to create a compelling brand positioning". Adding, "We believe that success for a country, city or region brand can be achieved by discovering, defining and channelling this chi into a brand positioning that reflects the core truths of a place."

This isn't really going to help much when one of the core truths about Scotland is that we famously have more pandas than Tory MPs. If we had a quid for every time someone's said that joke there would be no need for a sovereign oil fund. You'd have thought that a company heavily influenced by Chinese philosophy that's discovering defining and channelling Scottish chi would have known that already.

Another core truth is that making use of ancient Chinese religious philosophies which aimed to bring balance and health to the universe in aid of a bunch of self-aggrandising careerists who worship money is some pretty bad karma. But I'm sure Acanchi have a chant and some scented candles for that.

Anyway, I don't think we need to worry too much about a London PR company's attempts to use magic against us. This is Scotland. We invented druids. And they can curse.

And in other news.

I've just had a wee look at April's site statistics. Amazingly there were over 80,000 page views, and just shy of 20,000 unique readers. That's incredible for a wee blog written by someone who represents no organisations, no political party, and well - just takes the piss. It's obviously not just me who thinks the Westminster parlie is risible.

So hello to all the new readers, lovely to see you here. You come from all over the world, and a special hello to whoever it is who reads this blog in Mongolia. The dug gets into a yurt with a wifi connection. That's a 21st century grassroots movement for you. The independence message is even reaching the vast grasslands of the Mongolian plains.

Must be our chi.

And because we've got some shit hot druids.

3 May 2015
Untamed lawns

Ian Jack writes like he's a character in the movie Alien, who knows that at any moment an evil monster is going to burst out of their stomach, slaughtering them in a gruesome explosion of intestines and gore, and unleashing havoc on the world. In the meantime he's going to reminisce about how much better everything was in the sixties when people still trusted the Labour party and the mainstream media. It's the Guardian's version of Francis Gay going seven days hard with largactil.

On Friday, feeling quite cheery after successfully de-minging the toilet - although that may have been in part due to the fumes - I chanced upon Ian's musings in the Guardian about the woe that awaits Scotland if its media continues to decline. It was my own fault for clicking on the link. It's like inviting someone to your birthday party because you'd feel guilty if you didn't, even though you know they're only going to bend your ear for hours with graphic details of their last hospital visit. One that involved toenails.

Ian was worried about the dire state of the Scottish media. It's become so enfeebled that it's no longer capable of holding the powers that be to account. Ian thinks this could be a terrible problem in an independent Scotland, and we'd be at risk of turning into a one party state with a media that cowers in terror before an all-powerful Alicsammin.

Mind you, it's a terrible problem just now, where we have a media - including a state broadcaster we are legally obliged to pay for - which willingly swallows Better Together's line along with its hook and sinker, all with the aim of crapping all over the yes campaign from a great height. You only have to look at the aclarity with which the nodding doos of the Scottish media gobbled up the claims of the Vote Nob Orders non-campaign like a flock of rats with wings, without undertaking even the most cursory investigation of whether this new grassroots movement did what it said on its box of expensive Eezy-Lawn genetically modified seeds. Ian's own paper is one of the most enthusiastic Better Together seed peckers, and he doesn't appear averse to a bit of ornamental insta-lawn himself.

Print newspapers everywhere are in crisis. Sales are falling as the traditional media struggle to evolve a business model to keep them afloat in an era of mass digital communication where people are decreasingly likely to pay for their information. The problems of the Scottish media are not unique. However the media crisis is more acute in Scotland, the disconnect between the traditional media and public opinion has been exposed by a referendum campaign which has highlighted the media's role in the manipulation of information for the benefit of the established order.

As a direct response to this unsustainable state of affairs, Scotland has developed a flourishing new digital media. In fact, we have the BBC to thank for it. The unknown BBC executive who took the decision to clamp down on public commenting on the broadcaster's Scottish webpages inadvertently set off a chain of events which have destroyed the BBC's reputation north of the border. The BBC, and the rest of the Scottish media, are now reaping the long grass of the law of unintended consequences.

Once upon a time, there was a wee corner of the interwebbies called Blether with Brian, although it was always more "A blether while Brian's away getting the messages". There were a number of regular below the line commentators, many of whom were far more entertaining and informative than the vast majority of the BBC's output - and who often grassed up truths that the BBC was reluctant to broadcast. I was one of that merry little band of part time opinionators.

Then there was the Steven Purcell scandal. The leader of Glasgow Cooncil resigned amidst allegations of drug taking, inappropriate contacts with some seriously dodgy people, the bullying and intimidation of council staff and councillors, with even more serious allegations floating around in the background. It was well known at the time that an important part of Stevie boy's modus operandi was regular meetings in one of Glasgow's posher restaurants with the movers and shakers of the Scottish media, including, allegedly, executives from Pacific Quay.

Stevie poured a bottle of paraquat all over his carefully cultivated gardens and his cooncil leadership imploded in a shower of cocaine fueled insanity. The BBC's reponse, along with that of the rest of the Scottish media, was to invite the public to feel sorry for poor wee Stevie's battle with mental health issues. There was no attempt to investigate the murky goings on which lead to his self-destruction, because that would only have exposed his close contacts with the very people who claim to be the watchdogs of standards in public office. Not least of whom were the executives at Pacific Quay.

Over on Blether with Brian there was a bonfire of the commentary, the BBC's moderators zealously removed any remark which portrayed the disgraced leader of the cooncil in a less than sympathetic light. The story was clamped down on, and clamped down hard.

In response, a person who used to comment on Blether with Brian woke up one fine morning and decided that if no one else was going to challenge the inadequacies of the Scottish media, he'd do it himself. And so Newsnet Scotland was born. It was the beginnings of Scotland finding a different voice, one that wasn't controlled and directed by the powers that be. That unsung hero of the Scottish independence campaign was not me, but I offered to help out.

As ma mammy always said, if you want something done you need to do it yourself. We were going to do it ourselves. Without money, without resources. All we had were words.

And look what happened. Newsnet was not alone. Bella Caledonia, and a host of new Scottish bloggers were also sowing the seeds of dissent. The grass started to sprout up beyond the control of BBC gardening. Untamed words fell on the fertile Scottish soil, and it grew a carpet of wildflowers. Now it's a dense undergrowth of leafy growth, with tall trees and a diverse ecosystem of voices and opinions. Information in the wild, and no amount of mainstream mowing can keep it under control. How's that for grassroots Acanchi?

I've been immensely privileged to witness the contributions that hundreds of ordinary everyday folk have made to the Scottish digital revolution. Ordinary everyday folk with extraordinary and incredible talents, who have passion, skill and a firm belief that Scotland cannot sit back and expect its problems to be solved by those who have created them and fostered their continuation.

It was noticeable that Ian Jack suggested that state funding of newspapers might be the only answer to the shortcomings of the Scottish media. A measure he hinted might lead to a neutered and careful press that is not willing to challenge the establishment - like that's not what we had before.

However he's missed the point. Ian's trapped in the managerial solutions of the Labour party and their press pals. But the Scottish people are doing it for themselves, we no longer need it to be done for us. We have informed and educated ourselves. We've built up a huge movement without central control. We're everywhere. This movement is not going to go away. It's changed Scotland forever. The days of deference are dead, and the only ones mourning its passing are Jim Murphy and the rest of those who feel threatened by the new Scotland's confidence.

And that is why I have every confidence that an independent Scotland will be a successful and prosperous nation. We don't need the self-appointed self-described big boys and girls to do our gardening for us. When we do things ourselves, we can do anything.

And we do it with style.

5 May 2014
Revolving the Cringe

Scotland is uniquely incapable of governing itself. It's the only notable thing about us. We're not programmed to take decisions. Not like those Norwegians or Finns who are all six foot tall blond androids who come out of the factory with a preinstalled democratic decision making app. It's the same people who made Angry Birds. But no one is going to make a short ginger android, on account of the risk of it running amok and causing a worldwide cataclysm with its radioactive Irn Bru datacore and a death ray capable of frying mince from halfway across the solar system.

It's often interesting when someone presents you with an argument to turn it on its head and look at it the other way round. For decades, Scotland has lived with the argument that we're too wee, too poor and too stupid to be a normal independent country. No Unionist party has actually uttered the phrase, except to dismiss it as an invention of independence supporters, but it is an accurate summary of the thrust of the arguments against independence. The phrase is the distillation of the Cringe.

Too wee too poor too stupid means Scottish independence would have no effect on anyone apart from Scotland - and the effects on Scotland would be George Robertsonesque in their cataclysmassiveness. The rest of the UK would sail merrily on, ruling waves and waiving rules, scarcely noticing our absence except once a year when Bob Geldof presented a Band Aid concert to send relief packets of square slice and Mars Bars to the starving weans north of the barbed wire border.

The central claim of the Yes campaign is that Scotland is not too wee, that it's a wealthy country, and that the population of Scotland is no more nor less intelligent than any other collection of 5 million humans. The argument that Scotland is too wee too poor too schtupit is obviously false, but if the original argument is false, then it is no longer so certain that Scottish independence is a consequence free zone for the rest of the UK.

The British establishment scarcely notices Scotland - except as spot of Great British regional colour. Scotland's role in the pantheon of Britishness is to act as a tatty tartan lucky charm on the mantlepiece, rubbing it occasionally will magic away the contradictions in the belief that British nationalism isn't nationalism at all. It's Scottishness of the Rory the Tory I'm Scottish You Know variety, Scottishness as a form of heritage kitsch, a distinctive past but not a distinctive future. Safe, twee, and not something you give much thought to. Or in Rory's case, thought which is hopelessly deluded.

So they thought that winning the referendum would be easy. It was taken for granted that people in Scotland would also share their unswerving conviction that our future lies with Westminster. A museum replica of a Glasgow tenement single-end with no hot water and an outside cludgie is all very charming and poignant, but it's not like anyone would want to live there. Instead the referendum became an opportunity to score political points against Alicsammin, and finally manage what George Robertson promised when he said devolution would kill nationalism stone dead.

But they reckoned without the Yes campaign. An entire nation of DIY enthusiasts who are experts in renovating clapped out Glasgow tenements and turning them into attractive 21st century living quarters. Look, they said, we can't just live here, we can live here with style. Compared to the draughty corridors of Westminster where no one can hear you scream, modern living is a very attractive prospect.

But by gaining ground in this independence referendum Yes supporters are not likely to get a photo shoot in the lifestyle pages of the Guardian and gushing praise for our use of soft furnishings. Which is a shame, because we've got a really interesting Celtic twist on Scandinavian design.

Instead, in their eyes, we're the doing the equivalent of marching en masse into the chambers of the Palace of Westminster and the offices of the national media, and collectively baring our builders' arse cracks in their faces. During their lunch break. They're not best pleased by the intrusion and it's putting them off their tea.

On Sunday it got worse for them. A proper serious newspaper with a lifestyle section came out in support of independence. The anti-independence strategy depended from the beginning on minimising engagement and portraying independence supporters as a tiny minority of deluded and backward looking fantatics. Better Together wasn't having a whole lot of success with that before, it's got much harder now. The independence tenement is getting the glossy photie treatment. You don't get that with Better Together's 60 Minute Makeover.

And in the draughty corridors of an unrenovated Victorian institution, the shocking realisation is beginning to dawn on some that the unthinkable might happen. And that in turn means the Westminster parties must face up to the consequences that will have on their own plans. All the earnest discussions about Labour's polling figures, tensions between Davie and Nick, the rise of UKIP, the future of the UK within the EU, they've all gang agley. The British establishment is having an Oh-Fukkit moment, the feeling you get immediately after your foot slips on an icy pavement but before your arse hits the pavement giving you a very sore bum and a very red face.

A couple of weeks ago, the delightfully batty Benedict Brogan in the Telegraph said that a Yes result in the referendum would lead to David Cameron's resignation. Although Benedict also thought that it was all Gordon Brown's fault. Clearly the concept that people in Scotland might think that Davie Cameron and Gordie Broon are equally at fault hadn't occurred to him. And neither had the thought that we might just think him and his UK media colleagues might share a goodly portion of the blame too. Despite that, he was at least acknowledging that Scottish independence changes the Westminster game, and the rest of the UK will have their own DIY work to do. Still, at least we'll have a lovely photo spread of a renovated Edinburgh town house to show them.

Although other Tory voices have denied that Cameron would resign, the consequences of a Yes vote would be massive politically. Scottish independence doesn't mean the loss of another colony, leaving Westminster to carry on despite the loss of 37% of the territory it governs, 8.3% of the people who are its subjects, and 9.9% of its income. It means the potential loss of over 37% of the balance of trade, the renegotiation of EU opt outs which depended upon concessions of Scottish resources, and the urgency of finding a new home for Trident. The budget plans and manifestos they've spent months preparing for a General Election in 2015 will all have to be rewritten in a hurry. None of which has been prepared for. They'd even made a point of saying they weren't going to prepare for the possibility of Scottish independence.

It will have happened on the Coalition's watch. And worst of all they could have avoided it. They've been caught out by their own arrogance, short-termism, and lack of understanding of a country that's supposed to be an equal partner in the most successful union of nations in the history of the universe. If that's not a resignation issue for a Prime Minister, nothing in British politics is. It also tells us that if we want to get rid of David Cameron in solidarity with ordinary people in working class areas in Manchester, Liverpool, and Southampton, like Labour tells us, then the surefire way to do it is by voting Yes in September.

Scottish independence means the end of the Union of 1707. It means the end of the United Kingdom. The remainder of the United Kingdom is perfectly at liberty to call itself what it likes, but though the words remain the same the substance will have changed, and a whole range of Westminster's load bearing walls come tumbling down. It leaves them exposed.

A revolution is what happens when you turn an accepted way of thinking upside down. When the Cringe is turned around - it's the British establishment who are too wee in imagination, too poor in understanding, and really far too stupid to be permitted to continue in power.

6 May 2014

Pwned and poonds

Monday was a bank holiday, so it was a slow news day. We got treated to mair pish from the Guardian, this time a jokey wee article spunkily poking unfunniness at the audacity of provincials who think they can make grown up decisions. From the publication which gave us 76 reasons to make snide pretend apologies to Scotland, it's suggestions for a new name for a new Scottish currency from Tim Dowling, an American journalist now living in London. Snide remarks about buckie, bawbags and boak filed under politics. Seeing as how he's American, he thinks being told his copy is spunky is a compliment. In Scotland we know that means it's the product of a wank.

Spunky Tim clearly didn't get the memo, we're going to use the pound. Scotland was playing a game of currency chicken with Westminster, and they blinked first. That gemme is already a bogie son. It was a major splash in the Guardian, you'd think he'd have read his own paper. Mind you, Scottish correspondent Sevvie doesn't read it either, he seems to think the publication is neutral on the subject of independence. Bless.

The pound won't need a new name, unless Westminster does by some miracle ensure that Scotland can't use Sterling - possibly by sending in the SAS to swoop down on the checkout queue in Asda, forcing pensioners to pay for their messages in buttons and euro cent coins found down the back of the sofa. But in that unlikely event the rUK will no longer have North Sea oil to use as collateral, Scotland will have told the Treasury to stick its Bank of England issued credit notes up George Osborne's gimp suit, and it will be the pound which needs a new name. It will be known as "worthless", while its new German language name will translate as "bet you wish you'd joined the Euro".

And while we're on the topic, memo to Steve Bell, another Guardianista with a tin ear for funny where Scotland is concerned. If you want to write cod Scots dialogue in yer cartoons, at least get it right. It's not a "poond", it's a punn. It's even got a joke in the name. Just how easy do you want us to make this for you people? And you still can't raise a laugh in Scotland. Jesus wept.

It's just a bit of banter when an English publication mocks Scotland. When Scots mock anything English, it's both a symptom of a deep atavistic cancer eating away at the Scottish psyche, and the only culturally distinctive thing about us. The UK media presents a caricature Scotland defined by its supposed hatred of England. And so a resolutely non-ethnic civic nationalism which includes many thousands of English people amongst its supporters is defined as anti-English and racist. No matter how carefully a criticism is phrased, how accurately it is directed, it is interpreted as "Scotland hates the English."

I can't not get angry about being called a racist because I want independence. Homophobic UKIP supporters telling me I'm a bigot tends to have that effect. I spend most of my time and energy caring for an English man with dementia. I thought I was doing it because I love him, but apparently I'm merely extending his life out of badness so I can watch him suffer. I'm torturing him with comfy cushions and cake. It's all very Monty Python isn't it? So why am I not laughing.

Because the independence campaign has so far refused to provide the requisite amount of anti-English hatred, a new wannabe meme has sprung up. Quite possibly a product of the very same people who brought you the grassroots Vote Nob Orders campaign. It's that the word Westminster is just an evil fascist cryptonazi dog-whistle for "English".

This is an obvious nonsense. Westminster is Scotland's sovereign parliament too. Westminster is not an imagined "other" - yes we're looking at you David Aaronovitch - its influence reaches into every area of Scottish life, and its decisions are the final ones. All other political decisions in Scotland are conditional upon its power and authority.

So when independence supporters say "Westminster", we mean Westminster. Westminster is not England, we understand the difference even if some of the Guardian's more irritating hobbyist unionists don't.

Thankfully at least one UK media figure seems to have got it. Jon Snow published a decent pience on his recent trip to Scotland to report on the referendum campaign, and described the visceral hatred for Westminster that exists in the country. Scotland's independence debate is largely driven by Westminster, only not in the way that Westminster had hoped. Now that's funny, Guardian take note.

Jon understood that the term Westminster was not code for anything. It's the Cuprinol of Scottish politics, only on the list of ingredients on the back of the tin it says "Careerists, militarists, liars, idiots, nuts." There's also a sell by date of 1900.

Jon was impressed by the level of political debate in Scotland. But Scotland's own Unionist commentators are not so impressed, though this may not be unconnected with the fact that they're losing the argument. And badly at that.

David the Comb Torrance had a bit of a stropette in the Herald, and blew his cover as a sort of Unionist chase-me chase-me and make me yours. He was moaning that pro-independence blogs and websites, and Wings Over Scotland in particular, aren't doing the Unionist media's job for them. We should be criticising Alicsammin too.

Sorry Davie love, I can't speak for anyone else, but it's just that Westminster's basterts are much bigger basterts, and you know, you don't go cleaning up a bit of spilt milk in the kitchen when there's a steaming pile of turds in your living room. At least those of us who can't afford cleaning staff, which excludes most of those at Westminster. So I'll concentrate on getting rid of the turds first, then decide on domestic catering arrangements, if that's alright with you.

The thin piece was just an excuse to get a menshie in for his forthcoming booklet, pamphlet, leaflet, whatever, pressing for a federal UK. Davie didn't say who was going to deliver federalism in the UK. The federalism fairy perhaps. It's certainly not going to be the Westminster parliament. It's taken them over four years to devolve powers over airguns to Holyrood. You'd think a politics geek would have known that.

I shouldn't talk though. I'm only posting this blog piece to announce that I'm going to write a novel about a politics geek who lives in Narnia with his imaginary federal friends.

Davie and his comb then got pwned by Stu Campbell, which was highly amusing. Apparently pwned is a gaming term for getting your arse handed to you on a plate. It can be pronounced poond, which may be the source of Steve Bell's confusion. But the best laugh was Davie praising the CBI for their honesty in apologising for the "honest mistake" that some nameless minion had apparently made without authorisation.

He should write more for the Guardian. They need some decent comedians.

7 May 2014
Bedtime for a fairy story

I don't do Twitter and am the world's most reluctant Facebooker, being far too anti-social for social media. I've got a PhD in time-wasting as it is. Getting into Facebook or Twitter would be like persuading an alkie of the benefits of heroin. But people who do use Twitter report that David Torrance, subject of yesterday's och-whit-ur-you-like, has been complaining about the low standards of the debate in the Scottish independence referendum. He's not the only Unionist to voice similar complaints.

It's likely that wee Davie's beef is really that Scotland isn't having the debate that he wants us to be having. We're discussing independence. We're discussing the fact that the Westminster system is a rank and rancid Victorian gentlemens' club that's still suffering a hangover from the heady days of Empire. We're discussing getting rid of Trident, building a commonweal, and creating a land that has the powers and the will to confront its own problems. But we're not discussing Davie's pet Unionist project, the one that's going to take a wave of the sparkly wand of the federalism fairy to magic into existence.

We're not discussing lots of things. We need to up our game. No one has written a serious and intelligent report with footnotes on how the constitutional debate is affecting Scotland's loch monsters, banshees, kelpies, selkies or little folk. Do we really want to throw away all that mythology in order to become a modern 21st century nation? No one wants to talk about the brownies though, especially not Labour.

What about the pixies and elves of England - not to mention the gnomes of the City of London and the mental dwarfs of Westminster - should we not show solidarity with them? Why has no one mentioned Shrek? Will the M6 take us to the Magic Kingdom, or is London too far far away? These are serious questions that only the federalism fairy can answer.

Federalism in the UK isn't going to happen. Not now. Not ever. There is no will for it amongst the federalism fairies. Like the charming and suspiciously kitsch Edwardian fairies of Cottingley dancing in the rose garden in the sepia images, they were revealed as a hoax when Nick Clegg went into coalition with Davie Cameron in the rose garden at Downing Street. Ming Campbell took the photies for that too.

The Lib Dems are the only UK party to advocate federalism. They like advocating it so much they've been advocating it for over 100 years without ever managing to do anything about it. It's their version of Labour's Parliamentary Road to Socialism, which comes complete with its own little solidarity selkie. It makes plaintive noises and offers a nirvana of redistribution, only to drag you to your death in the deep dark watery gloom.

Tories don't really have a Scottish fantasy creature, since having one depends on being in touch with Scottish reality in the first place. They're just the ugly duckling that grew up to be an ugly duck. One that paddles in a moat you can get cleaned on Westminster expenses.

And then there are the zombies. You can't kill off a Westminster politician's career by voting him or her out of office. They'll just come back from the political grave and eat the brains out of Scottish devolution legislation in House of Lords committees.

So it is actually vital that we discuss the role of fantasy creatures in the independence debate, because from here it's looking like they've been the heart of UK government for decades. Could be that's the problem.

However on Tuesday we did discover that one particular fantasy creature is real. A Labour MP who takes a principled stand for fairness in the Scottish independence debate. One exists, there's even better photies than there are for Nessie. Paul Flynn, Labour MP for Maverickshire, was spotted on camera telling off a Commons Committee for a cheap stunt designed to embarrass the Scottish Parliament and preventing a proper investigation into whether Alistair Darling's pal Nick MacPherson had broken civil service rules on political impartiality. It was very easy not to mistake Paul for a dead log floating aimlessly, because that's what the rest of the room was doing. He was walking out in disgust. Pity he's not a Scottish MP, but that's probably asking for a bit much. If 'bit' is defined as 'bigger than the UK's national debt'.

Meanwhilein the Guardian there was an article about the political uncertainties faced by Cameron, Miliband and Clegg, and their respective bands of austerity munchkins. The article discussed the possibility that electoral plans might have to change if there's a yes vote in September. An anonymous MP admitted that the Better Together campaign was worse than crap. He bewailed:

"The Better Together campaign is just ramshackle. It would not matter if it was just crap, but it is nasty. All the threatening from Whitehall has been counterproductive."

In Scotland, at least amongst supporters of the yes, undecided voters, and quite a few who are leaning towards no - in other words anyone who isn't a member of a Unionist party leadership, channelling Alan Cochrane, or wishing upon a federalism fairy - this is a political insight up there with the realisation that Jeremy Kyle is only pretending to be a social worker.

This article also repeated the assertion previously made by Benedict Brogan at the Telegraph that a yes vote in September would certainly force Cameron to resign. Westminster's dylithium crystals cannae take the loss of Scotland. So voting yes is looking increasingly like the only sure fire method of getting rid of Davie Cameron. The Guardian was also of the view that Miliband would have to resign too, since Labour would be seen to share equally in the culpability. That's what independence supporters would call a hatrick.

And this within 24 hours of yet another Unionist commentator complaining that they are unhappy with the standard of the debate in the referendum campaign. It's no bloody wonder there's a low standard when one side of the debate is doing its utmost to prevent a proper debate taking place. Their jobs, careers, and reputations depend on it. Sometime in the future there's going to be an robot copy of David Starkey presenting a sneery history 3D live streaming about crappy prime ministers of English history. Davie's name will figure prominently. And there's another reason for a yes vote - it might one day produce a David Starkey history programme that's worth watching.

When the Westminster parties refused to consider any form of enhanced devolution as an option on the ballot for September - an option which would probably have secured a handsome majority and enabled them to avoid the issue of Scottish independence until they'd all safely retired - they all sneezed at once and finally killed the federalism fairy. Instead we got the cartoon monsters of Project Fear, and the realisation that Scotland is more likely to get devo-max or federalism or whatever devo tweak you like from Santa than we are from the Westminster parliament.

We're all up for a serious debate. But first the fairy stories have to be put to bed.

9 May 2014
Male pattern Westminsterness

In Thursday's papers we were told that Davie Cameron will not resign if there's a Yes vote in September's referendum. Which doesn't really come as much of a surprise, seeing as how shamelessness is part of the job description of a UK Prime Minister. Friday saw reports in which Cameron challenged those who said he should never have permitted the referendum to take place - as though it were somehow within his power to prevent it. He may arguably have had the legal authority to do so, but politically it would have been impossible to refuse. There is no written constitution in the UK, and no constitutional prohibition *a la catalana* on an independence referendum to give Cameron a fig-leaf of democratic respectability. A refusal would have guaranteed Scottish independence in short order.

But really the announcement was made because Davie doesn't want to give us any ideas about getting rid of him as a favour to our friends in England, which would be a demonstration of practical solidarity of the sort Labour can only dream about. It's a wee side effect on the side of the independence medicine bottle - warning, may cause the permanent loss of a Prime Ministerial career. Like male pattern baldness only you can laugh at it without feeling you're a bad and shallow person.

Unless your hair is already a fading memory, like mine, in which case baldies are fair game too. Once you've learned to embrace your inner Kojak as well as the one on your heid, you have licence to mock those who are still hoping they can comb their hair a bit differently in the hope no one will notice that Iain Duncan Smith is sneaking up on them. Which to be fair is a genuine reason for having nightmares.

So Davie's keen to rule it out, although short of a hair transplant he's stuck with the unrelenting march of his male pattern balding. But he won't be resigning. And I believe him. He'll be sacked by the rest of the Tory party instead.

Scotland's Prime Minister is in a bind of his own creation. Which is what makes it genuinely funny and a whole lot more wounding than cheap cracks about hair loss. He's damned if he says he would resign, and damned if he says he won't. Politically, the second is merely the lesser of two evils as far as Cameron is concerned. But not by much. They're both pretty evil.

Scottish independence is not the same as Her Majesty's Goverment graciously granting independence to a colony. It means losing 32.2% of the UK's area and 8.3% of its population to a peaceful and democratic movement which has just told the Westminster Parliament that its system of government so irredeemably crappy that we want no part of it and are swapping it for a new system that offers a better prospect of doing what the electorate tells it. That's not just a slap in the teeth, it's a broken jaw.

Then there will be the embarrassingly urgent problem of Trident. The French are going to be smug. The Russians will gloat. The

Americans are going to be reminded that British state incompetence isn't confined to Johnny English movies. The pure affrontment.

And even more urgently still for a Conservative PM, UKIP will be enjoying the bounce from electoral success in the Euro elections in England, and there will be the little matter of EU related negotiations to enter into. Whether Scotland is inside or outside the EU by the date of independence, Cameron's still going to have to sell a reduction in UK voting powers and influence to an increasingly fearful and dubious back bench. And then there's the thorny topic of negotiations with Scotland over divvying up the UK rebate. The rebate agreement lasts until the EU Financial Agreement expires in 2020, until then it's likely that other EU member states will prefer not to reopen the can of worms, and hope Holyrood and Westminster can sort it out between themselves. Afterwards it's open season on the UK's special EU concessions. And Davie's got a promised in out referendum on the cards. Not looking good is it.

In terms of blows to national prestige, this is all a very big deal. As Chairman of the Board of UK PLC, Cameron has ultimate responsibility for the fact that a significant chunk of his shareholders really dislike their country being referred to by a metaphorical reference to a business. Because Cameron is not our boss, he's our servant. We're campaigning for a country where politicians cannot lose sight of that fact. For Westminster public accountability was never more than a rapidly receding speck on the far horizon, which has now vanished off into the Magic Kingdom where the federalism fairy sups tea with the redistributive elves of the Union and the Scottish goose still happily lays golden eggs in a Treasury battery farm.

According to Cameron all of the above is less important than his commitment to hold an in out referendum on Europe. Placating UKIP voters is more important than Scotland, which is why Davie is willing to go head to head with Nigel but not with Alicsammin. We're just not worth bothering about. Not a good message to persuade Scotland to vote no, but it's a sign of just how weak Cameron's hand is that it's the best he's got.

This has all come to pass because staving off the issue of Scottish independence, at least until Davie was safely esconced in the House of Lords, would have required opening up hundreds of other issues which are really best avoided if you're a Westminster Parliament. A firm offer of something approaching devo-max from all three main parties as a second option on the ballot would mean opening up issues of Treasury accountancy to public view. It would mean dealing with the West Lothian Question, the Barnett Formula. And it would also require coming clean about the true state of central versus regional spending within the UK. People in the rest of the UK would also discover the extent to which they subsidise London and the South East, and would be unlikely to be as happy about it as Boris Johnson is.

Instead of facing up to these long standing and deep rooted problems in the structure of the British state, Westminster did what it always does, it went for the short term fix that promised an easy result. Let's batter Alicsammin into submission once and for all. Only a minority of Scots supported independence according to all the polls, and the same polling consistently showed that Scots ranked issues like wages and employment, education, health and housing far above constitutional matters in order of importance. How could they not lose?

But they misjudged it badly, and now the Yes campaign is gaining momentum and the polls are narrowing. The campaign strategy hasn't worked, its credibility is in shreds, and they've only just realised they've been fighting it the wrong way round all this time. They should have gone for positive before negative, then people might have paid more heed to the scare stories. Now few believe a word they say.

But it's too late now. Even if they do manage to rescue a No result, it will be a pyrrhic victory. Independence is on the horizon and getting closer. It's going to be the death sentence on Cameron's career, whether he resigns or not. No wonder he's losing his hair. There's no rogaine for the Westminster Parliament.

12 May 2014
Out for indy

I don't often comment on Guardian articles, but did the other day. It was in reply to a particularly annoying and persistent clueless

Unionist who wanted to know what independence supporters were "most insulted by". I replied I was most insulted by Unionist trolls who are all over the Guardian's Scottish comment threads like a manic depressive Ian Paisley at a Gay Pride march. The comment was removed, no doubt because it was considered an example of egregious cybernat monstering, or possibly was considered offensive to Ian Paisley, or both.

But I was telling lies, evil cybernat lies, lies of the sort you'll never ever find in the august pages of a respected national newspaper, oh no. Not the bit about Unionist trolls being like a manic Ian Paisley at a Gay Pride march, because that bit is true, it's the bit about being most insulted by the hobby Unionists who post below the article. All too often the article itself is way more insulting. This is especially true if it's a Guardian editorial, a paper which dishes out insulting flavoured with extra seasonings of hypocrisy and a crunchy topping of sanctimonious. I was being unfair to the troll, because whoever writes Guardian leaders is like Fred Phelps after snorting a line of speed the length of the M25. Which is also the circumference of a Guardian leader writer's mental universe.

On Friday the Guardian published an editorial which managed to squeeze into one short article just about every slur, stereotype and lie about the referendum campaign, and which - without any apparent shred of self-awareness - was entitled *Scottish referendum: Accentuate the positive*. It then went on to accuse yes supporters of whipping up anti-English sentiment, abuse, and general nastiness, praised the "grassroots" Vote Nob Orders astroturf, and called on Unionists to start making a "more" positive case. Which makes it sound as though they have a baseline of positivity to work from. Not that the Guardian's leader writer attempted to give a positive case, he or she was just making another addition to the increasingly lengthy list of politicians and leader writers who call on someone else to make a positive case for them. Now we know what a collective failure of imagination looks like. Just read a Guardian editorial about Scotland.

There's little point deconstructing the piece. It would be like deconstructing soiled toilet paper. You already know it's full of shit.

Poking through it only makes you feel dirty, even with marigold gloves and a claes peg on your nose.

Some people insist that printing such lies, misinformation and arrant nonsense is evidence of a conspiracy against Scottish independence. That's not to say that the British state is not secretly pulling whatever strings it can behind the media curtains, because it certainly is. But those with a direct line to secret services handler are relatively few in number. Most of the crap originates in the universal human propensity to focus on any auld shite that happens to confirm an existing prejudice and ignore everything that doesn't.

It's like the anti-gay bible bashers of Ian Paisley's and Fred Phelps' ilk, they scream verses from the Bible which prohibit marching down Bath Street waving a Rainbow saltire hand in hand with your same-sex beloved, but then they'll go to McDonalds and munch on a cheeseburger. The verses in the same chapter of the Bible prohibiting eating meat and dairy products together don't apply to people who think Jesus tells them to hate. Better Together works in a similar way and so its message is eagerly lapped up by those predisposed to believe it, and who have a vested interest in continuing to believe it - such as Guardian leader writers and certain Labour party cooncillors.

Ah but ah but, our Ian Paisley impersonating Unitroll would say - all that applies to independence supporters too. You just believe what that alicsammin tells you and he's a liar and he eats too many pies and wears tartan troosers that you've paid for with no currency because you can't use the pound so he can go on holiday with Putin and plot how to rid Europe of bearded Austrian drag queens who win the Eurovision Song Contest - because that's how evil he is and so must you be as well. Ah ha. Or words to that effect.

There may well be a small minority of people who would still prefer independence even if it did mean we'd all be living in caves without any friends. Not that I've ever met any. And I'm sure there is also a tiny minority of people who believe every single word that a politician utters. Not that I know any of those either, but they do exist. Usually they're politicians' grannies. Although with some even that's a stretch.

The real difference is that for most people who want independence, a belief in it is something that they arrived at after a period of doubt and questioning. They sought evidence, they compared sources, they reflected upon it and discussed it with people whose opinions they trusted. We've been lied to by the mainstream media and politicians so often and for so long that they no longer enjoy the authority they once did, and the Internet allows information to be searched for, sourced, and made accessible in a way that was never possible before. And then that information can be passed on.

The Unionist position is the default position. It's a position that went unchallenged for so long that those who hold it no longer realised it was a position at all. It was like heterosexuality. It was the normal against which everything else was judged abnormal. Scotland's learned that other normalities are possible. And achievable. While supporting independence is not like being gay, it is a lot like taking the decision to come out of the closet. It's taking a leap of faith in yourself and in your own possibilities. Scotland is the country that's coming out of the closet.

The Unionist media is reacting in the same way now as the homophobic editorials of old. The media demonisation of independence supporters is a surreal experience for those of us who have been here before. Gay and lesbian people lived through all this in the 1980s. Newspaper editorials then were full of wilfully ignorant fulminations about evil pariahs who wanted to break up the traditional family. Now take the preceding sentence and just add the words "of nations" - and you're describing 2014.

But when the establishment demonises and misrepresents you, when it issues increasingly hysterial threats and bluster about all the dire consequences that will come to pass, the wrath of Ian Paisley's God that will smite you for being a drag queen with a beard or a supporter of Scottish independence, it tells you something important. It tells you that you should not be afraid. You are scaring them. They are afraid of you. You are the powerful one in this equation.

I've made this point before, but it bears repeating. Gay and lesbian people are always going to be a minority, but we won the campaign for legal equality because we came out of the closet in large numbers from the 1980s onwards. We faced up to those who demonised us and refused to be afraid. And in turn that meant more and more straight people who previously had no reason to think about the homophobic attitudes of the law or social convention found that they actually knew "one of them", and were often related to "one of them". For the first time they had to examine their own attitudes. And that's what wrote a new normality.

Independence supporters are not a small minority. We're everywhere, we're in everyone's family. Independence supporters can be demonised in the pages of newspaper editorials and television studios. But they can't be demonised where it matters, in the social circles and networks of family and friends of independence supporters. Those are the people who're most likely to have a vote. The more of us who come out of the Unionist closet, the more we establish the new normality of a Scotland where other paths can be trodden. Where, dare I say it, we can dae it oor wey.

So say it loud, say it proud. I'm out for indy.

13 May 2014
Home made hope

The Kirk has announced it's to hold a service of healing and reconciliation after 18th September. The move has been broadly welcomed by a Scottish media which sees it as a Sign from God supporting their contention that independence supporters are unrepentant sinners who have rent the country in twain. We stand on the brink of lasting social chasms, other than those caused by the economic policies of Westminster governments. The War of Alicsammin is manifesting itself in foul new weapons hitherto unimaginable and shortly to be banned by the Geneva Convention. Scotland is a house divided.

George Robertson and Jim Murphy have been collecting the proof. They have found evidence of door chapping in Largs, people talking to their mates in Broughty Ferry, and ordinary people voicing political opinions in Penicuik. There was even a rumour that someone in Glasgow told a joke. Evil separatists promiscuously spreading the virus of nationalism with public meetings and human contact.

It's a biological weapon. People have been infected with hope. It's contagious.

And we quite like it. Hope is a novel experience for people in Scotland, we've had precious little of it. For a land so blessed with natural and human resources it's been in remarkably short supply for as long as anyone can seem to remember. Many of us thought that we were genetically programmed not to have any. This was the land of no gods and the precious few heroes who are all deid. But recently we've made the remarkable discovery that we don't actually need any heroes, because we're all heroes in our own way. We no longer need to hope that a hero will come and deliver us. The only deliverance is the one we create for ourselves. Hope is home made.

I've spoken to more people than I can count about Scottish independence within Scotland and outwith it, it comes with being lippy and opinionated. With a tiny handful of exceptions of an orangey persuasion - or if not orange some other member of the citrus family like soor lemon - none of those I've spoken to within Scotland oppose the idea of independence in principle. None have any emotional attachment to the Westminster Parliament. What they are attached to are vague and ill defined connections of culture, family and experience, connections which don't depend upon any Parliament to validate their existence, and which are not confined to the borders of the United Kingdom of Great Britain and Northern Ireland. The Union's roots are shallow, which is one reason why they've had to be covered with the artificial grass of the ironically titled Vote No Borders - set up in defence of the most isolationist state in Europe, one whose politics outside of Scotland are dominated by calls for more stringent border controls. Did that PR company really think this through?

Those who oppose independence overwhelmingly do so because they are misinformed about Scotland's potential, are fearful of the unknown, or because they still think of independence in party political terms. They are the ones who still have no hope. The task of independence supporters is to inform, reassure, and show how hope of something better is possible. We're doing that by talking, by discussing, by sharing information, creating music, making art, by engaging with people. Who knew independence campaigns could be such a good laugh.

We're having a independence campaign, and not only is it all entirely peaceful and democratic, it's overwhelmingly good natured and characterised by wit and good humour. This is not usual for an independence campaign. There is no civil unrest. There are no ethnic tensions, the yes campaign is resolute that Scottishness is a state of mind which can be acquired by anyone who chooses to live here. It's not about ethnicity or nationality. It's not about where you're from, it's about where we're going. People who are not Scottish by birth are equally represented in both sides of the debate. No one is getting shot. No one is being hauled away in the middle of the night by masked gunmen. There are no internment camps. No tortured bodies have been found in roadside ditches. No bombs have blasted shoppers in high streets. We should be celebrating that fact, screaming it from rooftops, because it is a testament to the immense maturity of Scottish democracy. Our media should be hailing Scotland as an example to the world of how the most politically sensitive of topics can be handled in a peaceful and democratic manner. This is praise not just for supporters of independence, but also for the overwhelming majority of supporters of Union. All of us, whatever our stance on independence, deserve great credit for this.

Instead we get carping in the media from Unionist politicians who are upset that someone called them a rude name on Twitter while blind to the rampant name calling from their own side. Calling people rude names is what Twitter is for. What do you expect when you're restricted to 140 characters, contextual analysis, subtlety, tact, and nuance? Disagreements on Twitter are bound by their format to be curt. So here's a Twitteresque suggestion - get a fucking grip and grow up.

If Westminster does manage to pull some fearful rabbit out of its hat, and scrapes home to a No vote, who is to be reconciled to whom? It will just be Westminster being reconciled with itself. When you've got two faces you can do that. It will be return to business as usual, without Caledonian distractions, a politics dominated by the struggle between the Tories and their bastard Thatcherite offspring in UKIP. They will hope that Scotland will return to its previous alienation, while they get on with the important business of widening social divisions and inequality as they seek to turn the UK into a mini-me Republican USA.

Meanwhile independence supporters will reconcile themselves to the fact that they've learned how to hope, and once learned that knowledge will never be forgotten. We'll continue to spread the message, only starting from a higher baseline. Home made hope can't be stamped out from on high. Nothing about the Yes campaign is an exercise in alienation and the creation of divisions, it's the opposite.

If there is a yes vote our task will be to show those who voted no that hope does not exclude them. And we can even reconcile ourselves to those politicians who spread lies and whipped up fear - although whether we're likely to vote for them again is a different matter entirely. There is no need for revenge, except by building a better, more prosperous, and more socially just society in an independent Scotland to show them that they were wrong.

The independence campaign is itself a healing process. It's healing the wounds of the past and teaching a nation how to hope again. That's worth celebrating.

13 May 2014
Nationalist nasturtiums and the new poll tax

A terrifying new development has occurred in the independence debate, conclusive proof of the Labour party's claims that Unionists are being subjected to a coordinated campaign of victimisation and intimidation. Alan Titchmarsh is on his way to Falkirk to report on the shocking news - the threat of nasty nationalist nasturtiums and anti-English anenomes to the Great British potted plant.

Without the slightest consideration for Unionists with hayfever, for the past 14 years the thoughtless followers of the Beechgrove Garden in the SNP's Falkirk branch have held an aggressively bullying sale of potted plants every year outside the town's Thornhill Road Community Centre where they foist secessionist sweet peas upon unsuspecting citizens.

Alicsammin has sent them orders to taunt the Union with window boxes. They make Labour committee members who've forgotten their anti-histamines cry, and the evil pruners of the Flowers of Union are doing it deliberately. That's just how vile these people are. They're even in alliance with Greens, although all the vegetables are firmly on the side of Westminster.

And to think that they're doing this at the same time as the Chelsea Flower Show, trying to take away attention from Great British Gardeners like Diarmuid Gavin and his inventive idea for a garden based on Labour's Scottish devo policy. It's wilted, colourless, and is in the shape of a maze without an exit which leads you on a devolution journey in an ever decreasing circle to a beartrap in the middle. Just follow the sign marked 'jam'. Once you go in, you never come out again.

What do you mean he's Irish? He can't be foreign, he's on the BBC furgodssake. Do you need any more evidence that separatists have no shame? The Daily Mail and the Guardian don't.

Speaking from a secret location, a Labour party member said:

"It was awful. We had planned to hold a Labour party committee meeting, but getting there would mean running the gauntlet of a bouquet of carnations and exposing ourselves to foul SNP abuse in the form of perfumed plants and the very real threat that someone might brandish a gladiolus. It was just too much for us to bear, what with that recent incident in Edinburgh involving a Yes sticker which vandalised Ian Murray MP's office door and covered up a part of his priceless collection of Edinburgh Young Team Ya Bass graffiti."

Between sobs, he added, "This campaign of terror against the reputation of the Labour party in Falkirk has to stop. First Eric, then Grangemouth, and now this."

When asked whether Alicsammin was going to apologise for the shocking flower display, a spokesperson for Yes Scotland said: "Whit? Oh grow up you idiot."

However our fearless reporter could not help but notice a menacing camelia on the desk, and slowly backed out of the door.

Next week, Glenn Campbell will present a special report on how wind patterns from Siberia are devastating British annual perennials, and how it's all the fault of Alicsammin and his pal Vlad.

Meanwhile, shocking news has surfaced about a new poll tax. Taxpayers have coughed up fifty grand for an opinion poll commissioned by Westminster. Polling into Scottish attitudes towards the independence referendum was reportedly carried out by IPSOS Mori in January, but never saw the light of day because for some odd reason IPSOS Mori only asked people who had not been pre-vetted by Better Together, and the results were skewed by normalcy.

Reports that the poll showed a strong surge in support for yes have been sidestepped by Nick Clegg, who's terrified that people will keep calling him a liar. You know he wants to deny it, but he's being being bullied by a pensioner from Leuchars who hopes his floral display of red white and lavender will get him a seat in the House of Lords.

Is there a reason that public opinion is a state secret? Can public opinion even be secret? Have Bertold Brecht's DDR commissars flitted from East Berlin to the East Neuk?

After the uprising of the Edinburgh Agreement
The secretaries of the Westminster Union
Had leaflets distributed in the Glesca Subway
Stating that the people
Had forfeited the confidence of the government
And could win it back only
By redoubled efforts. Would it not be easier
In that case for the government
To dissolve the people
And elect another?

15 May 2014
The four whored men of the Acrapolypse

The four whored-men of the acrapolypse, Warmonger Reid, Kiss of Death Murph, Pestilence Prudence Broon, and Wee Dougie who's starved of affection, are riding across Scotland to rid the land of worshippers of the demon Alicsammin in preparation for the coming of the Tory lairds and just in time for the release of the new Godzilla movie. Better Together is relaunching its campaign only this time it will be headed by Labour's own Godzillas - Gordie, John Reid, Murph the Smurf and Wee Dougie have all been fingered. Scotland's likely to reply with a pair of fingers of its own.

How many relaunches is that then? Wasn't there one of those last year? And another in February? By the time you get to three, it's no longer a relaunch it's what happens to a rubber chicken stuffed with a whoopee cushion when it's tossed out of the window of a London PR and rebranding specialist. Birds are after all the only living descendants of the dinosaurs, so it's appropriate really.

Labour's Big Beasts are exactly the same as the city wrecking version found in Japanese B movies, they went through several relaunches and rebrandings too. The only difference is that Labour's Big Beasties insist upon us paying for a glitter effect lavvy seat before they take a dump in the High Street. At least Godzilla takes care of his own toileting arrangements and isn't overly concerned with public donations. But it's not enough that John Reid got taxpayers to pay for his sparkly new bog sear, Labour wants us to kiss the arse of a man they loathe almost as much as disaffected Labour voters do.

There's a reason John Reid has hitherto not put in an appearance in the independence debate. And it's because the hatred that the rest of the Labour party has for him is exceeded only by his hatred for them. John never held on to his socialist principles, but he's got a PhD in holding grudges. He enthusiastically hitched his wandering red star to Tony Blair's warwagon because he wanted to be a cowboy. However he is a fortunate man, not only has he already got his bahoochy firmly planted on both a sparkly lavvy seat and a bench in the Lords, unlike Dougie he doesn't need plebs to love him. He's already blessed with a close and loving relationship. Every morning he gazes upon the face of only person on the planet that he truly loves and who loves him back, and then he has a shave. The only reason he's getting involved now is because they really are so desperate that they have to be pleasant to him.

His arch nemesis Gordon Brown has been 'entering the fray' ever since the fray started to unravel, which was before Better Together's stuffed rubber chicken was first hatched in a PR company's focus group meeting. Gordie pops in and out more often than a drunken knee trembler up a back alley. That always starts with a promise and ends in disappointment too. However Better Together's Tory strategists have managed to convince themselves that the sympathy we felt for Gordie when he was subject to blatantly anti-Scottish abuse at the hands of the Tory press somehow translates into respect for what he did while in office and a willingness to believe any of the tortured syntax that issues from his conniving gob. We felt sorry for him. But no one wants to vote for an object of pity, especially when the object of pity has made an extremely lucrative career out of preaching about poverty in luxury hotels and conference centres. They really should stop dragging him out. It's getting cruel now.

Wee Dougie Alexander needs to remember that the next time he does the puppy eyes thing and begs for us to show some solidarity. You know, like he did for his sister. Dougie only wants to be loved for being a clever little boy, but big sis was the one with the galaxy intellect. Dougie was left with the fun sized curly wurly and the task of masterminding Ed Miliband's 2015 general election campaign. At this stage in the proceedings, Her Maj's Opposition ought to be enjoying a commanding lead over a collection of clueless public school Tories and Lib Dems with a suicide note. But no, instead UK politics are dominated by a fight between the Tories and UKIP over which one of them is the true inheritor of Maggie Thatcher's handbags, and Labour is behind in the polls. Dougie knows that the only way Labour can get back into power is by showing they can wield Maggie's handbag just like the rest of them and by adopting the Iain Duncan Smith approach to statistics. So this one looks like it's going the same way as the last election campaign that Dougie masterminded, the one that gave the SNP an absolute majority in a system Labour had designed expressly to prevent that happening. How many bites has he taken out that curly wurly so far?

And then there's the Murph, skulking up from behind and hoping that no one with a vote will notice him. A cut price Jack Straw in an ill fitting suit conspiring against his party enemies in whispers. He was another devotee of Tony's. Tony is the great unmentionable of Labour's ProudScottery Promotional Department, the spectre and his 150,000 Iraqi ghosts at Labour's funeral banquet, whose name cannot pass the lips of Better Together in case the public remember that the four whored-men had sold themselves for that one too.

Better Together believe that disaffected Labour supporters in Scotland can be persuaded to place their trust in a party and a parliamentary system by the very same bunch who trashed that trust in the first place. They embody most of the reasons we're having this independence debate. They're not the solution, they're the problem. But they're going to come and lecture us about the dangers of alicsammin anyway. Which is why they will convince no one, it's not about alicsammin, Scottish independence is a non-prophet organisation.

Meanwhile details of the secret poll suppressed by Westminster have started to leak out. Rumour has it that when asked whether they thought that the intervention of Gordon Brown would aid the No campaign: 47% of respondents broke out into derisory laughter, 16% demanded he reimburse the losses they've suffered to their work pension plan, 21% said they they were too creeped out by his photograph to answer, 11% said there is nothing he could ever say now that they could possibly believe, 4.9% said 'Who?', and 0.1% said they were related to him and had to agree because they need to face him at family New Year gatherings and he's a kill-joy enough as it is.

99.98% agreed that George Osborne is an alien space lizard, and 0.02% are Ruth Davidson. Asked their views on his Sermon on the Pound, 62% said it made no difference because they never believed a word Osborne had ever said before anyway, 23.5% said it made them throw a mug of hot coffee at the telly, and 1130% said they couldn't give a shit about numbers and statistics and currencies because it's not about money, it's about democracy.

The only accountancy some of us are interested in is making sure our politicians are held to account. We can only do that with a yes vote. We can't do it with the four unaccountable accountants of Labour's love in with power.

16 May 2014

Attack of the Oomphaloompa

Since the negativity isn't working, Davie Cameron has come to visit for two days, painted his face orange to blend in with Scotland's last remaining North Britons, and wants to tell us all about oomph. Davie the Oomphaloompa promises that his bar of chocolate substitute really does contain the golden ticket to the Willie Wanker's Devo Factory. This is what passes for a positive case for the union in case anyone was wondering. If we vote no we'll get a bar of his special oomphy chocolate, and can open it up to find a big devo surprise.

There's one chance in 1.5 trillion of it actually containing any devo, or even any chocolate. More likely it will contain a letter from Iain Duncan Smith saying your chocolate ration has been removed because you refused the offer of a zero hours contract. Davie's not promising devomax then, just oomph, which is also a handy mnemonic for the speed at which devolution legislation passes through Commons committee stages: 00 mph.

We also put the Great into Britain. Which was nice of him to say. It's like oomph, but with nuclear missiles and submarine bases. That's what allows Westminster to be the Big Bawed Oomphaloompa of Europe, only because Brussels sprouts give them testicular envy and Davie would prefer to be firmly attached to the scrotum of the Pentagon they're semi-detached Big Baws. Which is possibly the first time ever that a hernia has been pitched as something to aspire to. That might explain the strained expression on his Davie's face then.

Got to keep that positive vibe going, and that's hard to do when you don't have anything concretely positive to say. The Oomphaloompa kept repeating the phrase 'best of both worlds', which his strategists had obviously told him was the theme du jour, apart from the oomph. It's unclear how any world can be described as best if it means having Oomphaloompa Davie as Prime Minister. But he does make a good impression of a Roald Dahl character, after all Davie and his pals throw kids down the waste chute too.

You'd think in at least one of those two best worlds the Prime Oomphaloompa of Scotland would actually talk to the little people in Scotland who were not either serving members of the armed forces under orders to treat him with deference, or tame journalists who do the same because it's part of their job description. He keeps carefully away from anyone who might point out that he's not actually a children's character proferring a bar of chocolate and a dubious devo lottery.

So he's definitely not for debating Alicsammin, even though he's a very naughty boy bent on gobbling up all Westminster's Scottish sweeties. A real Oompa loompa would have words with him. Or at least a wee song. Instead we got waffle about this great family of nations. The problem with that is that Davie thinks he's the daddy. He wants to tell Scotland when it's devo bedtime.

He also made what is quite easily the most asinine argument ever made in favour of the Union, and in that he's been up against very strong opposition. Not for Davie the simple ridiculous scare, the outlandish threat. Oh no, in his manic quest for PR content free positivity he took inanity to an entirely new level. The long awaited positive case for the Union is that the only way we can get more devolution is by voting no. If we get independence, the process of serving up more devolution stops. Davie wants us to know that we'll no longer have dinner to look forward to if we have a full plate of food and are able to feed ourselves.

We're having to arm wrestle him and his Labour and Lib Dem associates for the dinner one cold baked bean at a time, with only a hint that there may or may not be some chips too, but forget about ever seeing the steak pie. A pudding? You think there's chocolate too? There might be a stale cracker that Michael Forsyth, Iain Lang and George Foulkes have chewed on until it's devoid of any flavour or calorific value. And there's always the food bank.

You'll have had yer tea Davie. And now we're going to help ourselves to ours. You can get back to Willie Wonka's Chocolate Factory. We've had enough children's stories.

Oompha Loompa, de-vo-voo-doo,
Dave's got a devo carrot for you.
Oompha Loompa, de-vo-dee-lay,
If you vote no he'll whisk it away.

What do you get when you trust a Tory?
Trident, bedroom tax and austerity.
What is he at we can see through his crap.
What do you think will come of that?
And we don't like the look of it
Oompha Loompa dee-vo-dee-dum,
Vote yes to give him a kick in the bum
Then we'll live in happiness too,
Bye bye Oompha Loompa dee-vo-voo-doo.
De-vo-voo-doo

17 May 2014
Bhòt Bu Chòir anns an reifreann and annoy Nigel

I once nearly got accused of stalking when I lived in Spain, and to be fair, I was actually following the couple. How weird and creepy is that. But in my defence it's not because I was stalking them, it's just that I overheard them in the street talking in a language I'd not heard before, and I wanted to hear enough of it so I could work out what it was so followed them along the street for a minute. I'll admit to being weird and creepy that way, I love listening to the sounds of other languages.

Anyway, the language was probably Quechua, or maybe Aymara, which are spoken by several million people in Peru and Bolivia, and I hadn't been so excited since I overheard overheard a couple in a bus station in Utah talking in Paiute. At least I think it was Paiute, it might have been Shoshone. It might not get anyone else going, but for some of us it's like an auditory form of trainspotting.

This makes me the polar opposite of Nigel Farage, so I can't be that weird and creepy after all - and that was the best news all week. Nige doesn't like hearing people speaking furren on the phone on trains. Unless it's his German wife talking to her relatives. It makes him uncomfortable as he's convinced that they're talking about him and saying nasty things. And to be fair, they probably are. Spanish for bawbag is *escroto*, it's a word you may very well hear if Nigel is the subject of a Spanish language conversation.

The leader of UKIP objects to people speaking languages other than English in public spaces in the Yookay. He thinks it's terribly rude.

How dare foreigners come to this country and refuse to forget how to speak in their own language to their mammies. But the truth is that UKIP aren't very good at other languages, even those which have been spoken in the British Isles for a lot longer than English. Other languages force them to wake up to the reality that not everyone is a culturally insular little Kipper and that SHOUTING. AT. PEOPLE. SLOWLY. isn't the same as talking French.

They have as many problems with Welsh. Last year the Welsh language version of the party's website announced that it wasn't the United Kingdom Independence Party at all, it was Plaid Annibyniaeth y Du, which translates as "The Black Independence Party". Nigel hadn't suddenly come out as a supporter of Malcolm X, although UKIP members making black power salutes might have improved their chances of courting the ethnic minority vote. It was just a typo for the correct Welsh version - *Plaid Annibyniaeth y DU*. DU is the Welsh abbreviation for Deyrnas Unedig, Welsh for United Kingdom. Without the capitals, it's *du*, the Welsh word for black. They didn't notice the mistake until someone pointed it out to them.

But despite the window dressing of some Welsh language pages on website of the party's Welsh branch, UKIP isn't keen on any languages other than English, even those which aren't remotely 'foreign' at all. In 2012, the party's branch in the English county of Shropshire mounted an objection to the use of bilingual Welsh and English roadsigns in parts of the county close to the Welsh border.

Welsh isn't a foreign language in these districts, it's not even just the language of another nation in this greatest union of nations that the universe has ever seen (© Better Together). The administrative border between Wales and England does not coincide exactly with the boundaries of the Welsh language, and there are villages in the Shropshire border districts where people still speak Welsh - especially around the town of Oswestry, or Croesoswallt to give it its Welsh name. But UKIP's local activists thought that eliminating a part of their own linguistic heritage was something to celebrate.

But we shouldn't be too surprised. UKIP are a bit confused about the linguistic heritage of the country they claim to be defending from hordes of foreigners with their strange speech and suspicious food. They think Welsh and Cornish are forms of Gaelic - which is exactly like thinking that French or Spanish are forms of Romanian, or that English is a form of the same language Nigel's wife speaks with her relatives in Germany. Which is maybe why Nigel doesn't object to that. According to a policy document on "restoring Britishness" published in 2010, the party swore to *"enthusiastically support teaching of the various Gaelic languages and histories within the UK, in Scotland, Ireland, Wales and Cornwall"*.

Not that UKIP are enthusiastically supportive enough to give "Gaelic languages" any resources to allow them to maintain themselves. In 2013, UKIP's MEPs, including the linguistically sensitive Nigel, voted against the EU giving support to the minority and regional languages of Europe - languages spoken by people who are not immigrants who have willfully failed to learn English. Language like Welsh, Gaelic, Scots and Cornish, all of which have as much claim to be languages of the UK as English does.

UKIP members are typically the kind of people who are blessed with the power to hear people talking even when they're not in the same building. You know, the traditional complaint that Welsh people in pubs all start speaking Welsh to one another as soon as an English person enters. Which leaves you wondering just how the kippers knew what language the Welsh people were speaking in before the English person entered the pub. Or how the Welsh people knew that the person entering didn't also speak Welsh, because contrary to some stereotypes, speakers of Celtic languages do not all know each other personally. In fact Welsh people all speak Gaelic to one another in pubs just before an English monoglot Kipper enters and only switch to Welsh to confuse Nigel. Welsh for bawbag is *sgrotwm*.

UKIP are threatened by linguistic diversity. Not just the languages of migrant communities, but by any language which isn't English. The future they have in store for Scotland and Wales is one where our languages and cultures are kindly granted the status of hobbies. We'll be allowed to pursue them in our own time and at our own expense, but don't expect the state to do anything but preside over their slow extinction. Which is pretty much their view of devolution and Scotland's distinctive political culture too.

There are European elections on Thursday. They've not set the heather alight in Scotland, where we are more preoccupied with another vote later this year. But UKIP are likely to perform strongly in England on Thursday, and their malign influence will have a major impact on the strategies and policies adopted by the main Westminster parties. The UK is gradually drifting away into a fantasy land of Little Englandism where everyone speaks only English and thinks Thatcher was a Great British Hero.

Scotland's rich and diverse tradition of multilingualism is under threat. UKIP's attitudes are distressingly widespread enough as it is - the Scottish Government is not providing bilingual Gaelic and English ballot papers for the referendum.

Such narrow minded attitudes don't need any more encouragement, but if we don't put a cross next to the Yes box on our English language only ballot papers, that's exactly what will happen. There's only one way to protect Scotland's languages, and only one way to ensure that Scotland's migrant communities are encouraged and supported in their efforts to maintain community languages. Linguistic diversity enriches us all, it gives us a window on the world that we don't get if we can only function in English.

Bhòt BU CHÒIR anns an reifreann! Vote AYE in the referendum.

19 May 2014

Where are we going as a nation, and why are we in this handbasket?

You can't go to the shops for the messages these days without having to dodge the missiles being thrown by hordes of angry yes voters across a barricade of burning car tyres blocking Cumbernauld Road. Inside every shop there's an irate man with a blue painted face spouting anti-English insults and calling for the reintroduction of hanging for everyone who refuses to learn Gaelic. Meanwhile pensioners clutching poly bags run in terror past Parkhead Forge to escape the whirling blades on the wheels of a van bearing a Vote Yes sign. But you're not even safe at home. Throughout the land families cower in fear of the late night chap on the door, it will be an SNP fanatic who's going to stab you unless you agree to vote yes more quickly than a blink in Alistair Darling's eye. It's so bad that Better Together can't put forward any speakers for public debates, out of fear that their supporters will be dragged from the hall and stuffed into a wicker man to be set on fire to propitiate the ancient Celtic god Alicsammon, the sybil of secession. Even potted plants are biological weapons in this war. It's referendum carnage.

All of this must be true, because it's regularly reported in the media. But then, so are sightings of Nessie.

It's a strange thing. Apparently no voters are being terrified into cowed silence, too afraid to speak out despite having the support of the entire apparatus of the British state and most of the mainstream media. Love for the Union is the love that dare not speak its name, yet every day it's plastered all over the front pages of the Mail, the Telegraph, the Record, the Sun, the Guardian and the Scotsman, like a page three model with a come hither tease and a premium rate phone line. Better Together have helpfully provided an astroturf lawn for Vote Nob Orders picnics. The telly, and the BBC in particular, is chock full of the Joy of Great British Unionsex, demonstrating all the positions in which you can be shafted yet still convince yourself that you're in a partnership of equals. It's not like no voters are bereft of support, it's not like there is no one who wants to encourage them to speak out, it's not like there is no one to give them information and arguments they need to state their case.

What we're seeing now is what happens when a scaremongering campaign goes wrong. Better Together set out from the assumption that support for independence was the preserve of a relatively small minority. And back when the campaign started this was true. Opinion polls regularly showed that most Scots did not want independence, and most Scots placed constitutional issues quite far down their list of political priorities. So Better Together decided that it would win the referendum by ensuring that this state of affairs continued. No voters were to be taken for granted, in the way that Scottish voters are always taken for granted by Westminster politicians, and they'd concentrate on scaring the shiters out of the don't knows while demonising yes supporters as SNP fanatics that no reasonable person would wish to associate with. All that was required for this campaign to work was domination of the airwaves and the printing presses, and they had that.

But it didn't work as planned. What they didn't count on was an effect that they themselves had created - the widespread public distrust and outright hatred for our political classes. No one loves Westminster except those for whom it's the mainline terminus of the gravy train. If you had a quid for every time that Westminster broke a promise, you still wouldn't have enough to pay your English daughter's uni fees.

So across Scotland, people began to ask the question - where are we going as a nation, and why are we in this handbasket? Gradually the realisation dawned even on many who were predisposed to vote no that we're up shit creek and the paddle has been privatised. Previous no voters realised that voting against the continuance of the Westminster system isn't voting to end a glorious era, it's voting to end a greedy error.

The fearbombs were exploding on a daily basis in the media. And were getting more and more extreme, and less and less believable. There's only so long that people will accept being treated like idiots, do it long enough and those people are going to rush to accept the first chance they have of giving you an almighty kick up your smug self-serving backside. It's not like they had a high opinion of Westminster politicians to begin with.

The campaign broke out of the party political rut, where it could have been contained within the regular ding dongs of the licenced party trolls. It spread to non-party groups, it became a mass movement. But even that could have been contained. Containment and demonisation worked with the anti-globalisation protests, which helpfully assisted in their own demonisation by smashing up the centre of London. But these protests were also unfocused, a howl of rage against an unjust and unfair political and economic system, without a clear plan of action to take beyond the demonstrations.

There has been no campaign in recent British political history like the Scottish referendum campaign. Referendums* aren't commonplace in the UK, and when they do occur they are usually hedged around with qualifications, obstacles and ah-buts from the political parties. The farcical AV referendum was devised so that voters were offered quite possibly the only alternative system of voting that was worse than First Past the Post, and it was a vote carefully depicted in party political terms - embodied in the lying liar Nick the liar Clegg. Voting against AV was more a vote to kick the lying liar Nick the liar Clegg in his lying nads. Did I mention he was a liar? The result was a vindication of Westminster. And Nick's lying nads are still well padded. Westminster's backroom machinations behind Scotland's 97 and 79 referendums are well known. The independence referendum is a referendum whose terms have not been determined by Westminster, and for that reason alone it is is unique.

In the shape of the Scottish referendum, Westminster is faced with its worst nightmare. It's a referendum whose terms they have not set and did not control. It's a popular mass campaign beyond party politics, whose activists have little interest in party political point scoring. Alicsammin is a big fat liar you say? And this should bother me why exactly? I'm not voting for Alicsammin. I'm voting for independence. But worse than that it's a focused campaign, with a very clear political objective - a yes vote in the referendum. Political goals don't come more focused than a single affirmative word.

A focused mass movement in a campaign beyond their control - no wonder they're scared of us. Yes supporters should not be discouraged or even angered by the increasingly hysterical shrieks in the UK media. It means they're still losing.

It will get worse over the next few months. Expect all-out doomageddon on the one hand, and a red white and blue bunting-fest on the other when the polls start to show yes is in the lead. They have no other course of action open to them, but it will be self-defeating. The no campaign is already disintegrating - Labour MEPs confirm that Scotland will of course be admitted to the EU, Danny Alexander admits that there will be no border controls, the UK Government admitted that pensions will continue to be paid. One scare story after another is admitted to be false, and with every admission another little piece of Better Together's credibility dies. All that is left are the shrieks and the slurs, and the desperate attempt to rally the troops with the pageantry of wars long over.

The more they shriek, the more they attempt to diminish, abuse and demonise, the more they depict a reality that ordinary voters in Scotland cannot recognise, the more people in Scotland wonder how we can possibly be better together with a political system which holds us in such contempt.

We can step out of the handbasket, and decide on our own destination. It's a promise that comes with home made jam. That's a promise that Westminster cannot compete with. And yes will keep winning.

*Pedant's note: I refuse to stop banging on about this. The plural of referendum is referendums. Referendum in Latin is not a noun, it's a gerund, a part of the verbal system. Latin gerunds do not have plurals, and the Romans weren't overly keen on mass participatory democracy either. Neither is Westminster come to that, but that's by the by. English has gerunds too, and they don't have plurals either - although English confusingly uses its gerund ending -ing for a variety of other grammatical purposes which can sometimes be pluralised. In the sentence "I like monstering", monstering is a gerund, but in "I like a good monstering" it's a noun. You can pluralise nouns, or at least most of them, and some gerunds are also used as nouns. But you can't say "I like swimmings" in the same way, because swimming is only a gerund, or a present participle which can't be pluralised either. Referendum in Classical Latin was like swimming, not like monstering.

Gerunds in Latin take the same endings as neuter singular nouns. Referenda is what the plural of referendum would be in Latin if it were a neuter singular noun. But it's not a neuter singular noun, it's a gerund. The only reason a plural is required is because the word was borrowed into English as a noun and the rules of English grammar demand that nouns have plurals. So since referendum only requires a plural due to the demands of English grammar, not Latin grammar, the only appropriate plural is the English plural referendums. Referenda is bad Latin, and using it just makes you sound like a pedant who has mispedanted.

Boris Johnson gets it wrong, and he's an Eton and Oxford educated Classicist apparently. I went to a comprehensive in Coatbridge. *Sic id fellitā Boris*. That's Latin for 'So suck it up Boris', only ruder. Because we can do monstering in Latin too. Now go and write it out 100 times.

20 May 2014

Escaping plans for Nigel

In a desperate effort to get some headlines in a country where most people think the party leader's name is Bawbag, UKIP's top candidate in Scotland has accused the SNP of adopting sectarian tactics because of a recent visit to a mosque by Al-Iqsammin. Many UKIP members believe he is a secret Muslim just like Obama, and the minute after independence he's going to ban bevvy and pork sausages. You can write his name in Arabic letters and Al Qaeda will understand what it means - just how much more evidence do you need?

But if you're still not convinced, Donald Trump is going to make a video demanding that Al-Iqsammin show his birth certificate, which will prove beyond all doubt that he is in fact a gay shoplifting communist Roma Muslim Romanian windfarm engineer asylum seeker on benefits who can't be deported because he's got a cat. And I'm not making this up, or at least, I'm only making things up to much the same extent that UKIP and Theresa May do.

David Coburn, UKIP's Scottish candidate, is desperately hoping to get a seat, which he can only get if the SNP's Tasmina Ahmed-Sheikh doesn't get one. The polls aren't looking good for Davie. Unkind people might think that he was sounding a racist dog-whistle in making a sectarian song and dance out of 'party leader asks people to vote for his party shock horror'. Thankfully we're not unkind at all. Milk of human kindness we are Davie, and our milky nature means we can recognise that Davie's just sour because north of the Border UKIP's as popular as Maggie Thatcher the Milk Snatcher.

Standing on a milk crate, Davie pointed that if he appeared in a Catholic church people would accuse him of sectarianism. Which would only be true if you were singing the Sash at the time. However more realistically Davie would be unlikely to gain a sympathetic hearing in a Catholic church in Scotland because most of them are full of Scottish-Poles and Scottish-Lithuanians and the priest is likely to be Scottish-Nigerian.

UKIP's Scottish candidate doesn't have a high opinion of gay people either, and he is himself gay, so you can understand we've got some complex and murky personal psychology going on here. But it's fair enough, gay people don't have a high opinion of him. He thinks that gay marriage is "rubbing people's noses in it". Which is just silly. That only happens at Inuit marriages. Gay marriage is legal in Greenland and Canada, perhaps Davie Coburn spends a lot of time in the Arctic and was unfortunate enough to attend a gay wedding when he had a heavy cold. It's not nice when a bearded wedding guest reeking of whisky rubs noses with you and your snotters freeze him to your face. It's even more unpleasant for the other person, especially if he's a gay Romanian. However it would be a justifiable reason for Davie's nose rubbing traumas so let's not leap to the conclusion that he's just a bit of a bigot, the wee snottery lamb.

Nigel doesn't condone homophobia, not at all. Oh no. He just thinks that homosexuality makes most people over 70 uncomfortable. Which is peculiar, you'd think by that age they'd have learned the importance of a good lubricant.

UKIP is widely expected to become the largest UK party in terms of vote share in Thursday's European elections. In Scotland it's unlikely to gain a seat, although it will probably overtake the Lib Dems in vote share, Scots will still prefer Professor Pongoo, who did it first. Penguins don't even come from the UK, they come over here and gobble up our fish stocks. They should go back to Penguinia, which as the geographically challenged contestants on Dale Winton's In It To Win It know is right next door to Romania. This is convenient because such people are UKIP's target voters. Yet penguins are still more popular in Scotland than UKIP.

UKIP doesn't seem to have a policy on devolution. In its last manifesto it wanted to replace the Scottish Parliament with a glorified committee of Scottish Westminster MPs, but in August last year while on a visit to Wales Nigel the Bawbag said that was old outdated thinking and he told a reporter for BBC Wales that UKIP was about to unveil a shiny new devolution policy. He still hasn't told anyone what that policy might consist of however, apart from vague noises about federalism, although the possibility remains slim that Nigel is the Federalism Fairy David Torrance thinks is going to magically deliver a federal UK. This is despite the fact there's a Scottish independence referendum going on - you'd imagine that ought to have the effect of concentrating the political mind, but it remains uncertain whether UKIP has one of those either.

UKIP are the political bastard offspring of Maggie Thatcher and Tony Blair. Nigel is in no hurry to pin his party down to specific policy measures. In the meantime the party can be a convenient vehicle for voters in the rest of the UK who are disillusioned with politics as usual. The real danger from UKIP is that the other parties will tack even further to the right in a bid to prevent losing support, and as they do so they'll move ever further away from Scotland's priorities. If the party does gain the largest vote share after Thursday's election, the pressures on the Tories and Labour to shore up their dwindling voter bases will be immense. Expect a lot more 'tough talk' about benefits, more demonising of migrants and foreigners, and the looming certainty of a referendum on EU membership which could see Scotland out of the EU even if most in Scotland vote to remain.

Most of the results will be announced on Sunday evening, after the ballot has closed in countries where elections are traditionally held on Sundays. In Scotland however, we'll have to wait until Monday - the Western Isles votes won't be counted until then - by which time the gulf in political aspirations between Scotland and the rest of the UK will be starkly apparent.

In September we can vote to make Scotland a UKIP free zone, then we no longer need to worry about what plans are being made for Nigel, and we can get on with making our own.

21 May 2014

Plane tickets and devo journeys

Many of Project Fear's scare stories say nothing at all about Scotland as an independent state. They focus on the process of becoming independent - What currency will we use? Will the EU let us in? You'll have to renegotiate every single treaty the UK ever signed. In an independent Scotland there will be crisis meeting after crisis meeting as we realise to our horror that we're still at war with the Mughal Empire and the Emir of Zanzibar, we've not formally recognised the Greek royal family or unrecognised them after the Greeks got rid of them, and we'll have to set up a special committee to deal with our failure to ratify the treaty determining the border between Alaska and Canada.

It's a bit like warning someone not to take up an offer of a holiday in the sun because they might get held up in a queue at the airport. This is what is so crass about independence supporters being described as separatists, it's like saying people only get married because they want a big piss up and a fight to break out between the best man's girlfriend and the bridesmaid, followed by trip to the airport and a fortnight in Benidorm. They're not getting married because they love one another and want to build a life, they're just irresponsible airportists who want to cause arguments and unpleasantness for their own selfish reasons.

Travellers going via Alicsammin Domestos Airport will have forms to fill in, paperwork to complete, 10,000 treaty applications to make. Going to the independence airport will be worse than making an application for disability benefit, but thanks to Iain Duncan Smith only marginally. We'll have to undergo an ATOS assessment and get a letter from our GP saying that the Westminster parliament is sick in the head and not fit for work. That will be the easy bit, you only have to look at Westminster to realise the institution passed the point of senility a very long time ago. You'll need passports, copies of your grandparents' birth certificates in triplicate, a signed declaration from a vet that your dog doesn't have worms - and make sure you have translations available in Slovene, Estonian and Croatian or you won't even get in the queue for check in. Anyway you'll never get past security, not with that Spanish veto. You won't even be allowed into Benidorm that's just how little they think of you. And there's the uncertainties, will there be more surcharges than Ryanair, can men pee in the airplane lavvy without spraying it all over their trouser leg?

Why bother with independence eh? Forget about all those dreams you had of a better life. It's just big argument, a queue in the airport and piss stained trousers that you're missing out on. Who wants that hassle anyway.

Instead of an independence day party that's got a nation sized cake followed by an exciting life journey of independence adventures and making our own decisions about where we're going, we're promised a devolution journey. We don't get to choose the destination, and there's nothing on the road except a flattened hedgehog which Johann Lamont is trying to pass off as a radical new increase in tax raising powers for Scotland. The devolution road itself bears a suspicious resemblance to one of those wooden backdrops in Roadrunner cartoons which independence supporting Wile E Coyotes slam into at great speed - just in time for a Westminster gravy train to appear from nowhere and flatten them. It's a very old joke which has been repeating for decades, but it's nowhere near as funny as a Roadrunner cartoon.

Yesterday Alistair Help Me Rona Carmichael proudly unveiled some new roadkill on the devolution highway. After a no vote, he wants everyone to get together for a cosy chat over some shortbread and scones about what devo rodents we can all agree on, and we'll have none of that lip from Nicola. Then once we've decided that we'd quite like a small hamster, he'll have a wee word with a Davie Cameron who will not want to appear to give anything away to the Scots after they've voted no and he's got UKIP voters to woo so he can win a rapidly approaching General Election. They won't stand for English taxpayers footing the bill for a Scottish subsidy hamster, so he'll roll the hamster ball to a committee somewhere down a dark and dismal Commons corridor, where it will get flattened by a stampeding rush of Tory and Labour MPs. And that will be the end of the devolution journey until the next time Scotland can think of a way of forcing itself onto the Westminster political agenda by finding a rabbit to pull out of a hat again.

There is no devolution journey. There's a game of snakes and ladders with the dice loaded against you. No ladders but snakes aplenty, and no end in sight. It keeps us passengers occupied while the Westminster drivers privatise the motorways.

We're better off at the back of the bus with certainties you can trust, like the certainty that the CBI would be back to issuing warnings about the uncertainties of independence just as soon as they thought the upset over their registration as No supporters had died down. It's only been a fortnight since they swore blind it was all a terrible misunderstanding, that's how long they think your memory lasts. What do you imagine they think we'll forget between now and whenever they get round to delivering devolution, or a high speed railway connection to Scotland.

And while the UK media is quickly back to pretending that the CBI's interventions in the independence debate are entirely neutral and motivated by nothing but genuine concern for our well-being, they don't want to cover the storm that's brewing on the offscreen side of the BBC weather map. The National Union of Journalists is growing increasingly frustrated by the decision of BBC Scotland management not to end the Corporation's membership of the CBI. It's almost as though journalists on newspapers don't have any idea what's happening with their fellow union members at Pacific Quay.

They can't be reading Newsnet or Wings or Derek Bateman's blogs either - apparently it was pressure from the NUJ which led to the decision to include the online media in the round up of the papers at the end of BBC2's shortly-to-be-axed Newsnicht. Instead we're getting a radical new change in direction from BBC Scotland news and current affairs. Something presented by a woman with a famous faither that's going to have fitba in it. So like Reporting Scotland then, only later at night. Certainties that you can trust, just like the devolution journey and the CBI.

I'd rather get the first available plane ticket. There's a flight leaving on the 18th of September from Independence International airport. Let's go on a journey that we choose.

22 May 2014

The Gospel according to St Dougie the Wee Lamb

I. And verily it came to pass that the Elders of the Kirk did decide to hold a debate on the independence of the land of Caledon. For the campaign hath caused rent and division, thus is it written in Scripture in the Books of Dailimail and Gaurdion and must be True. And did not the prophets warn that thou shalt not call politicians rude names on Twitter, for it is an abomination in the eyes of the Gord. But the people payeth heed not.

II. Lo! said the Moderator, we shall not take a vote, for if we vote yea the worshippers of Union shall rend their clothes and raise a mighty wail that shalt reach unto the Kingdom of Haverin at Pacific Quay. If we cast a ballot, Better Together shalt refuse to send a speaker at the last minute, Ken MacQuarrie reporteth us not and we shall never get mair bums on pews. For is it not true the Kirk loseth enough to thae mad Wee Frees or long lies in on a Sunday as it is?

III. And thus guaranteed - or so did he think - that he would not suffer the slings and arrows of outrageous ridicule, Wee Dougie of Alexander, belovéd of Gord but not of his sister, did hear the call. A host of Magrit Currans and Ian Davidsons appeared to him in a dream, and did chorus: "Furfuxake Darling's lost it, and thou shalt get thy jotters. Thou best get thine arse in gear, and thou canst save ours while thou art at it. Gaun make like a Holy Wullie, for it is the only thing thou art better at than thy sister."

IV. And Wee Dougie packed his sub-galactic intelligence upon his Labour donkey and did pass unto the General Assembly whereunto he did speak upon a pedestal with his halo freshly polishéd with Mr Sheen. For was it not written by the Prophet Kokring of Telegraffos that in the End of Days Labour shalt lie down with the Tories and preach obedience to the One True Parlie? For yea it is a vengeful Parlie.

V. Dougie told the parable of the good neighbour, and proclaimed that the land of Caledon must show the loyalty to its neighbours that siblings have for one another. For are we not taught by Westminster that we must pool our resources, and share Scotland's oil, and deer estates, and grouse moors with our neighbours, or at least the rich ones.

VI. And Dougie sayeth, is it not true that Westminster giveth tax cuts to our rich men, for it is easier for a rich man to enter the kingdom of Sterling than for a Scottish camel to enter Threadneedle Street.

VII. And let us forget not that they allow us to look after their Trident missiles, which is the only potential boom we're ever likely to be granted.

VIII. All that is good and True is the bounty of Westminster, and we would be lost sheep without a shepherd if it were not for their wisdom and the guidance with which they lead our future to the abbatoir.

IX. Neighbourliness and community, preacheth Wee Dougie, these are the things we can only experience through communion with Westminster. It mattereth not that Westminster has been hell bent on destroying them for the past three decades. For that was just a phase. Honest, ye can trust me, sayeth Dougie. For he was out the room the whole time he was a cabinet minister under the Lord Gord and He Who Must Not Be Mentioned. And so were the two Eds. That unpleasantness is safely out of the way, and so we can return to the True Path to invisible jam in a mythical Jerusalem.

X. And is it not true that if the land of Caledon were to sunder to the demonic armies of AYEbernats we would retreat from the benificence of Westminster's multiculturalism. For Caledonians would then be foreigners too, but not in an exotic or interesting way.

XI. And is this not a very clever way of insinuating that wanting independence is racist but without actually saying so. See so I am so as bright as Wendy, thinketh Dougie the Smug to himself.

XII. But we must only pool with some neighbours, not foreign neighbours which follow the teachings of false parlies. For the One True Westminster is a jealous Parlie and refuseth to mention the Irish Republic.

XIII. Behold, sayeth Wee Dougie, the fruits of redistribution. Rejoice, for we are truly blesséd with the best of both worlds, and the weapons of mass destruction of one of them.

XIV. Yea, for it is not written in Holy BBC Scripture, but 'tis how better together we really are.

XV. And the people did laugh and mock. Except the Moderator of the Kirk of Scotland, who hath a contractual obligation to keep a straight face.

XVI. Then the people did reply - Aye but the neighbours keep voting Tory and UKIP, and we can't change that for them. For it profit neither them nor us for us to jump into a barrel of shite and drown with them, as thou knowest fine bloody well. But we can see why thou hast a different opinion.

XVII. And the people cried out, before did we think that thou wert just sanctimonious, but now thou hast taught us well the meaning of Pharisee.

XVIII. Thou getst not the irony dost thou Dougie son? It is a truth uncommonly told that Labour needeth independence far more than the SNP. For it is the only path to your political salvation and through which ye can regain the soul ye sold to your lord Gord and the demon Tony Blair.

XVIX. Thus endeth the lesson on 18 September.

24 May 2014

Voting none of the above

Here's the summarised results of this week's English cooncil elections, to save you reading through acres of coverage. Labour is screwed, the Tories are screwed, the Lib Dems are totally screwed, and UKIP's screwing everyone.

Despite Ed Miliband's glum face, which to be honest is hard to distinguish from his happy face, Labour actually won the cooncil elections - they gained the greatest number of seats and topped the poll in terms of the percentage of the total vote they picked up. But Labour even managed to turn that into a defeat.

The problem is they were starting from a very low baseline. Think of the belly of a snake, then dig downwards until you get to the special corner in the basement of Hell reserved for Tony Blair, that low. They're the student who hadn't even achieved an F in the exam they needed an A for to get into uni, so to prepare for the resit they had lots of late nights with cans of red bull, mammy and daddy flew in a very expensive strategy expert from the USA, they listened to lots of sermons from intellectuals of the party like St Dougie the Diminutive, they stared a lot at piles of very thick books on electoral tactics and formulating policy ideas in the hope that the knowledge might somehow get into their heads by sheer proximity alone, and they managed to improve so much that they scored a D minus.

Not close, and definitely no ministerial motor. It was made a lot worse when Ed had a series of car crash interviews. He dented a door panel when he revealed he didn't know how much the weekly shopping cost and then he dented it again as he made unconvincing attempts to rescue the situation. A short while later he reversed over the local Labour party's foot when he didn't know the name of the Labour leader in Swindon council, which he was visiting at the time seeing as how it's a key council Labour needed to win. That was bad enough, but then he went into forward gear and drove over a puppy when it became apparent that he didn't realise that Swindon was in fact a Tory controlled council, this being sort of the reason why it was a key council Labour had to win. He was hoping to drive off and hope no one noticed, but Ed Balls got caught doing that too.

Labour should be doing much better at this stage in the electoral cycle, which is like a mountain bike only you're more likely to fall off and batter yourself in the groin in ways which people will video on their mobile phones and send off to Harry Hill, where it will haunt and embarrass you for all eternity. Even more embarrassing is the fact they'll send in the video clips even without the TV offer of 30 pieces of silver in return. In England's local elections, Labour not only fell off the bike and battered itself in the groin, it also catapulted itself into a vat of manure.

We're told that an official party inquest has already begun, which is a polite way of describing a bunch of politics geeks screaming 'Fuck!' at one another as they decide who to blame. But Labour's real problem is as obvious to voters in England as it is to voters in Scotland and Wales. Throughout much of the 20th century, Labour was the workers' party, and the Tories were the bosses' party. Then Labour became the party of managing workers' expectations, and the workers largely put up with that. But then Tony Blair and Gordon Brown happened, and Labour became the party of explaining to the workers why the bosses are right. But we already had the Tories as the Bastard Party, Labour became the only thing worse, the Two-Faced Bastard Party.

Meanwhile the Bastards themselves hardly covered themselves in glory. The Tories lost seats, but the party of government always loses seats in local and by-elections, so they're not losing much sleep over it. They didn't lose as many as they feared they might. In Scotland we hate having Iain Duncan Smith, George Osborne, and David Cameron telling us what to do, in England they have to put up with them and with Eric Pickles and Michael Gove as well. So the Tories could have done a whole lot worse. Which is a bit of a worry if your ideal result in the 2015 General Election is a repeat in England of what happened in Scotland in 1997.

The Lib Dems tanked, but didn't tank quite as badly as some of us had hoped. If you're Scottish tanking Lib Dems counts as a proxy version of having Danny Alexander strapped into one of those machines that pour evil looking goo over irritating teachers in children's tv programmes, and we didn't get quite the flotilla of supertankers of goo we might have liked. Certainly not a North Sea's worth, which would have been poetic. The party did very poorly, but avoided a complete collapse.

Meanwhile UKIP gained a lot of ground, although not quite as much as they gained in the last round of English council elections. UKIP didn't do well in London, because it's full of outward looking non-provincial types who look down on narrow minded petty nationalism, so that's something else Londoners have in common with Scottish independence supporters. Out in the shires and the north of England it was a different story. UKIP took votes from all the three other parties.

UKIP have proven their main point, which is that they're an unpleasant fixture in UK politics, joining the three existing unpleasant fixtures. It's not so much UKIP itself which represents the biggest danger, it's the effect UKIP has on the other three parties. The centre ground of UK politics just shifted even further to the right, and further away from the aspirations of most in Scotland.

They have local elections every two years in England, it helps to spread the apathy more thinly. The turnout was a paltry 36%, the biggest winner was the None of the Above party. But None of the Above changes nothing, because it doesn't force any of the above to make serious reforms. So you get the frustration of UKIP.

When Scotland next goes to the vote, we'll be able to mark the YES box and make "None of the Above" mean something.

25 May 2014
E-numbers Ali

Alistair Darling has reappeared after hiding away for a wee while because everyone thinks he's rubbish, especially those on his own side. It must be a sobering experience to have a belief in your own abilities which is as great as the UK national deficit, only to discover that everyone else rates your worth as having less currency than trying to buy your weekly messages with two plastic Smarties lids. Plastic Smarties lids have long been abolished, along with any hopes of devo max or sensible arguments coming from Alistair Darling.

Alistair has popped up to give us a wee preview of the Treasury paper due out on Wednesday, which we're told is going to prove just how much money the UK throws at ungrateful Scots. Allegedly we're already spending all our Smarties lids along with most of those from everywhere else in the UK - Smarties subsidy junkies that we are - and we've still got rubbish public services and swingeing austerity cuts still to come. The only way we can guarantee a continuing flow of Smarties is to vote no, although we'll only get the blue ones. They're the ones that were banned in some countries because they contained suspicious E-numbers.

Alistair wanted to let us know that Scotland doesn't have the Smarties for an oil fund. Almost other country in the world with significant oil resources has established an oil fund, but Scotland can't afford to. The only other country which didn't establish an oil fund is Iraq, which was too busy spending its oil income on invading Kuwait, oppressing Kurds, and going to war with Iran, presumably illustrating the point that you can't establish an oil fund if you're hell-bent on getting involved in a lot of Middle Eastern wars. So just like Westminster then.

And we've even got our very own version of Chemical Ali. What Scotland's E-numbers Ali is saying is "Scotland can't afford to become independent because me and my pals have destroyed its economy. And because we reserve the right to invade Iran too." This is apparently a reason we're supposed to say no to independence and give them a vote of confidence. Then we can keep letting him and his pals destroy Scotland's economy and scoff all the Smarties. There you go, you wanted a positive case for the Union, now you've got one.

Alistair's figures are based on the usual Better Together sleight of hand, and make the assumption that an independent Scotland would continue with the same spending priorities and decisions that we have at the moment under Westminster. Scotland will not be able to afford an oil fund if we keep paying for Trident and a bloated defence budget, if we continue to contribute to supposedly UK national projects like the London sewer upgrade and London Crossrail, and if we keep letting the UK Treasury classify a significant proportion of Scottish revenues - like VAT returns from Tescos in Motherwell or Bridge of Don - as originating from a company head office somewhere in England.

Combined with the sleight of hand is the creative accounting. Creative accountancy bears the same relationship to proper accountancy as a Labour manifesto does to a jam exhibition in the village Womens Institute. The Sunday Herald has revealed that the Treasury paper is founded upon a spectacularly fictitious account of the costs faced by an independent Scotland. The UK Treasury has over estimated the costs by some 650%. According to Better Together, the cost to Scotland of setting up new government departments will exceed £2.7 billion, or approximately 173 billion Smarties - although we can at least be certain there won't be any blue ones.

But this figure is based upon the supposed cost of setting up 180 ministerial departments from scratch. According to the Institute of Financial Studies, each new ministerial department will cost £15 million in initial start up costs. The UK only has 15 ministerial departments, so why Westminster thinks Scotland needs 180 is not entirely clear. Perhaps we're so unruly we need much more governing. The figure apparently comes from the Scottish Government's White Paper, which mentions 180 Scottish public bodies, but this figure includes organisations like the quango which manages the Cairngorms National Park. These organisations are already up and running, and would not require £15 million in order to be re-established in an independent Scotland. Scotland already possesses a number of ministerial departments, and the number of brand new ones we're going to require would scarcely cover the bottom of a tube of Smarties.

E-numbers Ali was just copying the same trick used by George Osborne, when he ruled out a currency union with Scotland on the grounds that Scotland has a vastly inflated financial sector that's too much of a risk. Osborne only achieved his scary figures for the financial liabilities of Scottish banks by including all the banks' assets and debts located elsewhere in the UK - even though these would remain the responsibility of Westminster and the UK regulatory authorities after Scottish independence.

The Treasury fear bomb is ticking away, and is set to explode on Wednesday, just in time to clear the newspapers and the telly of headlines about UKIP's gains in the European elections. But it's already been debunked before it's even appeared. The UK Government is now trying to backtrack, claiming that it was simply a minor clerical error. That's what you get when you rely on the CBI for your financial scare stories.

26 May 2014

Euro pick n mix

The results of the European elections were like a bag of pick n mix sweeties someone else had got for you, a few of your juicy favourites and far too many soor plums and bitter almonds. The full results are not yet in as I write - at 2.40 am. See how I suffer for the cause? Ok, it's really because the other half has a wee chest infection and isn't sleeping well. Which naturally means I don't get to sleep either. He'll survive, so nae worries, although whether Nick Clegg can survive is another matter.

So let's start with the almond. The bad news is that it looks like Scotland's got a new party balloon. UKIP's David Coburn is Scotland's very first bitter nut to be elected representative for the Bawbag Party. 139,687 voters were sufficiently convinced by a party with no Scottish policies at all that they put their cross next to UKIP.

UKIP has no devolution policy, after Nigel scrapped their mad plan to replace Holyrood with a glorified committee of Westminster MPs. Dreaming up a new one is on his list of things to do, although it's a safe bet it doesn't rank high on his list of priorities. In fact UKIP aren't just missing Scottish policies, they have no policies at all, except wanting out of the EU and hating immigration. Or three if you count their imaginative proposal for a new BBC weather service - There's been an outbreak of sodomy in Shropshire, which will be followed by heavy showers. But they haven't answered the important question, which is whether they'll replace the weather map.

We can now expect crows from Unionist parties about how Scottish people are just as mean and narrow minded as everyone else in the UK, so we ought to vote No. "We're unpleasant and so are you" is the new positive case for the Union.

But here's a prediction. David Coburn has a distinctively UKIP brand of choobery and will serially embarrass himself over the course of the coming months and years. He's already started, describing Scotland as Alicsammin's "nasty little dictatorship".

So that's the bad news, and it's survivable. And somewhat tempered by the fact that UKIP only barely scraped home into the sixth seat with 10.5% of the votes. The party's best share of the vote in Scotland was in Moray, where they managed to gain 13.6% of votes cast. In England, their worst vote share was in London, where they got 16.87% of the votes cast. Their best Scottish result still lags far behind their worst English result.

It was hardly the ringing endorsement they got south of the border where they are the largest party by a considerable margin. In Scotland they came a poor fourth, quite some distance being the Tories. And we all know how popular Tories are. UKIP in Scotland are still short of a whole panda. It's a bitter almond, but it has a thin sugar coating.

Falling into the not so bad category, like a green jelly baby, is the fact that the pro-independence parties didn't make any gains. But on the other hand they didn't make any losses either, and their share of the vote was pretty much the same as it was the last time the country was struck with the widespread apathy which passes for a European election campaign.

The SNP came top of the pile, escaping the punishment usually received by a party which has been in government for seven years, and its third candidate missed beating UKIP to the sixth seat by the tiniest of margins. Not a great performance, but not a bad one either. And really not terrible at all when you consider that Al-Iqsammin has been public enemy number 1 in the entire UK media for the past year.

Labour got one of those chocolate covered raspberries with a gooey centre that's too sickly. The chocolate coating and the red colourant are entirely artificial and make small children and Labour MPs and MSPs hyperactive, but not in a productive way. The party gained in its share of the vote, but not by anything like as much as it needed to be certain that its support is recovering enough to win the next General Election. Mutterings within the party about Ed Miliband's leadership will only increase. Don't expect them to come to anything though. Labour's instinctive response to all and any crises is let's just ignore it and hope it goes away. Eventually Ed will go away too. What won't go away is Labour's continuing rightwards drift.

The Tories did bleh, in a marshmallow that's been sitting at the bottom of the bag for four days sort of way. They lost just 3% of their vote share compared to last time, mostly to UKIP. The Tories will now move even further to the right in order to ensure that UKIP voter return to the Tory fold come the General Election. And will start making louder noises about borders, immigration and EU referendums in order to attract non-Tory UKIP supporters. UK politics just got nastier.

But then there was the candied lemon of the BNP. They lost their two seats, which was nice to see. But the seats went to UKIP, the less fruity and full bodied flavoured fascism, which isn't quite so nice, but at least doesn't give you food poisoning.

And finally, a delicacy and a special treat to be savoured, a macadamia nut covered in dark bitter chocolate - the Greens pushed the Lib Dems into a humiliating fifth place across the UK as a whole, and into an even more humiliating sixth place in Scotland. The party looks set to have just one surviving MEP.

While being interviewed by the BBC's Dimbleperson, Danny Alexander - who'd offered to do the interview rounds since he's the only Lib Dem with less shame than Nick Clegg - said that the party needed Nick Clegg to keep doing the same thing only with more shouting and star jumps, only to be soundly bitchslapped by an irate Lib Dem who'd just seen his party wiped out tell him that Nick Clegg is the problem. But Nick Clegg isn't the problem. He's just a symptom of a party that no longer has the slightest idea what it exists for. The way it's headed, it won't be existing for much longer.

So what does all this tell us about the independence vote? Bugger all really. Except that when there's a turn out of just 33% all you can say for certain is that most people really aren't that fussed by the EU one way or the other.

Meanwhile in Spain, the elections saw the collapse of both the main Spanish parties, the Partido Popular (spit spit), and the PSOE. The PP's vote share fell from 42% to just 26%, losing the party eight seats. So that's eight fewer MEPs plotting against independence. The PSOE also saw their vote collapse, from 38.8% to 23% losing nine MEPs. The big winners were parties of the left, the newly formed Podemos (We Can), representing *los indignados* who protested against austerity cuts came from nowhere and took 5 seats.

The extreme right did poorly. So Scottish Tory Struan Stevenson's wee trip to Barcelona to help out his pal Alejo Vidal Quadras was to no avail. Vidal Quadras was key in building the Partido Popular's anti-independence alliance in the European Parliament. The arch-conservative left the Partido Popular in a huff because they weren't sending tanks to arrest the leader of the Catalan government, and went off and founded his own Spanish version of UKIP with added rosary beads, called Vox. But they were well and truly voxed, and failed to gain a single seat. Adios Alejo.

27 May 2014

The art of independence and the ashes of Ukipukia

The world is having a flashback from a tab of LSD it dropped in the late 1970s. It's either that or the UK has been sucked through one of those space-time vortex thingies that fill the centre of every science fiction plot hole and we're now in the Dark Universe of Star Trek where everything is upside down and the wrong way round - Captain Kirk cannae get a shag (I mean, William Shatner. Would you? I rest my case.), Scottie's being forced to hoard a warehouse of weapons of mass destruction for the Lizard Aliens of Wesminstron, and Neil Hamilton is the voice of the anti-establishment uprising.

Neil Hamilton. Lemme run that past you again. Neil ... Hamilton ... He's the deputy leader of UKIP and on Monday he was all over Newsnight on BBC2 preaching revolution and the downfall of political immorality. Satire hasn't been so bombed since Kissinger won the Nobel Peace Prize for plastering Cambodia in napalm and Agent Orange. In case of any confusion that's the chemical, not the community organiser of the only grassroots movement that Better Together's really got - although both are equally toxic.

Before Neil Hamilton and his jolly hockeysticks wife scraped a living as a comedy guest turn on chat show sofas, he was best known for being the Tory MP who in 1994 was caught taking cash in a brown envelope in return for asking questions in the Commons. Despite it being proven that Hamilton had serially accepted non serial banknotes in return for asking a series of questions in the Commons on behalf of Mohammed Al-Fayed and others, Hamilton refused to resign. He was the first wee drop in the shower of venal and unaccountable politicians which turned out to be a permanent monsoon of Westminster climate change, destroying civilisation by its denial. Now for the second time in his life Neil's on the leading edge of a wave of shite.

Although Neil refused to resign, because being punished for transgressions is something that only benefits claimants should face, at the following General Election he was defeated by independent candidate Martin Bell, the BBC reporter in the white suit who was going to clean up politics without the benefit of the Kissinger's worth of chemicals required to disinfect the Westminster Parliament and remove all traces of flesh eating microbial politicians. Bell's whiter than white clean up crusade melted like a snowman, and then evaporated away leaving nothing behind, not even a damp patch on Gordon Broon's troosers.

Back in the 1980s, Neil spent much of his time campaigning against a ban on lead in petrol. He'd spent his childhood licking lead paint and it never did him any harm. The proof is in the intellectual tower of moral rectitude and joined up thinking we see in Neil and UKIP today.

Now it's Neil Hamilton who has been entrusted with the task of cleaning up politics. It's like King Herod came back 20 years after that unfortunate incident with the first born and opened a creche. It was all just a bit of a misunderstanding really. You'll be able to entrust your children's future to Ukipukia with a similar degree of confidence. They'll be encouraged to play with sharp objects, it's character building. They're going to need it because they won't have any friends in Europe. That's where nasty foreigners live, people who are bilingual in jibberjabber but talk in English behind your back. UKIP MEPs are monolingual, they speak jibberjabber all the time.

Scotland's very own jibberjabberer was interviewed on STV before the election, claiming that Al-Iqsammin wanted to fill the Highlands with Pashtun warriors and Afghan warlords, who will be slotted in between the windfarms that are being built for no other reason but to destroy the property values of deer estates belonging to hard working multimillionaire hedge fund managers and investment bankers. And he said referenda, which is the only proof anyone should need that the man's a pretentious idiot. He needs to be encouraged to appear more often on the telly and in the pages of newspapers. Every time he opens his gob he reveals the selfish vacuity at the heart of UKIP's message. He's a walking talking advert for all that is wrong with the UK's politics. UKIP have no answers, except a return to an imaginary golden age when Britain stood alone against the world, a wet dream of Great British Contrived WW2 Angles as beloved by the BBC.

They're not the cure for what ails British politics, they're the feverish and delusional part of the disease, disjointed nostalgia and demonic nightmares in equal measure.

It's like this: Scotland used to have its self portrait hanging on the wall. It was never a very good likeness, and too many parcels of rogues had a hand in the brushwork. Then the rogues sold it to Westminster in return for a handful of coin, and Westminster painted itself over the canvas. People got used to it, some even considered it an old master. But it was always a work in progress, constantly retouched, touched up and touched for expenses by generations of political piss artists whose confidence in their untouchablity grew as their talent decreased. The less in touch they were, the more they convinced themselves they breathed the refined and rarified air of lofty heights - when it was in fact oxygen starvation eating away their brains. And now we've been left with something scrawled in crayon and elephant dung, art created by a committee of over-privileged five year old brats.

The political arsonists of UKIP want to throw the canvas on the bonfire and replace it with a photo of a typical British family at a royal event street party that they found in the September 1954 edition of Empire magazine.

The artists of independence want to take the canvas back and paint a new picture of Scotland instead. The art of independence, not the ashes of Ukipukia. We'll rebuild the School of Art, and we'll rebuild a just, democratic, and outward looking Scotland as well.

28 May 2014
Scotland 1974

I decided to do a telly review, and settled down with my deep fried Mars bars and Irn Bru chasers. BBC Scotland's brand new totally non-stereotypical cutting edge 21st century current affairs for a modern Scotland show had its debut on BBC2, and I wanted to get into the mood. I wasn't disappointed, it was the Daily Record with moving pictures. I was just waiting for Dougie Donnelly to pop up and tell us about indoor bowling from Coatbridge.

We shouldn't rush to judgement, this was just the very first show. We're promised fitba in future editions, and doubtless some wee cute kittens as well. But we got the murrderr so we're well set on the road to the Reporting Scotland hat-trick.

Titled Scotland 2014, it got off to a bad start by promising to "investigate the costs of independence" with no mention of any possible benefits, and deteriorated from there. It was a bit like the bastard offspring of the Alan Titchmarsh Show and Loose Women, but without gardening tips, cookery segments, celebrities, or any of Alan's insight into Scottish politics and current affairs. It's daytime TV at night, so you don't have to miss it even if you're so depressed by the asinine intelligence insulting offerings of the BBC that you can't crawl out from under your duvet until past 8pm.

The programme is presented by Sarah Smith, who apparently got the gig because of her hard hitting interviewing skills, and her comprehensive journalistic talents, but not because she's John Smith's daughter. The first two of those qualifying conditions were not on display this evening, which just leaves not being John Smith's daughter. I'm not John Smith's daughter either, and probably neither are you, but I don't recall getting an invite from Ken McQuarrie to show up for an interview. Perhaps it was in that Better Together leaflet I put in the bin without reading it, or in that leaflet from a frozen food shop. Come to think of it, it can't have been in the frozen food shop leaflet. BBC Scotland has never knowingly mentioned Iceland's economic recovery.

First up was what was billed as an investigation into G4S, the private security company that raked in a fortune in contracts in Iraq. But there was little about the dark and nefarious nexus between government ministers and companies that employ psychopaths and give them guns, instead it was a piece about a murrderr. By this time I was wondering if Dougie Donnelly had been delayed in a malfunctioning lift with Archie McPherson.

Ken McDonald, BBC Scotland's science correspondent, presented an ill advised jokey wee segment about the costs of independence, which was loosely based on the Swiss Tony character from the Fast Show. It managed to be both unfunny and uninformative at the same time, achieving in under five minutes what Sanjeev Kohli took half an hour to do, so kudos for that. The joke about Swiss Tony was that he was a misogynistic used car salesman left over from the 1970s. Ken really needs to be careful about that sort of thing what with all the cutbacks being imposed by the management at Pacific Quay. Ken's on a BBC reporter's salary but Scotland's very own UKIP MEP, Jibberjabber the Hutt, will cheerfully spout outdated 1970s social attitudes for free. After all, it's not like he's got anything else to do.

Ken really ought to stick to the science stuff, because political satire is clearly not his strong point. Maybe he ought to stick to doing jokey wee segments about topics he's more familiar with like - What's the difference between the Large Hadron Collider and BBC Scotland's referendum coverage? One is a ruinously expensive attempt to smash matter into nothingness, the other is a scientific experiment. See Ken, it's not that hard, and you won't piss off half your potential audience. Just some geeks in Geneva who'll zap you with a scary death ray and try to suck you into a black hole, but real comedy isn't without risks.

The headline interview with Danny Alexander quickly skipped over any mention of the criticisms being made of the UK Treasury report's figures by the very same people who researched and published the statistics the report relies on. Instead Sarah felt it was more hard hitting and investigative to let Danny Alexander waffle on unchallenged. So did Danny.

It wasn't just the dubious independence costs that weren't explored, Sarah didn't ask Danny about how the Lib Dem's remaining particle of electoral support was smashed into nothingness by the Large Hadron Collider of Thursday's elections, and the fissile matter of party leadership being destroyed in radioactive decay. That sort of science was best left to Ken, but he was off looking at a used Cortina.

Instead the closest we got to hard hitting was Sarah asking Danny whether he'd prefer UKIP or the SNP to have won the seat the Lib Dems lost, complete with an 'Am I not a naughty schoolgirl?' smirk. And Sarah had a wee smirk on her face too. Naturally this gave Danny the opportunity to claim that both the SNP and UKIP are nationalists, while Sarah didn't think to question him about his own ProudScot British nationalism either.

And then we had a Trending segment, in which we were helpfully informed what was the most popular story on BBC Devon. Sarah joined two random persons and they twittered about Twitter for a bit.

Swiss Tony would have said it was all like making love to a woman, you go through the motions while thinking about someone else then satisfy yourself before rolling over and going to sleep, but that's probably misogynistic.

I never thought I'd say this, but bring back Gordon Brewer. I'd far rather have Gordon's grumpy mug than this fluffy content free crap that passed its sell-by date 40 years ago.

And in other news, Scottish cinema chains have decided to ban political advertising from referendum campaigners because the Vote Nob Orders deluge of misinformation was being booed by cinema audiences and had attracted a record number of complaints. The astroturf campaign and its London based branding and marketing agency tried to align Westminster's dismal message of indy doom with Scottish chi but got chibbed instead, and the self-proclaimed 'thought leaders' of Acanchi got sent hamewards tae think again.

(Update: I made a wee alteration to the original piece, after it was pointed out to me by blog reader Nigel Mace that I'd missed Sarah asking Danny about the Dunleavy and Young criticisms of the UK Treasury's misuse of their research during the 30 seconds when I went for a pee.)

30 May 2014
A passport to a positive future

Have you got an annoying relative? We all have relatives whose politics are an embarrassment. I've got a relative who's a No voter. His case for a No vote is based on swallowing Better Together propaganda wholesale, and he considers it brow beating when his numerous factual errors and misconceptions are pointed out to him. It's bullying to give him facts which contradict him, and aggravated assault to give him non-Scottish nationalist sources for those facts.

Admittedly, he does have me for a relative, and that's a difficult gig when we disagree because I'm the family bitch-queen, but still …

I only said that if Scotland votes No, when we get screwed over by Westminster I'll be telling him "See, I fucking told you so" for the rest of his life ... That's very mild by my standards, but this relative claimed to take it as a threat. Which if you ask me is getting dangerously into the drama queenery I've got first dibs on. Oh yeah, and I added that he had the political intelligence of a three week old haddock, which was unfair. I meant lumpfish.

My relative has a severe case of confirmation bias. One way in which his confirmation bias operates is that he will come out with some statement which is not correct, even though it's been explained to him before that it's wrong. Then people get exasperated with him because they've previously pointed out that his information is wrong, and there's only so many times you can tell a person something without wanting to slap them with a lumpfish. But this then allows the person to go "Bullying nationalists!"

Recently my relative made the claim that he didn't want a yes vote because he likes having a British passport and doesn't want it to be taken away. However earlier this year the UK Government confirmed that no one will be stripped of their existing British citizenship as a result of Scottish independence.

It's not entirely my relative's fault that he clings to his myth of passport stripping independence, the claim has continued to be made by Better Together and the Unionist parties despite the fact it's already been ruled out by the Home Office. Magrit Curran keeps mouthing about how she doesn't want her weans in London to be foreigners. To be honest, even if this was true, and Magrit knows it isn't, if she's really going to feel alienated from her own children if they had different passports from her, that's not an argument against independence, it's an argument that Magrit is in serious and urgent need of family therapy and counselling.

So for the benefit of anyone with an equally misinformed but not quite so closed minded relative, or who isn't Magrit Curran, here's the citizenship story again.

The UK government admitted some months ago that existing UK citizenship laws will not be altered if Scotland becomes independent.

Citizenship law is complex, but the basic position of UK citizenship law is that if British citizenship is acquired at birth, it cannot be alienated - nothing you do later in life can alter the circumstances of your birth. Which is fair enough, otherwise it would be a bit like changing your star sign by deed poll because you'd rather have a star sign that didn't make you gullible enough to believe in astrology.

Even when a UK citizen is naturalised as the citizen of another country which requires the person to make a declaration renouncing any previous citizenship as a condition of naturalisation, the UK continues to regard that person as a British citizen. Stopping being British is a bit like giving up being Catholic. You can be a gay atheist commie (waves shyly), but the Catholic church will still regard you as one of the faithful, only just not a very faithful faithful. Nothing you do later in life alters the fact that you were baptised a Catholic when you were a baby. Britishness works the exact same way as Catholicism. The Orange Order is still struggling with the irony.

In fact Britishness is even harder to give up than Catholicism, and both are far harder than giving up smoking while trapped in a tobacco warehouse with a crate of rizlas and an annoying relative. If you manage to piss off the Catholic hierarchy sufficiently, you can in theory be excommunicated, but that isn't that easy to achieve nowadays. You'd have to actually sacrifice a goat to Satan during an orgiastic Black Mass on the steps of the cathedral before you're likely to risk excommunication, although even then you're just as likely to get a nice wee letter from a nun expressing thanks for your efforts at ecumenical outreach. But if you're born British there's nothing you can do to make the British government strip you of your citizenship. Even Guy Burgess wasn't stripped of his British citizenship after he'd fled to the Soviet Union.

If, as a lapsed Catholic, you decide you don't want your kids to be baptised, they will not be Catholic in the eyes of the Catholic church. But you'll still pass on your British citizenship to your future offspring, even if they will be born in an independent Scotland and you took up Scottish citizenship upon independence. The babies which are not yet even a twinkle in anyone's eye will inherit British citizenship by virtue of their parents being British citizens. If you've already got kids, they are already British citizens, and will pass their British citizenship on to your grandchildren.

It's only the children of children born after independence who will no longer be British citizens, the children of the first generation of Scottish citizens born into an independent Scotland. So not only have no children who will lose British citizenship been born yet, their parents haven't been born yet either.

Scottish independence will not change the fact that everyone alive today who was born in Scotland was born a British citizen. The new citizens of Scotland will not even have made a formal renunciation of British citizenship, yet my relative affects to believe that his British passport will be ripped from his hands. He says this even though people who have signed a legally binding document explicitly stating that they renounce British citizenship still count as British citizens, and even though he swears to anyone who will listen that he's determined to be British until the day he dies. And he will be, even in an independent Scotland.

For my own part, I'll view my British citizenship after Scottish independence in much the same way as Catholicism. I'll be very firmly lapsed, but not sufficiently motivated to go and sacrifice a goat to the Demonic Alicsammin on the steps of Westminster in an effort to get rid of it.

Unlike my relative, I don't require any parliament to validate my personal identity. Independence is a state of mind. I know who I am, and don't need a wee booklet to tell me - whether that's a Scottish or a British passport, or the latest propaganda from Better Together.

This is not a debate about identity. It's a debate about governance, about the future, about the kind of society we want to live in. It's a debate about how we can ensure that politicians are accountable and representative, it's a debate about democracy. It's about bloated defence budgets, about what role we really want to play in the wider world, are we a land of peace or a land of nukes.

And we're faced with a choice, not a choice of passports, a choice of futures. The future Westminster gives us whether we want it or not, hostages to the fortunes of a discredited political system, or the future we build for ourselves with our own resources, our own talents and our own skills. Getting a shiny new Scottish passport is just a bonus prize.

The only passport that interests me is a yes vote in September, that's a passport to a positive future.

31 May 2014
The independence train to better transport

Derek Bateman has been having a wee bit of a moan today about the general crappiness of Scottish public transport. He makes some very good points, public transport in the United Kingdom still suffers from the Thatcher effect. Maggie reputedly considered that if you were still taking the bus by the time you were 30, you were a failure in life. Maggie's policies condemned generations to sit at the back of the UK bus. The UK has been following her failure for over 30 years.

Although the quote didn't actually originate with Thatcher, it's a fair assessment of the attitude of successive UK governments towards public transport - which whether Tory or Labour only consider investment in public transport to be desirable if it benefits business travellers. They're not interested in the needs of a single parent who only wants to get to Asda. Our transport policy is decided by a political class that doesn't need to use public transport.

On the day that Edinburgh's tram service restarts after a 60 year hiatus, it's time to have a wee look at Scottish public transport, and whether we're really better together with the privatised routes to a closed terminus the country has been put on.

Public transport in the UK is the most expensive in Europe. When the Conservatives privatised the railways in the 1990s, we were promised greater efficiency and choice. Instead we got higher prices and reduced services on non-profitable routes. The average cost of a train journey is on average 50% higher than a comparable journey made elsewhere in Europe. According to the pressure group Passenger Focus, in 2009 the average ticket price for a train journey of three to ten miles was £1.85 in France, £2.52 in Spain, £5.08 in Germany, and

£6.92 in the UK. If our public transport was 50% more efficient, 50% quicker than elsewhere in Europe, or had 50% better density of lines than elsewhere, that might be a 50% worth paying. But it isn't. We pay more for less.

Thanks to the Scottish Parliament and the Welsh Senedd, rail transport in Scotland and Wales is cheaper per mile than equivalent journeys made in England. England has the most expensive rail transport in Europe. But with limited budgets which are determined by overall government expenditure in England, there is also a limit to how much the devolved administrations can ameliorate the damage done to a railway network which has been sent down the wrong track by successive UK governments.

An open return from London to Norwich, a distance of 117 miles, costs an eye-watering £108. The same ticket from Glasgow to Aberdeen, a distance of 135 miles, costs £67.10. However in Spain, an equivalent ticket for a journey between Madrid and the city of Valladolid - about 111 miles - costs approximately £30. The return trips work out at 46p per mile in England, 24.8p per mile in Scotland, and just 13.6p per mile in Spain - and the Spanish trip is a journey made on a brand spanking new high speed railway line.

It will take you up to three hours to travel from Glasgow to Aberdeen by train, but only 56 minutes to get from Madrid to Valladolid. The European high speed railway network stretches all the way from Málaga to London, but goes no further. The UK has only the vaguest of intentions of extending it to Scotland, sometime after 2030 maybe perhaps possibly, and none at all of extending it within Scotland. And this is in what they keep telling us is Europe's strongest economy and the greatest Union of countries the universe has ever seen. It's evidently a better together universe that hasn't got high speed trains. The only high speed vehicles Scotland gets from Westminster are the ballistic nuclear delivery systems based on the Clyde.

It's not actually that easy to dicover how much a train ticket is going to cost you in the UK. The traveller is faced with a bewildering range of websites offering special limited tickets which have to be booked a month in advance when the moon is in conjunction with Network

Rail. Travelling to Marr in Aberdeenshire is more complicated than a manned voyage to Mars. Or you can call for advice, and get through to someone in a call centre in Chennai who doesn't know where Aberdeen is.

We have a railway network which does not reach many of our important towns, and which does not connect to large tracts of the country. The paucity of available routes means that work on a line closes the system down as train services cannot be re-routed, meaning that buses bearing the destination "Choo choo I'm a train" are often more common than trains themselves. We're being systematically ripped off by UK transport policies, which eat up public subsidies for private gain. That's why they're called chew-chews.

Our roads are little better, a patchwork of potholes and cart-tracks. Work is only just due to start on the missing link in the M8 motorway linking Scotland's two largest cities - 50 years after the first motorway was opened the direct route between our capital city and our largest city remains incomplete. There are currently no plans to build a motorway connecting Aberdeen, Scotland's third largest city and the centre of the vital hydrocarbons industry, with the rest of the country. Meanwhile the Highlands are even worse served, in any normal country the A9 to Inverness should be the M9, an efficient and well maintained motorway. Instead it's a road which is single carriageway over much of its length and notorious for its accident blackspots. Kintyre and Cowal are regularly cut off from the rest of the country due to landslides blocking the A83.

Within our cities the public transport systems are not much better, the bus services do not integrate efficiently with commuter rail, and - Edinburgh trams aside - there are no light railway systems. Routes connect with city centres, but do not connect other parts of the city with each other. In Glasgow for example, there are plenty of east-west routes connecting the city centre, but you can't get a bus from most of the East End to Cambuslang, which face one another across the river Clyde, or from Easterhouse to Tollcross. Often you have to travel into the city centre and back out again. Integrated public transport systems are effectively non-existent in Scotland, that's a national disgrace in a country which aims to lead the world in combating climate change and reducing carbon emissions.

In an integrated transport system, you'd get a bus from the end of your street a short distance to the local metro station, and then using the same ticket you'd continue your journey to your final destination. In Scotland, following the UK's rampant privatisation model, trains, trams and buses all compete with one another instead of acting in concert.

Barcelona, the capital of Catalonia, has a extensive system of bus routes, a metro system with 11 lines, a number of commuter lines run by the national railway operator, two tram systems with three lines each (and a plan to connect the two systems through the city centre), and a number of heritage routes and funicular railways. The metro and bus routes are administered by a single body, and there are plans to integrate the tram systems and rail lines better with the rest of the system.

The greater Glasgow area is roughly comparable in terms of area and population, Glasgow has the second largest commuter rail network in the UK, a single line subway which has never been extended since it was first opened in 1896, and a system of bus routes which are only accidentally integrated with either the commuter rail or the subway. The buses, subway and trains are all administered separately. A bus ticket isn't valid on the subway, and a ticket for neither is valid on the local train network. To get from where I live in Glasgow to Byres Road in the West End of the city involves a bus journey costing £1.95 and then you have to buy a subway ticket for £1.40. The total cost is £3.35. In Barcelona an equivalent journey costs £1.75, you buy your ticket on the bus then use the same ticket on the Metro.

The lack of a joined up transport policy is a symptom of decades without joined up thinking in UK government which is only interested in public transport in London. Scotland's resources have helped to pay for the Docklands Light Railway, London Crossrail, and the new high speed line to Birmingham. Meanwhile we're stuck in the slow lane. Commuters in the north of England fare even worse.

Even small projects are delayed for years. The proposal for a Glasgow Crossrail service has been on the table for years, and is constantly delayed due to a lack of funding. All such a service requires is the construction of a short chord less than half a kilometre in length to connect the line to Queen Street low level with railway routes to the south west of Scotland. The project would open up the railway system in the West of Scotland allowing for direct and easy connections between Ayr and Edinburgh, and would make the Glasgow Airport link worthwhile. Funding the project must come solely from the Scottish budget. Meanwhile London Crossrail involves digging a tunnel 10 miles long underneath a densely populated city, the project counts as a UK national project and is paid for by everyone in the UK. That's the project which is underway, Glasgow Crossrail remains a distant dream.

Although transport policy is devolved to Holyrood, the overall budget is still set by Westminster. Cuts to transport funding in England have knock on effects in the Scottish budget. Independence offers the chance of a renaissance of Scottish public transport. Scotland doesn't have the powers to renationalise the railways or end the insanity of private bus companies creaming off the profitable routes. The country which once built trains for countries all over the world is now a rusty branch line. We deserve better, and Scotland is rich enough to afford much better.

A modern and comprehensive transport system is vital to boosting the Scottish economy. The only reason we have such poor and expensive services is because of Westminster. Our transport policies have been decided by generations of politicians who think getting a bus after the age of 30 means you're a failure in life. It's time to put an end to that. Let's wave goodbye to the traffic jam of Westminster, the independence train can take us on a journey to a properly integrated approach to Scottish public transport.

June 2014

1 June 2014

£he price of everything, the value of nothing

The No campaign is determined to focus on economics. No matter what the issue, it's going to be spun into the political equivalent of the guy displaying his bum crack in a dodgy repair shop who sucks his teeth and says "Oh It's gaunnie cost ye" before reeling off an incomprehensible list of suction flange regulators, pre-pressed titanium carburettor sprongs, and something that sounds like a sex aid which may be combined with a bum crack in ways which are still illegal in some US states. All of which is going to be ruinously expensive, and really not orgasmic at all. You only wanted a new headlamp, but now you realise that you'll have to convert your car to left hand drive in order to get one. It will be off the road for months, and there's no guarantee you'll get the parts from the Brussels office. EU regulations mate, says the Westminster mechanic.

The focus on economics does not actually have a great deal to do with Scotland's economic prospects after independence, and more to do with the fact that it's an ideal topic for polysyllabic waffle, but there's another reason why Better Together likes talking about the economy. They're spiritually Ukipped. UKIP has a pound symbol as a party logo, which has always been one of the things about the party I've found most unsettling. It's the perfect symbol for a bunch of people who know the price of everything but the value of nothing.

Better Together have been demonstrating that's all they know since the start of the referendum campaign. It must make it all the more painful for them that they've consistently been shown to be wrong about the price as well.

Most people know very little about currency unions, even fewer care about currency unions, but it's a topic that can easily be dressed up in a lot of scary sounding economics and made to sound like it's more dangerous than putting out an electrical fire by peeing on it. Using lots of long words in a discourse about topics most people don't understand and even fewer are interested in is a sure fire way of sounding impressive even when you're talking complete and utter bollocks. It works well in job interviews too, it's what gets a towel folder in Selfridges promoted to Chancellor of the Exchequer - that, and being very well connected socially.

Economics is like linguistics. They'd both really like to be proper grown up sciences that can make predictive theories, but neither are yet capable of giving a full explanation of the topic of their study, never mind devising a means of using current trends to predict future outcomes with any great accuracy. Linguists can tell you that the English spoken in the future will be different from the English spoken today, just as the English of today is different from the English of the past, but they can't tell you what the changes are going to be. It's possible that alicsammin will have completed its journey and replaced the word independence, confusion between the two is already rife in the UK media. America and Scotland will celebrate their Alicsammin Day holidays and we can expect future headlines like "Wales declares alicsammin" or "Westminster negotiates with Cornish alicsammin coalition". Pressure groups will be calling for an alicsammint regulator to sort out the bias in London based newspapers, and the BBC will insist that it preciously guards its alicsammin against government interference and is completely unbiased. Political parties will have to change their names too. "Alicsammin is at the very centre of the BBC's philosophy", the pensioned off UKRAP (United Kingdom Remnants Alicsammin Party) minister who's got the gig as chairballoon of the BBC board of trustees will intone. No one will believe them in the future either, some things will never change.

It's much the same with economics. It's the science where two professors once shared a Nobel prize for saying opposite things, which makes it a handy source of important sounding statements which can easily be spun into fearful warnings, especially because they involve money, lots of it. Bazisquillions of quid.

The scares rely upon a lack of knowledge. For example the often repeated claim that a currency union would only be possible if Scotland surrenders control of all its economic levers to Westminster relies upon ignorance of how currency unions actually work. The Bank of England would determine the base interest rate as it does now, and Holyrood and Westminster would negotiate mutually acceptable borrowing limits. Currency unions do indeed require a measure of loss of sovereignty, but that applies to both parties. Just now, Scotland is represented in the Bank of England by George Osborne and has no say at all. In a formal currency union Scotland would have formal representation. Scotland would have full control over its own revenues, its taxation policies, benefits policies, public spending priorities, and could decide that it wasn't going to invade some Middle Eastern country thank you very much. Claiming that this means Scotland would have less independence than it does under Westminster is the sort of bollocks that George Osborne came out with in his job interview. Or would have done, if he'd had a job interview. He just had a friendly chat with his friend Dave instead.

The truth is rather more boring. Scotland is currently a wealthy Northern European nation, and will continue to be so after Scottish independence, with or without a formal currency union. So after carefully weighing up all the economic arguments, and pondering the consequences at length, I've come to the considered decision that I really couldn't give a toss. Scotland will still be using Sterling, whatever, formal currency union or no. Pensions will be paid, trains will still be delayed, and life will go on as normal. There will be no fiscal paradise, but there will be no economic armageddon either.

I'm no economist, but you don't need to be an economist to spot the essential flaw in economic arguments against independence. If Scotland is indeed dependent upon the rest of the UK in order to maintain a standard of public services comparable to those of other northern European countries, then who is responsible for bringing this undesirable state of affairs about, and why are they not being held to account for it? Vote no so Westminster can continue to ensure the Scottish economy is so weak the country will never be able to stand on its own two feet is not a ringing endorsement of the Union.

Better Together chooses not to answer the really difficult questions by doing all it can to prevent them being brought up in the first place, and its main means of doing so is to go oooooh currency union no.

Other arguments for independence are unanswerable, and throw up questions which Better Together cannot answer. Questions like - getting a chancellor that the electorate of Scotland voted for and not George Osborne. Can you put a price on that? Like being able to vote politicians out of office safe in the knowledge that they won't sneak in via the back door of the House of Lords and continue to influence our laws and public policies - how many quid is that to you? Getting rid of Trident - how much is that worth to you?

Independence is priceless.

1 June 2014

More news the BBC doesn't want to report

So where shall we go today on our journey to independence? There's Jeremy Paxman and his conviction that we're only considering independence because we hate the English, UKIP's Scottish MEP for Kensington Jibberjabber the Hutt has been jibberjabbering about getting a Yes vote overturned because he's in love with neverendums, or it's tempting to have a bit of a dig at the BBC's favourite archaeologist who's been making windswept claims that Scottish people are sleepwalking into independence - when in fact we're paying attention to the independence debate, it's just his programmes we sleep through.

But the news today is news that the Scottish media, particularly its Pacific Quay branch, has decided hasn't happened at all. On Sunday there was a demonstration outside the BBC's Scottish headquarters at the end of what can only be described as a disastrous week for the Mickey Mouse McCorporation and its McDonaldsification of the referendum debate.

The new flagship news and current affairs programme has bombed after a launch that was hyped as much as the London Olympics. Sadly it didn't get a gold medal, or even a bronze. It was left at the starting block and limped off for medical assistance in the first qualifing heat. Almost 90,000 people tuned in to view the first edition of Scotland 2014, but by the end of the week that figure had plummeted to a mere 22,000, approximately the same number of people in Scotland who gave a shit about the Royal Wedding. There are more readers on this blog than that, and this comes to you without £5 million quid of your money being spent on it. Mind you, if someone wants to give me £5 million quid, I wouldn't say no. I'd spend it on bribes in exchange for a yes vote and suborn dog owners with doggy chew toys in the shape of Labour's devo-nono policy. That died without a squeak too.

Not that I'm bigging up the blog or its site stats, 29,000 unique readers and 110,000 page views last month isn't that huge or influential. This is not a national daily newspaper. (Although it gets almost three times the readership of the Guardian in Scotland. Ha ha Severin.) This is not Wings Over Scotland, Newsnet Scotland, or Bella Caledonia, just a quiet and quirky wee corner of the interwebbies full of Scottish political jokes - like the entire output of Vote Nob Orders - self-determination toilet humour, and the occasional foray into Iberian politics, Scottish languages and Glesca Corpie trams. Of course the numeric comparison is not exactly comparing like with like, but it does serve to illustrate an important yah-boo-sucks-to-Ken-McQuarrie rhetorical point.

This is just a wee pisstaking blog devoted to pouring a urine bottle of nasty smells over the Scottish media and Better Together and going HA! It is written by a full time carer during breaks between emptying urine bags and not a highly paid media professional with experience on UK national telly. Moreover this blog makes no effort to promote itself, yet it still gets more readers than BBC Scotland's flagship news and current affairs programme gets viewers. That alone tells you that there is something seriously wrong in the Scottish media. When viewers lose faith in a broadcaster, they seek alternative sources of information. Even Scottish referendum news junkies like me have switched off Scotland 2014 in disgust.

The failure of the programme comes as members of the NUJ at Pacific Quay have making rumbling noises about taking strike action, a political earthquake far more significant in Scottish terms than anything achieved by the ubiquitous Nigel Farage. Nige is never off the telly. After the European elections and the English local elections he's now billed to make daily appearances on Bargain Hunt where he'll scour antiques markets looking for 1950s social attitudes he can try and sell to the public at inflated prices. Then he'll be presenting the One Show as the cosy sofa based face of how very dare you call me a racist, and making guest appearances on the three programmes per day with Great British in their titles. So at least he'll be on the telly slightly less often than he has been of late.

The BBC has largely avoided any mention of its own difficulties, but the ramifications will be more significant in Scotland than anything from Nige or his pal Jibberjabber the Hutt. The staff and (most but not all of) the presenters at Pacific Quay are not the problem with BBC Scotland, they just produce and front the programmes and take the flak for the public manifestations of policies originating from BBC management. It's their professional reputations which are being trashed by Ken McQuarrie and John Boothman, and quite naturally they're not happy about it.

The NUJ had already forced BBC management to concede that the headline round up at the end of current affairs programmes was hopelessly biased because the papers are hopelessly biased, so online media headlines were included too. We have the NUJ and the professionalism of ordinary BBC staff to thank for that, not BBC management. Reeling from cuts and demoralised by poor leadership, staff disaffection was already crystalising around the issue of the BBC's membership of the CBI and the arrogance of management in refusing to recognise that there was any issue at all. Threats of industrial action were already in the air.

And then as the week ended, its new flagship programme gone the way of the Mary Rose, its rotten timbers sunk in the mud off Pacific Quay, BBC's management demonstrated yet again that they have the lightness of touch of an elephant on a steroid rampage, and the tact and diplomacy of Attila the Hun after he's trapped his bollocks in his saddle.

You do not have to be an admirer of the collected oeuvre of Gary Roberston to recognise that if any BBC employee has slogged his wee guts out on behalf of the Corporation, it's Gary. He's pulled long shifts and fronted radio shows in the morning and tv shows at night, all because BBC management have taken a lawnmower to their own grassroots staffing. And for his pains, Gary's getting his jotters because his bosses would prefer to bring up expensively paid journos from London who are clueless and out of touch with what's been going on in Scotland since they high tailed it south in search of career prospects. We're all being short-changed. One Isabel Fraser is worth 3000 James Naughties.

Yesterday Gerry Hassan tweeted that Gary's sacking was "directly linked to outgoings of six fig salaries of Jim Naughtie & Sarah Smith. BBC Scotland management in deep crisis."

He's got that right. BBC staff are up in arms. There are calls for strike action, and the BBC itself is now very firmly centre stage amongst important referendum issues despite the careful efforts of management not to report on the Corporation's own newsworthiness. Boothman and McQuarrie are in for a shock, far more people care about the BBC than care about currency unions, or watch the intelligence insulting Scotland 2014.

The people who should be getting their jotters are John Boothman and Ken McQuarrie. They couldn't even write a successful blog, never mind run Scotland's national broadcaster. It's not the staff or the presenters, not even the most biased amongst them, who has brought this about. We're all biased, the fact that some BBC presenters allow their biases to show is the fault of poor management. But far worse than that, BBC management have brought the organisation to the brink of strike action during the most important referendum campaign in Scottish history, a campaign which could have profound implications for the BBC. That is management failure of the most spectacular kind.

At this juncture in Scottish history, above all others, BBC management should have been keeping its eye on the ball, unfortunately Ken and

John think that keeping your eye on the ball meant they should give us mair bloody fitba instead of intelligent news and current affairs analysis.

Keep Gary. Sack John and Ken.

2 June 2014

¿Por qué no te callas? Juan Carlos shuts up

For those of you who don't speak Spanish *¿Por qué no te callas?* means *Why don't you shut up?* It will be the lasting legacy of Spanish King Juan Carlos of the House of Bourbon, who announced his abdication today. It was the closest thing to a catch-phrase that he had, the Hispanic equivalent of 'We are not amused'.

Juan Carlos uttered the words to Hugo Chávez during an international conference of Spanish speaking nations, when the late Venezuelan president had embarked on one of his speechathons. The event was held shortly after the Spanish government had supported a coup attempt against him, so Hugo wasn't best pleased with the Spanish delegation. Juan Carlos is always uncomfortable when involvement in coups is discussed, and wanted to go and do something more interesting, like shooting endangered species in Botswana. For a while *¿Por qué no te callas?* became the most popular ring-tone in Spain, and across the land mobile phones went off to the sound of the King saying "Gaunnie jist shut it?"

The King used the familiar pronoun *tu* in addressing Chávez, which in Latin America is normally reserved for speaking to small children and social inferiors. The inappropriate use of *tu* can be considered deeply insulting. In the Spanish of Spain people are more likely to call one another *tu*, but whatever variety of Spanish you speak when you address the president of a country during an official summit as *tu* instead of the polite and formal *usted*, it's going to be interpreted as an insult. Chávez had words to say in reply.

Today Juan Carlos has shut up. He's announced his abdication, citing health issues and his age. The truth of course is that Juan Carlos resigned before he was pushed, as the Spanish royal family is mired up to its well upholstered neck in the morass of corruption scandals which have stripped the Spanish establishment of what little credibility it had left.

The official mythology about Juan Carlos was looking tired and tattered long before his daughter the Princess Christina was implicated in the corruption charges being faced by her husband Iñako Urdangarín. According to the official story, Juan Carlos was instrumental in ending the attempted coup in 1981 and so is personally responsible for keeping Spain a democracy. The tale is about as believable as the claims in the UK media that Willnkate are an ordinary young married couple, because ordinary young married couples always live surrounded by sycophants in a palace with a staff of flunkies that your taxes paid for.

In 1981 when Spanish democracy had only recently been re-established after decades of military dictatorship, members of the paramilitary Guardia Civil attempted to take over the Spanish Parliament and reinstate military rule. As it became clear that the plotters had failed to gain the backing of the majority of the armed forces, the king appeared on national television and appealed for a return to democracy. He was then credited with saving the nation. However the truth is rather more murky.

In 2012 the German newspaper Der Speigel published a report claiming that during conversations with a German diplomat, Juan Carlos revealed that he had considerable sympathy with the plotters. Although few seriously believe that the King had an active role in planning the coup attempt, allegations continue to circulate that he knew about the plans beforehand and guarded his silence until he was sure the coup had failed. The allegations were fuelled by the widespread public knowledge that Juan Carlos was besties with some of the more senior and shadowy plotters from when they attended military college together.

After the economic crisis struck Spain, leaving thousands jobless and facing dispossession and eviction, the King naturally wanted his subjects to know that he felt their pain. He demonstrated this pain by falling downstairs and breaking his hip in a luxury safari resort in Botswana where he'd buggered off on a freebie so he could go and shoot elephants. He'd declared just a few days before that he spent all his time worrying about the fate of the 55% of young Spaniards who were unemployed due to the financial crisis.

Juan Carlos likes shooting things, in 2006 he was subject of controversy after shooting a drunk bear while on a junket to Russia. The tame bear had reportedly been drugged with alcohol laced honey and released in front of the royal party's guns. A later official Spanish investigation claimed that the bear had not been shot by the King himself, but rather by some other member of his party, so that made it all OK then.

However by and large Spaniards were prepared to overlook Juan Carlos's affection for killing things, hunting with guns is a hobby which does not have quite the same upper class image in Spain as it does in Scotland. They were even prepared to overlook the numerous allegations of serial wick-dipping, one common nickname for the King was *el Rey de Suiza* 'the King of Switzerland' because it was rumoured that he spent more time there in the company of assorted actresses and female members of the minor German aristocracy than he spent in his official residence in Madrid. It is well known that relations between the King and his wife Queen Sofia have been strained for decades. There are persistent rumours that he has a number of offspring who are not officially recognised. The King is facing two paternity suits, which until now the Spanish courts have refused to look at since the King is above the law. It's unclear what will happen now he's abdicated and is no longer King, and presumably no longer above the law.

People in Spain overlooked a lot, but what they were not prepared to overlook was the King's hypocrisy. He made a big play of suffering with the Spanish people in their time of economic crisis, but there he was going off on luxury freebies with German princesses. And at the same time members of his own family appear to be up to their necks in the financial sleaze that's a characteristic of the Spanish political establishment. Public revulsion was reaching a pitch, and so the King decided to abdicate before he was pushed. It's the only way he was able to secure the succession for his son Prince Felipe, who will now become King Felipe VI.

Paul Kavanagh

Meanwhile Catalonia continues on its path to a referendum and independence. As one Catalan commentator noted, the first Spanish Bourbon monarch to rule Catalonia was Felipe V, and the last will be Felipe VI. Catalans are still determined that the Spanish monarchy will shut up for good.

El rei ha mort, visca la república catalana!

2 June 2014
The Kezia Dugdale Show

I wasn't going to do another post today - youse have had two already within the past 24 hours, and there are other things which need to be done. But then I made the mistake of having a wee look at Bella Caledonia's take on the BBCrisis, my jaw hit the floor, then continued on its downward trajectory and at the time of writing is passing through the central core of the planet on its way to the Antipodean Islands.

It was already rumoured that BBC management had decided to axe the popular Headlines programme on Radio Scotland, presented by Ken McDonald carefully avoiding any references to Swiss Tony. Today Bella Caledonia have inside information that the BBC managers in their immense wisdom, and with their sensitivities towards accusations of arseduppery at the McCorporation finely honed after a week of disasters, are going to replace Headlines with the Kezia Dugdale and Andrew Wilson Show. That Kezia Dugdale. Labour MSP for listseatshire, former aide de camp of George Foulkes, Lord of the Dance with Polis.

You'd think Kezia would be far too busy to take on a new gig at the Beeb. She's already got a job as an MSP and burns the midnight candle writing articles for that stout supporter of the Labour party and resolute campaigner against the evils of homophobia and racism, the Daily Mail.

On the talk page of her Wikipedia entry it helpfuls informs us that the article about Kezia is of "low importance". So's Kezia, and if her public profile was in any way commensurate with her talents that's how she would remain. BBC management and the Daily Mail beg to differ.

After all the ordure BBC management have caused to fall upon Pacific Quay over the past few years, and at the end of a week when they've sunk so low that even Nick Clegg could lecture them from the moral high ground, facing strike action and on the brink of institutional collapse, at the very time they need to do something, anything, that might just start to stuff toilet paper into the gaping chasms that are sinking the ship of the national broadcaster - they get rid of another experienced Scottish broadcaster and give us Kezia Dugdale.

In the surreal imaginings of BBC managers, Kezia is going to be a new, neutral and totally unbiased presenter during a referendum campaign. Wrap your head around that. Go on, I dare you. So in the words of the BBC's last remaining icon, the brand new Doctor Who, the Time Lord from Planet Thick of It - What. The. Fucked. Fucking. Fuckety. Fuck.

At the very time the BBC in Scotland is crying out for responsible in-depth reporting of the referendum by competent journalists, they're replacing the last remaining Radio Scotland programme which enjoys a modicum of respect with the semi-articulate Labour MSP Kezia Dugdale as its amateur journo.

But the new show is being balanced by Andrew Wilson, the former SNP MSP who is decidedly on the right of the party. So that makes it all OK then. And won't create the impression in any potential voter's mind that a vote for indy equates to a vote for the right. Or that the referendum is just another political party ding-dong. It really is all about alicsammin then. Let's turn the programme into an audio book version of the Scotsman's comment pages, that will really interest the listeners.

Imagine thinking BBC managers would countenance such a thing. Evil cybernats.

Actually they probably didn't countenance it, because that would imply they exercised a degree of thought that would have passed through "Kezia Dugdale you've got to be joking" long before it had got as far as page one in the introduction to the Machiavellian playbook of radio scheduling. They just didn't think at all, except to note that

Paul Kavanagh

by axing the Ken show they'd save money on expensive staff salaries which is better spent massaging Jim Naughtie's ego. They just didn't care about anything much else. Public perceptions? They're not paid to consider what the little people think.

When faced between possible explanations for a disastrous series of events, it's invariably the case that it's going to be a cock-up and not a conspiracy. BBC management's lack of management skills are such that they've managed to transform a cock-up into something that is indistinguishable from a conspiracy. You have to start off with a natural talent for incompetence and then go and take special remedial classes in order to get that bad. But they are effectively unaccountable.

We didn't need any more evidence that BBC management do not give a toss about public opinion. But just so we get the message we've now been presented with the splattered corpse of the BBC's reputation, fairness dripping into the gutter amidst bloody gore, with a smoking gun and Ken MacQuarrie and John Boothman standing there holding the trigger, the brains of BBC viewers and listeners splattered over their suits. And in an expensively tailored pocket is a handwritten statement saying "We done it, it was us, and we don't care" signed by the pair of them in their own excrement. They're just taking the piss now.

Sack them. Sack them now.

But they won't be sacked. So instead ponder this. This is the broadcasting system that the Unionist parties tell us is us getting the best of both worlds. Which is utter nonsense. Catalonia has several tv networks and numerous radio channels, including a 24 hour news channel of its own.

I've made this point several times before, but it needs to be shouted from the rooftops - Gagauzia has its own national broadcaster - and no-one even knows where it is. Gagauzia is a tiny self-governing scrap of territory in the poorest corner Moldova, the poorest country in Europe. It's the homeland of the Gagauz people, a small community of Turkish speaking Orthodox Christians about 150,000 strong. Gagauzia has fewer people than Aberdeenshire. But unlike Scotland, the Gagauzians are allowed to decide their broadcasting policies for themselves.

The parlous state of BBC Scotland has little to do with not enough money being available - the money is available, but it sure as hell isn't being spent on Scottish broadcasting. Scottish broadcasting has been reduced so low entirely because of political decisions made by the Westminster parties. They like to keep us ill-informed and stupid.

All three Unionist parties have now revealed their devolution plans, and every single one of them has explicitly ruled out giving Scotland the same degree of political control over its own broadcast media as is enjoyed by the Autonomous Territory of Gagauzia.

There's only one way that the state broadcaster in Scotland can ever be held to account, and the smoking gun held to the head of senior management to force them to improve their Scottish output - and that's to vote Yes and get a Scottish national broadcaster. This embarrassing farce has gone on too long.

3 June 2014
Resetting the debate dial back to stupid

Ok, time to be calm and tranquil after yesterday's traumas. It's all a bit eek at times this independence campaign isn't it. Every day the no campaign manages to find a new way of insulting your intelligence. There can be no nation on the face of this planet which has been collectively patronised as comprehensively as Scotland is being patronised by the UK media. It wouldn't be so bad if the UK media was inhabited by sage geniuses and wise elders, but it's actually populated by shrieking hysterics and navel gazers whose sole claim to intellectual and moral superiority is that they are commenting on venal and self-serving UK politicians and a kleptomaniac business class.

And they're still at it. A new ogre has entered the scare story steeplechase as several of the existing monsters fell at the fence of public opinion, broke their legs and had to be shot. Or at least we're being told it's a new ogre.

Following up on the wreckage of the CBI, which took a tumble at Credibility Gap giving itself several compound fractures and its jockeys a severe headache, comes Business for a New Europe. A new business organisation with a new way to scare you anew. They have Business in their title, which means that they're serious people with serious money and we ought to sit down like good little worker drones and say well that's us telt then.

According to BNE, Scotland is faced with years in the Eurowilderness and it will be "next to impossible" for Scotland to join the EU on the same terms as the UK - which will of course sail on unperturbed because it hasn't occurred to anyone at either Business for a New Europe, the UK Government or the UK media that Scotland might mount a legal challenge to the rest of the UK's dubious claim to be the sole continuing state.

But the new scare story is not actually very new at all. The new BNE report - if that is what it is - is essentially the same as a report written by the very same Dr Daniel Furby over two years ago, which had already been dismissed as an "error strewn fantasy". The same basic errors are in evidence in today's media stories too. For example BNE claims that Scotland would find it "very hard" to negotiate an opt-out from the Euro, which completely ignores the essential point that Scotland doesn't have to negotiate a formal opt-out from the Euro at all.

There's no need, as Czech Prime Minister Petr Nečas pointed out in January 2012 - before he was forced to resign in in a corruption scandal - saying that his country doesn't need a formal opt-out from the Euro. "No one can force us into joining the euro ... We have a de facto opt-out," he said.

Nečas was referring to requirement to join the ERM for two years before a country can join the Euro. Membership of the ERM is entirely voluntary, and EU members are at perfect liberty to delay membership of the ERM for as long as they see fit and can delay membership indefinitely until the times and circumstances are suitable for them. The Czech Republic doesn't think there will ever be a suitable time or circumstance. It's a de facto opt-out available to all EU member states, and is also the route chosen by Sweden, which likewise doesn't wish to adopt the Euro. Scotland doesn't need a formal Euro opt-out either. You'd think EU expert Dr Daniel Furby would know that. He probably does, but it doesn't suit the Better Together narrative to mention it.

Better Together keeps wanting to reset the independence debate dial back to "stupid". The BBC and the rest of the UK media are their willing accomplices. It's much easier than actually doing some research when you want to write a news story.

Nowhere in today's reports in the UK media does it say that the BNE story is a reheated scare from over two years old which has already been discredited, debunked, and thrown on the scrapheap of Project Fear rejects. I won't bother debunking it all again here, Newsnet Scotland published an article debunking it in March 2012.

So why is Business for Europe and its error strewn EU fantasies popping up again now? It couldn't possibly be because the CBI now has less credibility on Scottish independence than BBC 1970s presenters have on child welfare, and Project Fear is in desperate need of a business organisation whose name isn't going to provoke guffaws and derision in order to pour cold water on the aspirations of independentistas.

Business for a New Europe is another of those completely apolitical and totally neutral think tanks cum lobby groups which just happen to be run by a personal friend of senior Westminster politicians. The chairman and founder of Business for a New Europe is a certain Roland Rudd, whose first job before he founded a PR company and made a fortune was as a policy advisor to David Owen and the SDP. He later developed links with New Labour, and worked closely with Peter Mandelson. Roland invites Nick Clegg and his missus round for tea, kindly offered to help Tony Blair's son out with his first Saturday job and advised Tone himself after he finally gave in to Gordie Broon's temper tantrums and pondered what to with himself in retirement in between giving interviews to the Guardian denying he's a war criminal. Roland's family are politically well connected too, his sister is a Tory MP.

Amongst its board of advisors, Business for a New Europe boasts such luminaries as Leon Brittan the former Tory Home Secretary in Thatcher's government, Roger Carr the former director of the CBI, former Chef de Cabinet to Neil Kinnock and ex-UK senior civil servant Andrew Cahn, a former British ambassador, and a veritable roll call of individuals who've stepped out of UK public service into well paid jobs on the boards of companies. None of whom have any other interest than telling Scottish voters the truth.

So quite a lot like BBC Scotland and the UK media then.

4 June 2014

Alive and awake in the dreaming time

There's a wee meme, more a baby memette, in the Unionist media, that Scotland is sleepwalking into independence. And there was us thinking that we were running so fast we were all windswept and interesting. Except Neil Oliver, who's just windswept. But do a wee check on Google for the words Scotland, independence, and sleepwalking and you'll pull up Michael White in Monday's Guardian *Scottish independence: Are we sleepwalking to the brink?* in which he warns us that we're sleepwalking towards doom and disaster, *Scotland in danger of sleepwalking into independence* from the same paper last November, and in the same month *Is Scotland sleepwalking into independence* from the Telegraph and on and ZZZZzzzzzz walking on.

The doom and disaster towards which we're sleepwalking is apparently a legacy of lasting bitterness. This is because there are people in Scotland disagreeing with one another. Shocking, isn't it. I always thought that disagreeing was a defining characteristic of Scottish people, and it generally involves swearie words. Put six members of my family together in one room and you have 36 arguments. Disagreeing is kinda what we do, and we do it quite well with remarkably few incidences of stabbing. Perhaps Michael finds this odd because he has one of those stiff upper lip Great British families where you don't actually know if relatives are on speaking terms because they don't talk to one another anyway. We can only speculate. It's something else we can disagree about.

However, I know for a fact that no one in my family has ever tried to commit grievous bodily harm upon another member since that unfortunate incident with my mother's cousins, a bottle of Eldorado, the TV scheduling, a walloping over the head with a lawn mower, and a dozen stitches in A&E. And that was so long ago that there were only two black and white channels to argue over. But some people get quite obsessional about the Beechgrove Garden, so you can appreciate why passions ran so high. We've all kissed and made up since. Although the patio was concreted over, come to think of it … and no one ever did see that garden gnome again. It had black eyebrows, white hair, and a heart of stone.

We're having a lawnmower free independence debate though. Haven't seen much sign of Westminster's ornamental garden gnome recently either. Aren't they extending the patio at Westminster when they renovate it at a cost of squillions? Hmmm... Just keep your eye open for Gordie Broon with a lawnmower.

If your only source of information about Scotland was the UK media, you must think that the place is full of undead folk with their eyes shut and deaf to all warnings, doing the zombie walk. It's almost as if the Guardian and Telegraph political correspondents have confused Braeheid Shopping Centre with the House of Lords. Which is unfair, as there are strict laws preventing the shops in Braeheid from touting decrepit products long past their sell by date.

Scottish voters, at least according to the UK media, are clearly not thinking things through, by which they mean we've heard what UK politicians and the UK media have had to say, and we're not convinced by it, because by and large what they're saying is childish tripe. It's our fault for not listening, not their fault for not having a convincing case. How dare we persist in thinking this isn't about Alicsammin.

But what comes across most strongly in Mikey's lament is his sense of propietorship. Scottish independence for Michael represents his "losing an essential part of himself", even if that's a part that exists only in his imagination. Scotland is the essential part of Michael's self that allows him to espouse British nationalism without realising he's a nationalist. We're the multinational windowdressing in the Westminster shop of horrors. We're not the ones sleepwalking, but Michael is complaining that we are rousing him from his slumber.

Michael seems to be irked because he's suddenly got issues with his identity, so this is supposed to be a debate about identity, and Scotland's not cooperating. We're not having the debate he wants us to have. Stop with that civic stuff. Scottishness is monodimensional, it's only Britishness that can act as a container for the kaleidoscope of identities which we all possess. It hasn't occurred to Michael that you can be a hyphenated Scot without the other side of the hyphen being occupied by British. There are Asian-Scots and Polish-Scots, Franco-Algerian-Scots, and Anglo-Greek-Scots. Me? I'm Scottish all the time and Irish when it suits me.

Scotland did the identity debate a generation ago, when we took a long hard look at what it meant to be Scottish in Britain. Artists and thinkers took apart the tartan bedecked Haste Ye Back souvenirs and the red white and blue Silver Jubilee memorabilia and realised that it is the Britishness that's the confused and confusing part of the identity question, not the Scottishness. It's Britishness that obscures and Scottishness that illuminates the answers. But that was a debate that scarcely impinged on the consciousness of people like Guardian politics correspondents. The referendum debate had scarcely impinged on their consciousness either, until the currency fear bomb exploded in George Osborne's face and the opinion polls went the wrong way.

They're playing catch up, trying to rush their way through 40-odd years of constitutional, political and cultural debate in the dwindling time between now and 18 September. They're still stuck on the identity question, Scotland has long since moved on. The Guardian and Telegraph correspondents of this world look around the independence debating house for answers to their own questions, they see only an empty identity entrance hall and think we're still in bed. We're in the living room, living and having a ball, and we're about to open up the patio doors and let in the international air.

The UK media is for the most part missing out on the real debate, so it's effectively not happening as far as they are concerned. This revolution is not being televised. The real Scottish revolution is happening in countless conversations in the pub, in jokes between friends, in families sitting around the telly, in laughs and shouts and smiling faces, in walks in the park in the rain, in the privacy of our own thoughts and hopes. It's a very Scottish revolution, and it's unlike anything that's ever gone before. This is the revolution of the pie and pint, the revolution of tea and scones. And we've got our eye on the jam too.

But Michael, ah Michael. Michael will have had his tea.

Sleepwalking? This country has never been more alive. The crusty crud of Westminster has fallen from our eyes and Scotland is awake to potentials that had previously been closed, shut away in the dark closet of the cringe. Now our eyes gaze upon vistas undreamt, our voices have a range we never knew, and for the first time in our lives we've learned how to hope. There's a pathway through the mountains, and we know how to climb. And it feels so good.

We're excited at the countless possibilities that are springing up like Scottish bluebells after a long cold winter of the soul. We're not sleepwalking to independence, we're casting off our crutches and getting up on our own two feet, we're running towards the future with hope in our hearts, we're dancing towards it with our own rhythm, we're singing dreams into being with our own tunes. We're following the songlines to a future we seize in our own hands.

It's good to be alive in the Scottish summer, and it's even better being awake. Alive and awake in the dreaming time.

5 June 2014

#UkDividend

Danny Alexander's mythical £1400 UK Dividend will buy you -

1. Enough Lego to build a model aircraft carrier with planes, or one rivet on the two aircraft carriers the UK is building without planes to put on them.

2. Remedial classes in Government Work for Dummies for Danny Alexander because he doesn't know the difference between the Foreign Office and the cleaning rota in the giftshop in Cairngorm National Park.

3. Alistair Darling's mortgage interest repayments on his second home.

4. Build a Lego foodbank.

5. Study at an English University for a fortnight.

6. 50 hours of grief counselling for Nick Clegg after the last election results.

7. 500 Lego people so you can have your very own House of Lords.

8. Pay for a publicity agent who realised that mushy peas aren't a Scottish thing - but it's all Oop North when you're an upaid intern on your gap year between private school and Oxford.

9. Pay an ATOS assessment team for a day.

10. One threatened doing from Ian Davidson.

11. A five minute TV interview with Nigel Farage.

12. Enough drugs to make you forget for a few days that Lego comes from a small independent country that's doing much better for itself than the UK will ever do.

13. A tax cut for a millionaire for a week.

14. Two square metres of flooring tiles in a new London Crossrail station.

15. A lifetime of being patronised by politicians who think we're children.

16. The week's wages of a low ranking civil servant who will invent statistics to order.

17. Cleaning up radioactive particles from a beach towel sized area of Dalgetty bay.

18. 2.5 seconds of Scottish Questions in the Commons.

19. Half of the funeral bill for a person who commits suicide after their benefits are cut.

20. 1% of the production costs of a TV programme with Great British in its title.

21. The plane ticket and hotel bill for one night so a UK civil servant to go to Spain and solicit foreign involvement to influence a democratic Scottish debate in favour of a No vote.

22. 0.3 seconds worth of UK annual national debt.

23. A new telly after you broke the last one by throwing a cup of coffee at it when George Osborne talked down to you.

24. 0.04% of Margaret Thatcher's state funeral costs.

25. Donate it to the Yes Campaign and end this farce for good.

Of course it won't buy you anything at all, because Danny Alexander just pulled a number out of his backside. Vote No for an imaginary dividend that only exists in Wee Danny's lying mind, or Vote Yes and get the priceless dividend of being in control of your own destiny and politicians you can vote out of office when they patronise you - and you can be safe in the knowledge that their pals won't be able to give them a seat in the Lords as a booby prize.

6 June 2014

The Obamaniacs of the UK press

I didn't rush to make a blog post after the Obombashell news that the American prez has made some anodyne and highly qualified comments about Scottish independence. Because the truth is I don't really give a toss what Obama said, and I expect you don't either. In this we are merely expressing the equivalent Scottish view to the widespread public opinion in the USA regarding Scottish independence. They don't give a toss either, the only difference being that whereas we've all heard of Barack Obama, very few people in the USA are aware that Scotland is holding an independence referendum. The number of people in the USA who know about Scotland's referendum is probably lower than the number who think we're already independent. It may be a higher number than the number who believe Scotland is a part of Ireland, but that's a bit of a coin toss.

This is actually, believe it or not, a positive. The only way that the Scottish independence campaign would impinge upon the consciousness of yer average truck driver in Arkansas or a shop worker in North Dakota would be if members of the McTaliban were kidnapping US servicepeople and force feeding them the Collected Works of the Prophet Al-Iqsammin. Scotland's US obscurity is a good thing - it means we're not causing any upset. "Down with the Great Satan USA" is not a pro-indy campaigning slogan in this referendum.

Obama recognised this. The way he phrased his comments was significant, and careful. The US prez said that "from the outside" the UK seemed to be working, refraining from any comment about how it seems to be working from the inside. He did not have to add the "from the outside" qualifier, but he did.

Obama's the American president, he only is where he is because he's negotiated the snakepit of Democrat party infighting, and the brutal slugathons of two presidential campaigns. American politics is all about dressing up tiny little policy differences and pretending that they're significant. Since there is possibly even less difference between the two main US parties than the fag paper separating Labour from the Tories, window dressing is all they've got. It's not the shop contents that matter from the outside, it's the window dressing. Obama is very well aware of the difference between how a political system looks on the outside and how it appears on the inside - knowing that is his job. As far as Scotland is concerned he's on the outside, which means he can safely file it under "not my problem".

But he went further. Obama twice stated that this vote is for the people of Scotland to decide, and it was significant that he did not explicitly urge Scottish voters to stick their cross in the Nope to Hope box. The truth is that the USA can live with the result whatever way it goes. Not that this was apparent from the hysterical coverage given to the Nope to Hope comments by U-Kok-Upists.

Can you imagine the uproar there would have been in the UK media if Obama had said something along the lines of "Go for it Scotland. Wipe the smug look aff thon Davie's face. We don't think much of the lightweight either." It was never going to happen. That is not how international politics works. The diplomacy rule is that when asked about a contentious decision whose outcome does not have a great impact upon you either way, you do your best to minimise the impact of any comment you make and you don't do anything to embarrass your hosts. That's especially true when your hosts have explicitly asked you to say something about the situation. That's pretty much what Obama did. He has no control over the hysteria of Better Together and the wild dog pack of the UK press.

In the US coverage of the Obamaplea the headlines were more interested in his much stronger comments about the UK remaining united with the EU. Oddly these comments didn't receive much comment or publicity in the UK media. Perhaps they wouldn't have gone down too well with the swivel eyed readers of the Telegraph. The Wall Street Journal's headline on the speech screamed: *Obama says UK should stay in EU.* And in much smaller letters the sub heading said: *As for the Coming Scottish Independence Vote, President Says US Satisfied With a 'United' UK.* Spot the difference in importance rankings?

Meanwhile the right wing Washington Times reported: *Obama: hard to see UK benefiting from leaving EU.*

Here's what Obama had to say about the prospect of an in-out referendum on the UK's membership of the UK:

"And it's hard for me to imagine that project [the EU] going well in the absence of Great Britain. And I think it's also hard for me to imagine that it would be advantageous for Great Britain to be excluded from political decisions that have an enormous impact on its economic and political life ... I'm sure the people of Great Britain will make the right decision."

That's a much stronger statement which comes as close as possible to an outright plea to vote against leaving the EU without actually saying "For God's sake don't listen to nut-job Nigel." But it was scarcely mentioned in yesterday's focus on his bland comment about Scotland.

Did anyone seriously expect anything different? Just look at how the equally anodyne comments of Mark Carney of the Bank of England were spun. A studiously neutral speech saying that the bank would do whatever politicians told it to do became a warning of economic armageddon if Scotland continued to share the pound with the rest of the UK.

Intriguingly, although amidst the welter of UK press reports yesterday I can't track it down now (perhaps a reader can supply the link - this is citizen's journalism after all, so you're expected to do some of the legwork yourselves) there was a wee menshie that the Scottish Government was surprised by Obama's intervention. They were not surprised that he'd said something blandish in support of not giving the US more changes in international relationships because they've already got their hands full, they were surprised that he'd said so now - the Scottish Government hadn't been expecting anything from him until much nearer the vote. The fact it's happened now means that it will be lost and forgotten by the time September arrives, and Better Together has already shot the bolt of the biggest celebrity endorsement it's going to get.

All that Obama's comments showed was the Scottish media is not fit for purpose. But we knew that already, and it's one of the reasons only seen from the inside that led us to this independence debate in the first place. All that really happened yesterday is that the voters of

Scotland got more confirmation that if we want to live in a country where grown up and informed debate is possible, we need to vote yes in September.

7 June 2014
Visibly reducing the appearance of Danny Alexander

So you can't buy any Lego figures with your UKDivvie after all. Lego has written to the UK Government to tell them to remove all images of their product from the Treasury's daft political adverts. The most iconic brand name from a successful independent northern European country of 5 million people does not want to be associated with a campaign to prevent another northern European country of 5 million people from becoming successful and independent too. Lego has complained to the UK Government that its figures were used without permission and without its knowledge, and their use runs contrary to the company's policy of political neutrality. Lego has pointed out that they make toys for kids to help them learn through imagination and play, not political propaganda. The Treasury has difficulty seeing why this is a problem, since all the adverts were doing was playing political games with imaginary money.

Unlike real Lego adverts, the Treasury Lego adverts are paid for by the very people who are being advertised to. They're taking your money, and spending it so they can persuade you to keep on giving them your money. You might say that's exactly the same as real Lego adverts, which are funded by the profits made by the company which in turn come from people buying Lego. But at least Lego buyers get tiny plastic people who appeal to children in return for their money ... Oh ... I see what you mean ...

Commercial advertising is legally prohibited from making claims which are untrue, which is why they're so often hedged about with statements like "visibly reduces the appearance of wrinkles" which is what you put in an advert when you want to say "reduces wrinkles" but the sciencey bit won't back you up. "Visibly reduces the appearance of" doesn't actually mean anything specific. You can visibly reduce the appearance of wrinkles by putting a paper bag over your head.

It's a lot cheaper too. They could just as equally say "visibly reduces the appearance of Danny Alexander", which would probably do much more to guarantee increased sales although it still wouldn't get him off the telly talking pish about non-existent UKDividends. Mind you, in Danny's case we'd all prefer the paper bag over his head. That's a look that would definitely work for him.

But really unlike real Lego adverts, political adverts are not bound by the advertising standards code. They can say any auld bollocks that they like - as long as it's not defamatory or incitement to commit a criminal offence. It doesn't matter whether they're produced by a Government department, a political party, or an astroturf campaign funded by rich Tories outside Scotland and designed by a marketing and branding specialist which was clueless about the market in question. Adverts produced by parties and campaigning groups during an election or referendum campaign are not regulated by the Advertising Standards Authority. You can complain to them all you like, but they'll act like your appearance has been visibly reduced and you've got a paper bag over your head.

This is not actually a bad thing. We live in a democracy and it's a fundamental human right to make a clown out of yourself in a public place. You can't legislate against vanity and shortsightedness, and you can't legislate against vain and shortsighted people voting. Or standing for office, as a quick perusal of most elected politicians will demonstrate. When you combine vanity, shortsightedness, and a whopping great dose of self-interest, you produce a situation where even theoretically intelligent people will come out with the most stupid of claims. Claims whose relationship to reality started off as tangential, before corkscrewing out of control into some fantasy land inhabited by people who say they believe in a federal Britain and are prepared to vote for a pig in a poke. Which brings us back to Danny.

Danny Alexander, and the rest of Project Fear, are under no obligation to tell the truth. And in a functioning democracy there can be no obligations put on them to tell the truth. Otherwise it threatens our own right to make clowns out of ourselves in public places. But the UK isn't a functioning democracy because there's no one doing the sciencey bit. A healthy media sector ought to be broadly representative of the society it serves. The media is supposed to investigate the claims made by political parties and campaign groups, to uncover inconsistencies and highlight falsehoods, and where it the media sector as a whole is representative of the entire population, that happens successfully. That's the sciencey bit in political advertising. And it can even be done without resorting to made up words that you've trademarked.

But instead the traditional UK media is a campaigning group themselves. The problem arises because almost all the media outlets have the same stance. Positive news for the Yes campaign is sidelined or ignored, while there is little or no investigation into the inconsistencies and falsehoods of the No campaign. It's perfectly fine for an individual publication to have a stance. Dante Alighieri said that the darkest places in Hell are reserved for those who stayed neutral during a time of moral crisis. Having a open and publicly stated stance is in many ways more honest than attempting to be neutral, whose only saving grace is that it's more honest than pretending to be neutral. State broadcasters hadn't been invented in Dante's day, and he hadn't considered the possibility that the darkest places in Hell might have a sub-basement with a BBC Scotland studio.

But on further investigation it wasn't Dante who said that the darkest places were reserved for the neutral. It was JFK misquoting Dante. This is precisely the sort of investigative reporting that's not being done in the UK media. You should always investigate what a politican tells you, even when it's JFK or Barack Obama - never mind Danny with a paper bag over his heid. The only investigation the UK media likes to do is to investigate ways it can be spun into a blow for Alicsammin.

The missing check to the missing balance is the sheer impossibility of holding politicians to account. When they belong to the established UK parties, voting them out of office doesn't work. They just get a seat in the Lords as a consolation prize. You'd imagine that after pissing off the electorate to the extent that the voters kick them out of office would mean it's the voters who are in need of consolation, but in the

UK it works the other way about. He'll just become Baron Danny of Paper Bag.

Danny Alexander is so dumb even his imaginary friends want to play with other kids. Even Westminster's imaginary Lego friends don't want to play with them any more. And these are the people who want to make all the rules for the rest of us. These are the people who are quite happy with a media that doesn't investigate their idiocies and ensure that's all we get.

Let's vote yes in September and take Danny's toys away from him. It's the scientifically guaranteed method of not only visibly reducing the appearance of Danny Alexander and the rest of the plastic figure princes and princesses of Westminster, but giving them them sack for good.

8 June 2014
The shamelessness of John Reid

John Reid, before he got a peerage for services to Tony Blair, insisted on being called Dr Reid. Now he's Dr Frankenstein Lord John Reid Baron of Warmongering UKOK - and he's very upset that nasty independence supporters are abusing poor defenceless politicians. The abuse here is not a reference to John being felt up in a dark alley by a strange man who's offered him a bagful of security consultancy sweeties, he's complaining that people are saying rude things about him. Like calling him Dr Frankenstein Baron of Warmongering, or wondering aloud if you can barge your way through to the front of a crowd at the scene of an accident shouting 'let me through I once wrote a thesis on the slave trade in 18th century Nigeria'.

John wrote a thesis on the evils of the Atlantic slave trade in the 18th century, which saw millions of people kidnapped, transported across the Atlantic in chains, and held in brutal captivity on Caribbean islands, making a small number of rich and privileged American and European plantation owners even richer and more privileged. Nowadays John does work for the Chertoff Group, a company founded by Michael Chertoff the former US Secretary for Homeland Security. John Reid's boss had a key role in running the US detention centre at Guantánamo - kidnapping people, transporting them across the Atlantic in chains, holding them in brutal captivity on a Caribbean island, and making a small number of rich and privileged American and European security company directors and consultants even richer and more privileged. But it's probably abusive to point that out, unless you adopt managementwankspeak in which case it's synergy.

John's made a career out of abusing voters' trust. He doesn't think that we should be allowed to complain about it, he doesn't think that now he's no longer in elected office he should cease influencing our laws, and he's upset that he's not being accorded the respect given to Dr Frankenstein - although if a horde of Transylvanian peasants bearing torches and pitchforks were to turn up at his front door John would be the first to complain that they'd been sent by Alicsammin.

It's a funny thing respect. When you demand it, it's a guarantee that you're not going to get any. Especially in Scotland where the answer to the question "Do you know who I am?" is "I know *whit* ye are." Respect cuts two ways, you only get respect when you show respect. John's career has demonstrated that the only respect he has is the respect he demands from others in order to compensate for his lack of self-respect, or indeed his missing sense of shame.

Now John is attempting to link his own demands for respect to the respect due to those who fought and died on the beaches of Normandy. You can accuse John of many things, but the ability to recognise when you're being crass isn't one of them. Today in the Scotsman there's a report that John has been criticised for linking the commemorations of the D-Day Landings to the independence referendum. He claimed that the landings showed that "men and women drawn from Scotland, England, Ireland, Wales – ordinary men and women [...] did extraordinary things and did it together" with the clear implication that it's only possible for ordinary people to do extraordinary things under the aegis of the Westminster Parliament.

John's comments are an insult to the memory of those who died on the beaches of Normandy - it is not for him or anyone else to tell modern generations what the personal motivations of the fallen were. My Irish republican grandfather served in WWII, he took no part in the D-Day landings and thankfully he survived the conflict, but he was not fighting for King and Country, he was fighting against fascism. Those who died on the beaches of northern France died for noble personal reasons of their own, we mourn them because they were humans and individuals, and the war cost them their lives. They are no longer here to tell us what they did it for or what it meant to them. That's why we mourn and commemorate them John, not because the event glorifies the corrupt and venal politicians we're lumbered with today.

John Reid's remarks are also an insult to the thousands who fought and died on D-Day who were not Scottish, Irish, Welsh or English. The Canadians, Poles, Americans and the rest who fought and died were not doing so in order to preserve the Westminster Parliament's rule over Scotland. They were fighting against the evils of the Nazi regime. The D-Day Landings were not a Westminster affair, they came about because of co-operation between independent democratic nations who freely chose to act in concert against fascism.

There is no positive and substantial case for the Union. John Reid is reduced to doing what he and his ilk accuse independence supporters of - resting their case upon emotive and selective misreadings of a past that is long past. D-Day will remain in history, whatever happens in September. And Scottish people will continue to mourn the loss of the brave and noble servicemen and women from all over the globe who came together to fight against a great evil.

And hopefully, in the future, the politicians in a Scottish Parliament will not employ that sacrifice to make a cheap political point in a democratic debate. If they do, we'll be able to express our displeasure by voting them out of office and removing them from public life. Westminster does not give us that option with John Reid - and that John, is why we are having this independence debate now.

9 June 2014

100 days until the door opens

There was a nice wee story from the Basque Country that got lost amidst the Obamahoo and the AndyMurrayha that's dominated the press over the past few days. Last week final year students in Basque high schools sat their university entrance exams. In the maths paper there was a question related to Scotland.

The students were asked to calculate the confidence levels in an opinion poll about the Scottish independence debate. According to the poll cited in the exam question, 600 people had been questioned of whom 450 were going to vote yes. Pity it wasn't a real poll, but it was still nice to be noticed in a Basque exam paper.

The independence debate is often framed in terms of uncertainties, but it must be certain that Scotland has never enjoyed such a high profile in the world as it has right now - and that is entirely due to the fact that we have embarked upon a peaceful and legal campaign to recover Scottish independence. Across the world, people are paying Scotland an attention that they never paid this small, damp northern European country before. We're in Basque exam questions, in headlines in Bolivian newspapers, and in current affairs in Canada. Basques, Bolivians and Canadians are talking about us, but you won't find the BBC saying so. They only report the men from DelMonte and the manufactured astroturfing of the No campaign.

And it's not kilts, whisky and the Loch Ness monster that they're talking about in far flung places. They're talking about 5 million people who may just possibly challenge the right to rule of the traditional political elites, and who will do so entirely peacefully - without a shot being fired, without riots, without civil unrest. We need to thank ourselves, we need to pat ourselves on the back. We need to tell ourselves just what we've achieved here. This is truly a precious and beautiful thing. The most contentious political debate imaginable, an independence campaign - a debate which usually starts in violence and ends in war, and Scotland is doing it her own way, a peaceful way, a democratic way, a way filled with laughter and smiles. We are ordinary people, we do extraordinary things. And we do them far far better than our closed minded and narrow visioned political class could ever do. We're showing them how politics should be done.

All over the world people are paying close attention to this debate, yet here in Scotland most people have little idea just how remarkable the events of the Scottish Summer really are - because our media is full of the complaints of politicians, bewailing rude names on Twitter as harbingers of the end of civilisation, likening growls from wee mongrel dugs to the devastation of Hiroshima. The litany of negativity never ceases, the pre-arranged scares and concerted fears ramp up ever higher into the stratosphere of surrealism.

There's 100 days to go before 18 September. An independent Scotland will not be a paradise, we will have challenges, we will have set backs, but Scotland will decide her own destiny. The fate of this country will lie in the hands of its own people. The Yes campaign is creating a picture of the Scotland that is being born - a colourful collage of Celtic knotworks, Asian floral patterns, Italian masterpieces, English miniatures, African prints and Polish design. A people in movement, moving towards the world and open to it. We're looking to the future, we're making it up as we go along, and we're making something beautiful. This is what we can do when we put our minds to it when we step outside the pencil box that Westminster has put us in, a box where the only pictures are grey still-lifes, frozen and fearful.

100 more days of the No campaign, po-faced and pettit lipped, lost in past glories, tellers of scare stories, the warmongers, back hander bungers, benefits cutters, ifs and butters, Iraq-invaders, Trident cravers, casino bankers, Thatcher thankers, clueless dopes, killers of hope, asset strippers, swivel eyed Kippers, nay-sayers, truth slayers, BBC junkies, peerage monkeys, dependency touters, ProudScot doubters, expenses blaggers and privatisers, poison daggers and boardroom misers - lecturing Scotland on our antisocial behaviour while they tell us to vote for No future, a future that goes from crap to crappier. The best they can offer is that things might just get back to being crap again.

Compare and contrast. What sort of country do you want to live in. You can live in a land of hope, or you can live in the land of the po-faced and the pettit lip. A country where you're told what's good for you while the rich get ever richer and inequalities widen, where emigration in search of work is described as a Union benefit. Or an independent country governed by people who live here, people we can vote out of office if they do not live up to our expectations.

A Slovene friend once told me why he supported independence for his small country. He said: I love my country because it is small and harmless, and it needs people to look after it.

This small and harmless country is ours, and we will look after it because it is our home. Westminster politicians said that they wanted to turn the country into a land of owner occupiers when they sold off the family silver, we will answer them by telling them we'll be the owner occupiers of our own land. All that interests them is how they can use our resources and our talents to further their own careers. Let's make the future of Scotland our priority, the future of our children, our grandchildren, and generations yet to come. Let's show the world what a small and harmless country can do, and be a voice for peace and justice in this world.

The key is in our hands. 100 days to go until we open the door and step out into the fresh clean air.

10 June 2014

The clunking fistula

The clunking fist has clunked again. Gordie's gone and punched above his weight right through the middle of Alistair Darling's carefully contrived strategy to frighten seven shades of shite out of Scotland. BBC Scotland's Westminster correspondent has been speaking to Labour MPs, and they're not best pleased. Not displeased about Ali trying to terrify their constituents, they're fine with that. Scaring the ordinaries is part of the job when you're an unaccountable Labour MP in a safe Scottish seat, the worst that will ever happen to your career is getting bumped up to the Lords. No, they're displeased that Gordie's stuffed himself like a buttplug in the diarrhoea production plan.

Some have tutted. A couple raised an eyebrow. But largely they screamed traditional Scottish miffednesses - most of which start with words beginning with f, and contain words starting with a c and ending with a t. Someone said Gordie was a bit silly. That was probably St Dougie the Diminutive, because it would spoil his Holy Wullie image to swear at a reporter. He is however looking up Bible verses containing references to arses.

The reason for the ire is that Project Fear ignored Alicsammin's repeated demands that it was only reasonable that the First Minister of Scotland should debate with the Prime Minister of Scotland, and had ridden out the resultant fireworks. Gordie's just relit the blue touch paper by doing the unthinkable - conceding that Alicsammin might actually have a valid point. This breaks the first rule in the Project Fear playbook, which was carefully written out by Alistair in green crayon large enough even for Gordie to read it. But Gordie was too busy hiding under his sulking rock and wouldn't come out until he was offered a speaking engagement where he got star billing.

The calls for Davie Cameron to get kicked from one end of a debating chamber to another by Alicsammin now have Gordie's voice in support. The guy who was in Davie Cameron's job before him thinks that Davie ought to man up and sacrifice his dignity for Britain. Lots of people in Scotland think that too, but mainly because we relish the prospect of witnessing Davie the PR man having the P ripped out him and rammed up his Rs.

The Labour party is now frantically seeking a stool softener for Gordon. Anything, in fact, that will help to flush him away, even a loo brush would do but Alistair has refused to supply the badger hair even though diving into toilets in search of putrid rot is his sole area of expertise outside expenses maximisation. Gordie has taken it upon himself to be the Saviour of the Union and to point out all Alistair's errors in the process, and everyone else's. But mainly pointing out Alistair's, because getting one up on an entry on his ever lengthening list of Them What Done Him Wrong is how Gordie understands politics.

It is conceivably possible that Gordon Brown and Alistair Darling are the same person. They never appear in the same room together, and rumours persist that Gordon is what Alistair turns into after he's been hit on the heid by a flying Nokia. What's harder to conceptualise however, is how Gordon thinks he can be the reasonable Dr Jekyll to Alistair's nasty Mr Hyde when both of them are equally monstrous.

Gordie's been making some very unhelpful statements. In his interview with whoever believes he still possesses a nanogramme of credibility - essentially Gordie, his wife, and the UK media - he demonstrated his usual out-of-touch sensitivity to anything that he can't take credit for himself, saying:

"I think the nationalists want people to think it's Scotland versus Britain or Scotland versus England. And I think sometimes the government itself has fallen into this trap."

Which isn't actually true. It's the No campaign that wants independence supporters to make out it's about Scotland versus Britain or Scotland versus England, and Labour is caught up to its scrawny neck in the maws of that trap just as much as the Tories. They're really quite upset that the Yes campaign hasn't obliged, so they've decided to act as though it was true anyway, in the hope that it will become true if they repeat it often enough.

This is a tactic which is doomed to failure, as anyone who has stood in a newsagents shop clutching a worthless scratchcard will realise. It doesn't matter how may times you assure the shopkeeper you have won the jackpot, it doesn't alter the fact that your card shows only a lemon and an unlucky number. The only payout you're going to get is a Labour MP worded expression of miffedness and an instruction to leave the premises and go and commit an auto-erotic sexual act, which is pretty much the payout Scotland's voters have been delivering to the No campaign.

But the big problem faced by Project Fear is that Gordie, one of the starring ogres in the Unionist Horror Show, has decided that he'd prefer to be played by Shrek in the slasher movie version - Mike Myers being possibly the only Holywood actor whose Scottish accent is less contrived than Gordon's. Gordie believes that Project Fear needs to be less ogresome, and should try to persuade Scots of the benefits of a diet of mouldy slugs instead of scaring us with claims that there would be no slugs at all after independence.

So as a result, and as if No Future wasn't unconvincing enough, Scottish voters are faced with four competing versions of nawness.

There's the devonotatall of official Labour, the devohaha-we-out-devoed-Labour-and-it-wisnae-hard of the Tories, the federal fairyland of the Last of the Lib Dems, and now Gordie's endogenous devo growth theory - which grows like a bleeding polyp up Alistair's bum. There is theoretically a fifth version, but Nigel Farage hasn't told Jibberjabber the Hutt what it is yet - although it promises to be a version of the Lib Dems' federal fairyland but set in a Narnia that Romanians need an entry visa for.

The only commonality all four possess is that they have an equal chance of successfully negotiating the Commons and the Lords and passing into law, as much chance as the four flavours of ogre icecream, Gordie's mouldy slug, Alistair's sour grapes, Tory spoiler and the Lib Dem's no-we-are-still-here-actually, have of surviving the mince-frying glares of an increasingly impatient Scottish public.

The No campaign was already hopelessly divided and at odds with itself. Gordie's just opened up a new crack in the not-so-united front. Poor Gordie, he used to have a reputation as a clunking fist, now he's a clunking fistula.

11 June 2014
The No Slogan Slogan Paradox

Better Together has unveiled its new campaigning slogan because "better together" just wasn't working for them. It's difficult to make the claim that you're better together when your own campaign team refuses to appear in the same room, Labour and the Tories hate one another, Alistair Darling and Gordon Brown hate one another, everyone hates Danny Alexander, and John Reid hates everyone. They want us to hold fast to the Union, but they themselves are only able to hold fast to their grudges.

Worried that Scottish voters have begun to ruminate on the philosophical contradictions of a better together campaign composed of separate pieces which are not only independent of one another but have declared open warfare, and which is nominally led by a man whose grasp of the campaign is as reality based as Colonel Walter E Kurtz, panicking party leaders have decided on a change in tactics.

Better Together vehemently deny that they're in any difficulties, not at all, the No campaign has been going as swimmingly as a drowning man. They've changed their slogan because they're doing so incredibly well that they only want to experience the minty freshness of a newly coined slogan all over again.

So now they're saying No Thanks instead. Contrary to the rumour that the new slogan is based upon the answer received every time someone in Better Together suggests that Gordie and Alistair ought to kiss and make up, it was instead a product of the No campaign's very own branding new grassroots movement, Saatchi and Saatchi - famous for advertising standards greats such as "Labour isn't working" illustrated by a dole queue the length of the billboard. The slogan won Thatcher the 1979 General Election whereupon she proceeded to lengthen the dole queue off the billboard, down the street, and right up the M6 taking in a scenic tour of job centres in every industrial community all the way to Wick. Saatchi and Saatchi, no thanks.

In keeping with the 1980s post-industrial wasteland vibe, the new slogan looks like it was ripped it off from another famous campaigning slogan of the 80s, Nuclear Power No Thanks. Only that doesn't really work for Westminster either does it. Trident missiles, no thanks. Tory governments, no thanks. ATOS disability interviews, no thanks.

Patronising Guardian editorials, no thanks. Nicolas Witchell, no thanks. BBC weather map, no thanks. Or to give it its correct technical meteorological designation, fuckin BBC never heard of Equal Area Projection ya cartographically illiterate designwanks weather seen from London diarrhoea coloured map, no thanks. Although admittedly that last one is not such a snappy Yes slogan.

Other possible No slogans were ruled out by Saatchi and Saatchi as they didn't play well in focus groups. Naw no noo nae need was briefly considered, but that sounded uncomfortably like an ambulance was arriving and was thought likely to cause needless upset amongst elderly Tories with angina. This threatened to obliterate half the No campaign's grassroots membership, leaving them with only Labour cooncillors and people who want to be Labour cooncillors to rely on. However some of those were uncomfortable with the proposed new slogan too, as it brought on incidences of Post Traumatic Stress Disorder after some mistook it for the sound of a polis car on its way to investigate some dodgy property deals. The only enthusiastic support it got was from George Foulkes, who said it reminded him of a dance invitation.

After ruling out the sound of an ambulance, the Saatchi team thought it might be just as well to go the whole hog and adopt the catch phrase from Mork and Mindy. Naw noo naw noo. Which might have worked, although it does bring up the uncomfortable reminder that the comedic pratfalls of naive spacecadets from another planet is quite a good description of the No campaign. But then other catchphrases from the programme were considered, and Naw noo naw noo Shazbut just didn't sound like a ringing endorsement of the Westminster Parliamentary system.

Better Together has a tin ear for language. The English language - that's supposed to be a Union benefits lads and lassies, and they cannae even use that right. Irony is meant to be such a British value too. For shame. They're making Michael Gove upset, and that's supposed to be Al-Iqsammin's job. But you require a tin ear for words when the words you utter are at such variance with truth that even the most shameless liar would cringe internally when they opened their gob, at least if they weren't comedically clueless aliens from planet Nawnoo Nawnoo.

As a lover of words and snappy slogans, it's immensely puzzling to me why the No campaign persist in choosing slogans that are so easy to subvert. This is all the more puzzling since these campaigning slogans are supposed to appeal to the inhabitants of a country which is famous for its verbal subversion. Scotland even invented an entire genre of poetry devoted to slag offs in verse, the fine art of flyting. And we also gifted the English language with the word fuck. It's a Scottish word, first attested in the poetry of Dunbar - makar, versificator, flyter and piss taker for the Scottish crown - in 1503. So it's not like we don't have previous for taking the piss and swearing a lot.

But to be fair, it's very difficult to come up with a decent no slogan. Just say no makes you sound like the kids from Grange Hill channelling Nancy Reagan. However the real reason for the difficulty may be explained by the very word slogan itself. It's a loanword into English from Scottish Gaelic, a mangling of the phrase *sluagh ghairm* which means "shout of the host". This is not how to say "last orders" in Gaelic, host in this instance is a more polite and twee Walter Scotty type word for "uncontrolled horde of very pissed off Scottish people". In Gaelic the term referred to the battle cries of the clans.

Since a whole horde of shouty uncontrollable Scottish people is the philosophical opposite of all that Better Together stands for, you can appreciate their *sluagh ghairm* difficulty. Westminster prefers its Scottish people silenced and under control, and it's difficult to come up with a good popular and catchy rallying call to action for a message whose essence is "Shut up and sit down". It's the No Slogan Slogan Paradox, coming soon to the collected works of a Scottish philosopher that Dougie Alexander can misunderstand.

Independence, yes please.

13 June 2014

Not caring

There have been a number of interesting developments in the independence debate over the past few days. Gordie Broon drove his clunking fist through the middle of the tissue of lies, wishful thinking, and self-delusion that passes for a case for the Union by calling for Davie Cameron to debate Alicsammin and delivering a rebuke by proxy to Alistair Darling's strategy. Meanwhile, Alistair was caught in clear agreement with the proposition that the yes campaign is "blood and soil nationalism", seemingly in the belief he's actually participating in the D-Day Landings up against Nazis; Danny Alexander and the UK Treasury's legomen have gone back into their wee box after being caught out trying to illustrate fantasy figures with fantasy figures; the Tories have out-devoed Labour - the self proclaimed party of devolution has been outdevoflanked by the heirs of Michael Forsyth just ponder that one for a few minutes; Obama came, he scared and no one really cared - and then we discovered that Obama had only said anything at all because Number 10 had specifically asked him to and had specifically briefed a BBC reporter to ask him about it; Better Together has tacitly acknowledged its strategy was failing and has been forced to rebrand itself with an uninspiring nonslogan which was immediately subverted by Yes voters; the BBC continues to lurch from one PR disaster to another. It goes on and on in a litany of failure, of incompetence, and collapse. And it's hardly being reported in the Scottish media.

The big stories this week? A very rich person who has been an open supporter of the No campaign since there ever was a No campaign gave them a lot of money, and is upset because of childish insults on the Internet. And an ordinary carer is upset because of abuse on Twitter and Facebook. Alicsammin is being personally blamed.

But there's worse. Far worse. Someone said one of the most abusive things to come out of the indy campaign - and even me, with my penchant for swerrie wurds, hesitates to say it. It's just pure venomous evil. So for purely illustrative purposes mind, and please don't anyone get upset, because honestly no one is being accused of anything, but [gulp] here goes : "See you. You're related to a former Lord Provost of Glasgow by marriage."

That one cut to the quick with me, because I am actually related to a former Lord Provost of Glasgow, and not even by marriage - we share

DNA, at least a couple of toes' worth. The shame eh. Thankfully we're only distant relatives and we've never met, otherwise I'd be curled up in a wailing ball of tears with a snottery nose, too traumatised to type. But as it is I'm mortified and actually glad for once that I can't get out the house to face the boos and jeers that come with being related to a former Lord Provost.

Now this is not to say that it is not news that someone received abuse on the internet. Internet abuse and bullying is unpleasant. Unpleasant in the childish way of weans slagging one another off in the school yard and with pretty similar consequences. Although it is peculiar that yet again no substantive evidence of this horrendous abuse has been presented and forwarded to the polis.

I've had far worse and got over it. In fact I've had far worse and ignored it, and I'm an ordinary fulltime carer too. One who doesn't receive any care relief so I can go off and attend Labour Shadow Cabinet meetings. I'd love to have someone come in and take over my caring responsibilities for a few hours - even if it meant I'd have to go and talk to Johann Lamont. I really do get that desperate for a break sometimes, and if that doesn't make you feel sympathy for the plight of full time carers nothing on this planet will.

Some of us ordinary full time carers are stuck indoors day in day out because we're caring for people who cannot be left unattended and our Labour local authority will only pay 80% of the cost of 2 weeks of respite care annually, and won't pay for care relief for a few hours a week so you can go out and do ordinary things like going to the bank to sort out problems with an account, or go and buy a new bed because you can't share a bed with your partner any more and have been sleeping on the sofa for the past six months. I can only get out if I can find someone to sit with my partner, whose care needs are such that he needs a properly trained carer. You can't just ask a random friend or relative to deal with some of the things that need to be dealt with. So I spend my days cleaning up shit and piss, only to sit down for a cup of tea and a rest and see nothing but shit and piss on the news. That's the glamorous life of the full time ordinary carer.

Care relief isn't easy to afford when it can cost up to £15 per hour and you only get £60 a week Carer's Allowance to live on. I've had to turn down a number of invitations to attend Yes events because I can't afford care relief. A social life is a dim and distant memory. Then I see Labour's ordinary carer spokesperson appearing on telly and at high profile events. It's nice for her that she can get out and develop a public persona, a career and a life that's not filled solely with changing incontinence pads and cleaning up piss. I'm glad she's escaped the crushing social isolation that so many ordinary carers are trapped in. I'm happy for her, and pleased that carers get any sort of attention at all.

Meanwhile Labour has rubbished the Scottish Government's proposals to increase Carer's Allowance by a measly tenner a week if we get independence. "Who's going to pay?" screams Labour. The carers will always pay. Always. We pay in worry, in stress, in the loss of our careers, in our isolation and loneliness, in our flesh and our creaking bones and aching backs. We're the ones who shoulder the burden for the party of British redistribution, along with the disabled, the poor, the disadvantaged, and the marginalised, so the People's Party can continue to sook up to millionaires and City bankers.

Just saying like, as an ordinary carer who hasn't been a member of the Labour shadow cabinet for the past two years.

It is news of a sort that a carer has received abuse on the internet. It's just not especially surprising news, and neither is it especially informative news unless you find it surprising and informative that some people say childish and stupid things on the internet. Magrit Curran says childish things every time she opens her gob, but the BBC still takes her seriously.

However we are being told that this is a phenomenon specific to the independence campaign, when this is very far from being the case. Some of the worst instances of online abuse, name calling, threats, and bullying I've seen online were in a forum devoted to model trains. Some people take the detailing on the latest Hornby model steam engine very seriously. The abuse doesn't come solely from model train enthusiasts who support Scottish independence. Model train enthusiasts are clearly malevolent.

It's all a part of a very clear strategy, to demonise supporters of independence in an effort to dissuade undecided voters from engaging with arguments for independence. That was always the strategy all along, only now it's reached a fever pitch because the polls are narrowing and canvass returns on the ground show a much stronger position for Yes. The No campaign is losing, and they know it. There *is* a concerted and organised campaign of abuse and vilification, and it's coming from Unionist politicians and the mainstream media.

All this is unpleasant and upsetting, but it doesn't get me down. I've dealt with worse. When you spend your days dealing with real shit, invented and non-consequential shit is of no great concern. The reason it doesn't upset me much is because it's not going to work. Campaigns of demonisation and vilification can only have any chance of success when the targets are a tiny minority. If you don't know any members of that tiny minority then you'll believe the demonisation and vilification, it will affect your perceptions.

But that's not the case in Scotland's independence debate. Just about everyone in the country knows independence supporters, in their families or amongst their friends. We are not a tiny minority. We are everywhere. Personal contacts vastly outweigh media reports in terms of their influence. The number of independence supporters is greater by at least an order of magnitude than the number who are likely to be persuaded to vote no because of media slurs and smears. And that number is smaller than the number of people who will be disgusted by media misrepresentation of a campaign whose members are known to them personally. All that it will achieve is yet another nail in the coffin of mainstream media credibility. It's simple arithmetic.

And the reason I'm so confident? Because I've been here before, as I've pointed out in a previous blog post - Witch hunts and who's afraid of who. Unlike independence supporters lesbian and gay people are a relatively small minority, we were subjected to a similar campaign of media hatred and vilification during the AIDS crisis of the 1980s. And look what happened there - we won.

The hatred and distraction techniques are a sign we are winning. Don't be afraid, don't be discouraged. Don't care. And always always remember - when someone demonises you, it means they are afraid of you. And that means you are the one with the power, the power of the

Scottish nation in movement towards a self-determined future. Face to face, conversation to conversation, we're changing minds, we're changing history.

And there's nothing they can do to stop us. That's why they're so scared.

14 June 2014
Searching for a miracle

Better Together No Thanks, shortly to be rerebranded as BeTNoTh because the perfect brand image for the Union is casino capitalism presented by a BBC weather announcer, are in a spot of betterbother, again. This time it's so egregious that even the Scotsman is having a hard time putting a positive spin on it. So it must be really bad then. Because that's like your doting granny admitting on national TV that you are, in fact, just a wee bastert.

It turns out that Better Together - remember when it was still Better Together, ah the nostalgia - made their annoying cinema advert in BBC Scotland studios with a BBC crew. Oh what a tangled web they weave when they're politically neutral at the Beeb. The advert, the Scotsman primly tells us, was "divisive" amongst cinema audiences, which is apparently how booing, cat-calling and throwing popcorn at the screen are described in the doucer parts of Edinburgh. So another quality production from BBC Scotland then. Actually that's unfair, it was all very professionally done. It was the content that was shite, and that was entirely down to Better Together.

The nice wee deal between Better Together and the BBC was, we are assured, a perfectly normal commercial transaction of the sort that the BBC often negotiates with film production companies. A film production company pays the BBC commercial rates to make use of BBC studios and crew and it's all perfectly legitimate and above board. Or in layperson's terms, Better Together used money raised to finance the production of pro-Unionist propaganda, which was paid to the BBC so it could finance the production of its own pro-Unionist propaganda, and pay its membership subs to the CBI. So that's alright then.

The BBC's own guidelines don't just say the Corporation has to remain neutral. They also say that the Corporation must not do anything which might look as though it is not neutral. This looks like it comes as perilously close to breaking the BBC's obligation to remain politically neutral as setting your Honda Civic on fire, dropping a 15 tonne block of concrete on the smouldering remains, and recycling the wreckage into a crackly radio receiver that can only pick up Kaye Adams, looks like it comes perilously close to scratching your car's paintwork.

It's all looking to be as big a flustercluck as the launch of Scotland 2014. BBC Scotland has been teetering on the brink of strike action for weeks, demoralised staff are deeply unhappy at the damage being done to the BBC's reputation by their own bosses. This latest episode in the Pacific Quay soap opera may lead staff to take strike action. Ken MacQuarrie and John Boothman are about as popular as JR Ewing with the cast of Dallas. They're hoping that once the referendum is over they will wake up and discover the events of the past 12 months have all been a dream. It used to be speculated that BBC Scotland might fall apart after the independence referendum, now it's looking increasingly likely that it will fall apart beforehand.

Better Together, or is it No Thanks? Or is it Acanchi's Vote Nob Orders or have they died a death like United with Gordon? Still think Vote Nob Orders was a good brand name then? And what happened to that Vote Nob Orders supergroup? Did anyone ever actually listen to that song all the way through? It's hard to keep up with the rebranding and the relaunches. What is the No campaign called this week? No Campaign, No Name. At least that's kind of snappy and alliterative. And they're led by a bunch of no-marks, so there's a sort of cosmic balance about it - don't chi think? Someone ought to tell them that it's hard to take uncertainty warnings seriously from people who're uncertain what their own name is.

But then it's hard to take any sort of warning seriously when it comes out of the mouth of Alistair Darling. Alistair's got a special way with words. In his own mind he's quite right to say that the Scottish independence campaign isn't civic nationalism at all, because Alistair's got a neighbour who votes SNP and he definitely doesn't drive a Honda. It's a German car, although it does have very badly damaged paintwork. And he can't understand why people are getting upset over the blood and soil reference. Yes supporters are up to their elbows in soil and blood. It's well known that SNP Falkirk maintain a crack squad of Beechgrove garden fans who terrify innocent Labour party committee members with displays of nationalist nasturtiums. And just the other weekend at Yes in the Park, evil followers of that even eviller website, the one with a logo that looks just like a German eagle if you take your glasses off and scrunch your eyes up, were making rolls and black sausage. Black sausage, made from blood that is. In German it's called Blutwurst - blood sausage. You need more proof than that? And they were flaunting their nationalist rolls and black sausage quite shamelessly. Some people even got accused of being related by marriage to a former Lord Provost of Glasgow. It's carnage out there.

Anyway, in other news, the No-whitever-they-call-themselves-this-week campaign have now also got the very tough sell to the Orange Order that they're marching behind the Pope. And just before marching season too. So that's ... eh ... a blessing.

Or at least the Pope is against Scottish independence if you pay heed to Unionist politicians, which isn't the same as the real world. Project I'm Afraid I Can't Remember My Own Name are clearly praying that the news can be spun into a deffo threat of excommunication if you dare to vote yes. They've already got the fire and brimstone courtesy of George Cataclysm NoCulture Robertson, now they want the eternal damnation as well.

However Pope Francis didn't actually say that he thought Scottish independence was a terrible idea, he just pointed out that independence campaigns tend to be somewhat fraught, and that each country is unique and deals with different issues. Both of which are what you might call rational and sensible observations, and not exactly revelations from God that voting for independence will result in plagues of boils and toads. Danny Alexander is a one man plague of boils, so at least Westminster's already got that one covered.

However when you go and read the original interview, given in his native Spanish to the Barcelona newspaper La Vanguardia, the Pope hasn't actually said anything in support of Nob Orders No Thanks. La Vanguardia, although published in Barcelona, is a Spanish language publication owned by commercial interests in Madrid. Intriguingly, three Catalan newspapers owned by non-Catalan commercial interests have recently had new editors appointed by their owners, all of whom are opposed to Catalan independence, one of whom is the new editor of La Vanguardia. Possibly that's a miracle, but the Pope wasn't asked to comment. But it's interesting to note that the reporter on La Vanguardia asked the Pope a very leading question of the sort usually found in Better Together sponsored opinion polls. The exact question to which Pope Francis was replying was "Does the conflict between Catalonia and Spain worry you?" To which the expected answer was naturally "Oh God yes."

But that's not what the Pope said. Here is his reply in the original Spanish, followed by my translation.

Toda división me preocupa. Hay independencia por emancipación y hay independencia por secesión. Las independencias por emancipación, por ejemplo, son las americanas, que se emanciparon de los estados europeos. Las independencias de pueblos por secesión es un desmembramiento, a veces es muy obvio. Pensemos en la antigua Yugoslavia. Obviamente, hay pueblos con culturas tan diversas que ni con cola se podían pegar. El caso yugoslavo es muy claro, pero yo me pregunto si es tan claro en otros casos, en otros pueblos que hasta ahora han estado juntos. Hay que estudiar caso por caso. Escocia, la Padania, Catalunya Habrán casos que serán justos y casos que no serán justos, pero la secesión de una nación sin un antecedente de unidad forzosa hay que tomarla con muchas pinzas y analizarla caso por caso.

"All division worries me. There is independence by emancipation, and there is independence by secession. Examples of independence by emancipation are the Americas, which emancipated themselves from European states. The independence of a people by secession is a break up, sometimes it's very obvious. Let us think about the old Yugoslavia. Obviously, there are peoples and cultures which are so diverse that they cannot be stuck together even with glue. The Yugoslav case is very clear, but I ask myself if it is so clear in other cases, in other peoples which until now have been joined. They must be studied case by case. Scotland, Padania, Catalonia. There will be cases which will be just and cases which will not be just, but the secession of a nation without a prior history of forced union must be handled very carefully [*the Spanish idiom is 'taken with many clips/tweezers'*] and analysed case by case."

This is scarcely a Papal Bull ruling in favour of Westminster. It is a bit of a shame that the interviewer didn't think to ask the Pope about Las Malvinas, because it would have been fun to watch the UK media spinning that one. However it may be worthwhile to point out at this juncture that the Catholic church in Scotland is entirely independent in its organisation from the Catholic church in England and Wales.

The independence of the Catholic church in Scotland was assured in 1189, when a Papal Bull was issued recognising the Church in Scotland as a "special daughter of the See of Rome", meaning that Catholic bishops in Scotland were directly answerable to the Pope alone, and not to the Archbishop of York as was asserted by the Norman monarchs of England. It was an affirmation that the Kingdom of Scotland was not subject to the Kingdom of England. The Catholic clergy were outlawed in Scotland during the Reformation, but in 1878 the Catholic hierarchy was re-established as a special daughter of the See of Rome. In the eyes of the Catholic church and Canon Law, Scotland is an independent nation already. Which is an interesting Osservatore Romano on Pope's comments on the Scottish independence campaign.

If they were looking for a miracle to raise their cremated campaign from the dead, the Pope has not obliged. It's looking more and more as though Scotland will excommunicate Westminster.

But not to worry, God himself will shortly intervene directly on behalf of the No Really You Need To Tell Us What To Call You Campaign - just as soon as Tony Blair gets back from his speaking engagements on the directorship lunch circuit.

Update: I've been asked for a clarification of the Spanish phrase 'tomar con pinzas' the Pope used in his interview with La Vanguardia. Its literal translation is "to take with tweezers", and in the Spanish of

Spain it can be used as an equivalent of "to take with a pinch of salt", however it lacks the same negative implications found in the English phrase. This is the choice of translation used in the Scotsman, and it gives the incorrect impression that the Pope believes that Scottish or Catalan independence are in some sense unbelievable or unacceptable. That's not what he meant at all. In Latin American Spanish (and the Pope is, remember, Argentinian) the sense of 'tomar con pinzas' is better expressed by the English idiom "to handle with kid gloves" - in other words it means that the topic must be handled with great care and sensitivity. I translated it as "to handle very carefully" as I thought this was the most neutral translation.

15 June 2014
Groupthink

There was an interesting interview with Scottish journalist Iain MacWhirter published today in the Basque newspaper Deia. In the interview, Iain talks about the decision taken by the Sunday Herald to support independence, and explains that if there is a No vote, a distinctive Scottish media has no future. The Scottish press is overwhelmingly owned by commercial interests outside Scotland, and if there is a no vote, Iain fears that Scotland's media lose any claim to being a national media and will continue its descent into becoming a tartan branch of the English regional press.

Talking about the role of the Scottish media in the referendum campaign, Iain described it as groupthink. Scottish journalists and Scottish Unionist politicians inhabit the same small world, all have the same world-view which they characterise as reality. This leads to heavily biased coverage of the referendum, coverage which the Scottish media is convinced is neutral and even-handed. Severin Carrell of the Guardian's quaint and charming belief that he's a neutral player in the referendum is a case in point.

There was a perfect example of such groupthink displayed on the BBC's Scottish Politics Show today, when journalist Kirsty Scott made the jaw-dropping assertion that it was unreasonable for Alicsammin's press officer to point out to the press that ordinary mum and carer Clare Lally was in fact a member of the Labour shadow cabinet.

If I had only known that being a full time carer exempts you from all and any scrutiny or criticism, I'd currently be resting louchely on a chaise longue, dressed in an embroidered smoking jacket, waving a cigarette holder and dispensing bon mots, while Torcuil Crichton did all the housework wearing nothing but a gold spangled thong and Alan Cochrane in arseless leather chaps fetched my slippers. Bend over Alan, you've been a very naughty boy.

And Kirsty Scott could do something useful with herself, like taking an evening class in plumbing and waste management. She clearly doesn't believe that her job involves investigating the claims made by political parties or the private companies involved in health and care provision, so she's obviously underemployed. At least if she learns plumbing she'll be able to do something constructive to help flush out the sewer of Scottish journalism in which she works.

Kirsty has previous involvement in journalism about carers' issues, in 2011 she wrote a puff piece for the Guardian bigging up a subsidiary of a private equity company, Care UK, which has a number of local authority contracts to provide care services. Care UK has benefited immensely from the creeping privatisation of health and social care services introduced by Labour and enthusiastically promoted by the Tories.

But all is not as rosy in the private equity care garden as Kirsty would have us believe. In 2010 Care UK were the subject of controversy after it came to light that they had been making sizeable donations to the private office of Tory health spokesman Andrew Lansley - who then went on to introduce more back door privatisation in the English NHS.

The previous year, 2009, Care UK was also in the news after losing a number of contracts with local authorities in England following a series of complaints about inadequacies in the company's service provision. Not that Kirsty thought to mention any of this in her hagiographic Guardian article a year later. Her Guardian puff piece was rightly met with outrage in carers' blogs and forums.

So it seems that Iain MacWhirter's fears that Scottish mainstream journalism risks descending into an amateurish occupation filled with folk writing puff pieces for private companies have already come to pass. Since her Guardian piece was published, Care UK have gone on to attract yet more government money, courtesy of the Tories' creeping privatisation, and have come under fire for their tax-avoidance strategies.

PatLallyInlawGate has attracted considerable interest amongst Scotland's carers. You can't talk about a "Caring Community" though, because none of us can get out of the hoose long enough to commune with one another over tea, scones, and sympathy. But I have managed to talk to some other carers and care assistants about the events of the past week. While, as fellow carers, more than anyone else we understand, appreciate, and respect what Clare does as a carer, no one I've spoken to has been impressed by her response to the online abuse she received. The attempts to blame Alicsammin's press guy for nasty online comments made by random punters are unconvincing and clearly politically motivated, as was Clare's refusal to accept the man's apology. Refusing to accept the apology was undignified, and that was the point at which Clare lost the moral high ground in the eyes of many of Scotland's carers. But it's also obvious that had she accepted the apology, the story would have died - and that's not in the interests of the Labour party or the Scottish media groupthink.

It is interesting to contrast this episode to a similar episode during the General Election campaign of 1992, the War of Jennifer's Ear. In an election broadcast, Labour made a big play of the story of a young girl who had waited a year for a simple operation for an ear condition. But it turned out that Labour was misrepresenting the issues. In the brouhaha which resulted, the original question of health care was lost and the media focused on an investigation of Labour's attempts to use a vulnerable person as a political tool to misrepresent and manipulate the narrative of an election campaign. Labour went on to lose the following election and we got another five years of Tory government.

In the War of Clare's In-Laws, the media is not talking about carers and carers' needs - they're talking about an entirely mythical orchestrated campaign of online abuse from evil cybernats and its supposedly unique role in the Scottish referendum campaign. And we're being told by Scottish journalists that it's unreasonable to investigate Labour's attempts to use a vulnerable person as a political tool to misrepresent and manipulate the narrative of the referendum campaign.

We live in a country where private companies take profits from the funding provided for care provision, then use some of that money to donate to politicians who promote greater private sector involvement. Meanwhile Scotland's journalists write puff pieces about the companies and praise the creeping destruction of a comprehensive state system of care provision, while condemning attempts to investigate the claims made by politicians about carers' issues. It's the ordinary carers and cared-for who suffer the consequences. And no one speaks up for us, except the demonised cybernats. You want a reason for independence? There's one right there.

Labour will go on to lose the Scottish referendum campaign. The Scottish media has already lost it.

16 June 2014
The great Caledonian rain forest

The Unionist parties are getting together to issue a "declaration of intent" on extra powers for the Scottish Parliament in the event of a no vote. It's a non-binding, non-specific, non-statement, because they can't agree on what powers should be devolved. But what they can agree upon is that transferring extra powers is terribly complicated and requires loads of consultation, it needs to be considered in Commons committees and Lords debates. We will give you more, they say.

They have to think carefully about what UKIP and Tory voters elsewhere in the UK think - you know, those folk that the Unionist parties have been telling that the Scots are ungrateful subsidy junkies who are dependent upon their largesse and taxes. They're hoping that these people whose votes they need in order to win the 2015 General Election won't mind about loads of constitutional freebies being delivered to those Scots - the nation they've told their constituents is composed of evil English-haters.

Any proposals the Unionist parties put forward now will go the same way as the Calman Commission - gutted, filleted and delivered late like a rotten fish that cramps your stomach. And Scotland will have had its chips, but no supper of powers. How many years to ban airguns? How many more before we can ban Trident? Vote no for dependency, vote no to be a client. Vote no to be silenced. Vote no to be told what's good for you. Westminster is sovereign, it will tell you what to do. Be fearful and obey.

Isn't it odd, how the Unionist parties are suddenly falling over themselves to make non-binding non-specific promises of devo-jam. These things they offer they could have offered years ago. But they didn't. They've spent the past few years asserting there was no demand, or it would be politically impossible, or that it would be more complicated and more difficult than building a working Large Hadron Collider out of Danny Alexander's lego men. Couldn't be because they're crapping themselves about a Yes vote could it? They promise more powers, they promise to pay heed. But you must surrender the only thing you have that will make us pay you any attention - the dream of independence, the dream of self-determination. Vote no, and let's have no more talk of doing things your own way. They will tell us what is good for us. It's what is good for them.

So how much do you trust the Unionist parties? The referendum is not a choice between trusting in the Unionist parties or trusting in the SNP. It's a choice between trusting the Unionist parties to decide what is best for Scotland, or trusting the people of Scotland. I know who's been lying to me. I know who's been patronising me. I know who's been telling me that we are nothing. It's not ordinary Scottish people.

Today the Scottish Government unveiled the provisional constitution of a new Scotland. It's a road map to a final constitution, one that all of us will be involved in writing. Rules that we have made, not rules imposed upon us. We will be the monarchs of our own glens. The first line of the new constitution : In Scotland, the people are sovereign.

It's the ordinary people of Scotland that a Yes vote will empower, with a written constitution that enshrines popular sovereignty. It's not about Alicsammin. It's about you. It's about me. It's about our families and friends and those we love. Scotland can be a state which is of the people, by the people, for the people - or it can be a province governed by the sovereignty of Westminster and subject to its grace.

Then look at Magrit the Stairheid Rammy Curran, Ian Ye Want a Doin' Davidson, Danny Lego man Alexander, John Let's Invade Iraq Reid. How much grace do you see? As much as a dinosaur with an inner ear infection dancing on broken stilts as it denies the knowledge of its impending extinction. They campaign in TV studios, in the pages of newspapers, behind the closed doors of boardrooms, bossing the bosses to boss us, telling us that we are nothings who have nothing.

So who do you trust? Trust yourself. Trust your family, trust your friends. Trust your children can have a better future. Trust the ordinary people of Scotland.

The Yes campaign doesn't have a grassroots movement. The Yes campaign does not own us, we own it. The grassroots have grown up, grown out, grown beyond anyone's control. It's people of all parties and none. It's a Scottish rain forest filled with diversity and life and laughter. The austerity axemen of Westminster get tangled in its vines, they trip over the undergrowth, bewildered, scared, lost in the forest of Scotland.

The Coed Celidon of the ancient poets has regrown, fresh growth springs all over the land. The time of lamentations is over Aneirin, the lost children of the Gododdin have found their way home to the forest. The mighty Scots Pine pines for them no more. Birds sing the new dawn in its branches, the bounty of the woodland brings life and hope. It is a place to dream, a plan to plan, a place to think of a bright future. Our green shoots reach to the skies, our roots stretch out from the Northern Isles to the Rhins of Galloway. The Great Caledonian Forest is alive again, its mighty trees nuture, and its canopy shelters the land. We are breathing. We are living. We are here. This is our place. This is our time. This is our rain forest.

Trust in home. Embrace the forest. Hug a Scottish tree. Vote Yes.

18 June 2014

Starstruck irrelevancies

Davie Cameron got his Chinese takeaway on Tuesday. The Chinese premier Li Keqiang is on a state visit to the UK, and it was predicted last week by some cynical independence supporters that he would make a statement expressing a wish that the UK remains united.

Number 10 is asking everyone and anyone they can think of to say something in support of the Union in a desperate effort to make up for the fact that no one in Scotland who's not a Unionist political hack, a millionaire, or a casino capitalist, can be arsed. Which is peculiar when you consider that they have the support of all the papers except the Sunday Herald, and the BBC's definition of neutrality is similar to that of Italy's in WW2. That's Great British Neutrality that is, there will be a series on BBC2 about it very soon.

Davie's team have clearly had a wee word in Mr Li's ear, or more accurately a spot of pleading. Li Keqiang - it's pronounced kerching - obliged with some anodyne comments a la Obama. However the Chinese leader added, "We will certainly respect the choice you make." He's clearly not that bothered about the prospect of Scottish independence, and he didn't threaten to take the pandas back or close down every Chinese takeaway in the country. So Scots will still be able to partake in that traditional Chinese dish, chips with curry sauce. That's one scare story that didn't happen then. Count your blessings.

The No Hope campaign, who still haven't clarified what their name is, are growing increasingly desperate. They're looking to add as many names as they can to their list of celebrity endorsements and can now add the Chinese prime minister to their wee list which started with Janette Krankie and ended most recently with the Pope. Mind you the Pope's endorsement only counts if you believe the Scotsman and its risible Google Translate version of what the Pontiff actually said, but it's as close as they're going get to having Jesus campaign for them. Still, they figure they can always fess up to their liberal interpretation of doctrine in the privacy of the confessional box afterwards. But it's only if there's a yes vote that they'll have to pay penance, on their knees staring damnation in the face.

The No Chance campaign were hopeful that support from Jesus would multiply their one stale loaf and a wet fish grassroots campaign into something which can feed the masses, but the miracle is not going to happen. Anyway, Scotland's still got the chips and curry sauce. But never fear, negotiations are underway for the No Mark campaign to get endorsements from the Buddha, Allah, Zeus, Moses,

Thor, Krishna, Papa Legba the Zombie Maker, and the Earth Mother - if by 'negotiations' you mean 'throwing yourself helplessly on the mercy of your god and begging'. It must be a bummer for them that deities don't tend to look kindly upon entreaties from unrepentant sinners. Deities send you to UKIPHell for that sort of thing, where you'll spend eternity surrounded by Romanians with mobile phones, trapped in a train carriage that's delayed for all time by flooding caused by an outbreak of gay weddings. Except if you worship Papa Legba the god of zombies, who is reputedly content with a sacrificed chicken. The House of Lords catering department can't cope with the demand.

Failing proper religious edicts or holy writ to keep us in the Union, the fall back tactic is to write letters to Santa Claus, although they're going to have to lie through their back teeth about being good little boys and girls. The tooth fairy has already ruled out making an intervention in support of Westminster, saying she was upset about the Conservatives' plans for dental health services. Rumour has it she's a yes supporter - yes voters being the ones with the toothy smiles.

You know they're getting desperate when the definition of celebrity is stretched to include John Reid, although why they believe anyone is going to be persuaded to vote no by John is uncertain. John and his bully-boy style of unaccountable politics are one of the reasons Scotland needs independence, his reputation was crushed into dust a very long time ago, caught between Iraq and his hard face.

He's been grimacing his way through TV and newspaper interviews, telling us that independence is a fantasy. A bit like those weapons of mass destruction in Iraq then John. Unfortunately for him, independence is the one which exists in the real world. John's not even yesterday's man, he's yesterday's warmonger, and he's been frantically sacrificing chickens to Papa Legba as he waits for the findings of the Chilcot Inquiry. Someone's going to have to be Tony Blair's sacrificial lamb and take the blame. After all, isn't that how the Westminster system works? It's either him or Jack Straw.

On Tuesday we had a wee visit from former Tory PM John Major. You may not remember who he is, he's the one between Thatcher and Blair who managed to fall into obscurity while he was still in office, and is reputedly the only man in history who ran away from the circus to become a chartered accountant. John wanted to warn us about irrelevancy - he knows a lot about being irrelevant. Apparently after independence what the people of Scotland want will become irrelevant to the likes of John, although how this differs from the current situation he didn't explain.

John, more commonly known by his full name "... Eh... John?... Isn't It?" , has had one of those road to Damascus experiences, although not one involving going to war with some Middle Eastern country this time. The outbreak of religiosity amongst the No Faith campaign is quite remarkable. The scales have fallen from Eh... John?'s eyes and now devolution is not after all the worst thing since the Ringling Brothers scoffed at his plan to perform double entry book keeping in a cage full of ravenous savage beasts. So he became Thatcher's chancellor of the exchequer instead, as it was the next best thing. After the Tories got rid of Thatch he got the gig as PM because he was the only one that no one in the Tory party hated. But that was only because they couldn't remember his name either.

Anyway, when he was PM, Wossisname refused to countenance devolution in any shape or form, and described the 1997 devo legislation as the worst thing since he'd witnessed the horror of an arithmetical error that had led to a shortfall of thruppence ha'penny. Now however, he's promising loads of lovely Halleluiah I See The Light devo jam. But being a private, indeed obscure, man, he's not telling us what led to his conversion. Possibly that's something between him and his god.

Back in 1994, he railed against the devolution plans being put forward by Labour and the Lib Dems, and asked :

"What happens at some stage in the future if the Scottish National Party were to have a majority in a Scottish parliament and asked to leave the United Kingdom?"

Thingummy is finding that out now. The Scottish Parliament will be asking that very question if there is a Yes vote in September. And what happens is that Westminster runs out of chickens and the whole zombie edifice comes crashing to the ground, at least for viewers in

Scotland. We get rid of Trident, get control over our own resources, get a written constitution with proper checks and balances to ensure that governments remain accountable and which states that the people are sovereign. And we get governments for whom the people of Scotland are not irrelevant. That all seems pretty relevant to me, unlike the opinions of forgettable politicians who've long been forgotten.

19 June 2014

Bring me the head of ... who?

There was a wee segment on Catalonia on Scotland 2014 last night, so I watched the programme for a change, at least that part of it. And it has to be said that the piece was not as unbalanced as I feared it might have been. Mind you, that didn't stop Sarah Smith saying that opinion in Catalonia was divided on independence like it is in Scotland. Which isn't actually true when you look at Catalan opinion polls, which show a large majority in favour of independence. The reason the Spanish government is so determined to prevent a Catalan referendum taking place is because everyone already knows what the result will be.

In the hoary tradition of BBC neutrality, the segment featured very short sound bites from Alfred Bosch of the Esquerra Republicana de Catalunya, a left wing pro-independence party, Muriel Casals of the pro-independence pressure group Omnium, for the opposition we got Juan Mocoso of the PSOE, who got all of 10 seconds, and then the centre piece interview with the big bad Spanish politico who was going to tell us we're eurobanned.

It had been touted beforehand with BBC Scotland saying that they'd been speaking to Spanish politicians who might make it difficult for Scotland gain EU membership, and a part of me was hoping it would be Alejo Vidal-Quadras Roco, who is the Spanish political version of one of those Hollywood blockbusters that consists of piss poor dialogue but lots of CGI spectaculars of a city being wiped out by alien monsters. Fun to watch the fireworks, but you know the movie's crap and is of no significance. Vidal-Quadras left the PP in a huff earlier this year, then failed to get re-elected to the European Parliament when he stood for the Spanish version of swivel eyed UKIPPERs. PPescadores, possibly.

So instead of the Spanish version of Nicholas Fairbairn, because some of us are old enough to remember when Scottish Tories managed a spot of eccentric colour along with their raving lunacies, the centrepiece of the segment was an interview with a very boring party drone of the Partido Popular who refused to be drawn on questions. Far more interesting was that it was prefaced with a statement from the presenter that the Spanish Foreign Ministry had refused their request for an interview.

The Spanish government will not go on public record making any official pronouncement about the Scottish referendum for a number of reasons. Reason number one being that they have no intention of vetoing Scottish membership of the EU, and reason number two being that any attempts to hinder or put obstacles in the way of Scottish membership will cause the Partido Popular and the Spanish government enormous domestic problems. Like they don't have enough of those as it is. So they're not about to say *¡Iros a la mierda!* to Scotland, which is one of those phrases they don't teach you in conversational Spanish classes at the community centre. But there's already plenty of voters in Spain saying it to the PP.

So instead, BBC Scotland interviewed someone called José Ramón García Hernández. And I said: "¿Quién?" Which is Spanish for "Who?" So I asked a Galician friend with whom I was chatting online at the time, and who is very clued up on Iberian politics. Tell me about José Ramón García Hernández, I asked. And she said: "Quen?" Which is Galician for "Who?"

Then I asked that trusty Spanish speaking friend, Google.es. Bring me the head of José Ramón García, I said. And it told me that José Ramón García is a Venezuelan baseball player and to stop making smart arsed references to low budget Westerns. In a normal universe, you can immediately rule out the notion that BBC Scotland is interviewing the Venezuelan Michael Jordan* in the mistaken belief that he's really the Spanish Foreign Minister. But this is Referendumland, where we get Daliesque surrealism from the No Grasp on Reality Campaign on a daily basis.

But thankfully for the rapidly diminishing credibility of BBC Scotland referendum coverage, he wasn't a Venezuelan baseball player, he was really a Spanish Partido Popular politician after all, albeit of the low-budget Paella Western variety. Phew. Mind you, I say "rapidly diminishing credibility," but that needs to be understood in the same sense that Attila the Hun has a rapidly diminishing credibility as a roving UN Peace Ambassador, or that John Reid has a rapidly diminishing chance of being thought of as a lovely man.

So let's try and put this into some sort of UK context, in order to give you a standard of comparison. Have you ever heard of the Rt Hon Sir Richard Ottaway? Chances are you haven't, it's not like he's a household name or that anyone in Scotland is especially interested in his opinions. Richard Ottaway is the veteran Tory MP for Croydon South and is chair of the House of Commons Foreign Affairs Committee. He's actually got some influence on UK foreign policy. Not a huge amount, but he's got influence. The kind of influence Scotland could do without, but then we can vote on that sort of thing on 18 September.

José Ramón García Hernández is far less consequential than Richard Ottaway. He was only put forward as the BBC interviewee because everyone else in the PP is mired in corruption allegations. He's the newly appointed backbencher for Marginalseatshire, a list member for Madrid who was bottom of the Partido Popular list, and was only appointed to take the place of a departing PP parliamentarian in April this year. He's the Partido Popular's party secretary on international affairs, an internal party position, not a Spanish Government position. He has about as much influence on Spanish foreign policy as the BBC interviewer who was trying to pin him down on an answer to the question - will you veto or put obstacles in the way of Scottish membership of the EU.

Even a minor PP functionary didn't want to commit himself to anything specific. Partly the reason was doubtless a peculiarly right wing Spanish version of Schadenfreude, Schadenfreude in Spanish is *regodeo*, in case you were wondering. Amongst Spanish right wing circles *regodeo* directed at el Reino Unido is usually expressed as "Ha Ha. It serves you right for Gibraltar." Contrary to what No I Still Can't Believe It's a No Campaign would have you believe, there is in fact considerable support for Scottish independence, even amongst the Spanish Partido Popular, and it's only partly due to the *regodeo* thing. It's hard to express to Scots whose experience of furren pairts is limited to two weeks on the beach just how insanely popular our wee country is amongst those who've actually heard of us. Which to be honest, isn't everyone.

But a more substantive reason can be found in the fish counters of Spanish supermarkets. Consumers in Spain consume vast quantities of seafood, a not insubstantial percentage of which comes from Scottish waters. Much of the catch is brought in by the Galician fishing fleet. The fishing industry is the largest single part of the Galician economy, and Galicia is a stronghold of the Partido Popular. The Spanish Prime Minister Mariano Rajoy is a Galician PP representative - can you guess who is the largest single contributor to his local and regional party funds? Oh yeah, that would be the Galician fishing industry. Mariano only has his job because of Scottish fish.

Delaying or putting obstacles in the way of Scottish EU membership puts the access of the Galician fishing fleet to Scottish waters at risk. It further puts at risk their access to Norwegian waters, as access to these waters depends on an agreement for reciprocal Norwegian access to EU waters - and the only EU waters that interest the Norwegians are the Scottish ones. Rajoy's not going to risk pissing off the PPescadores.

But there's another reason, which was alluded to by Patrick Harvie who commented on the piece afterwards. He made some very good points in his usual calm and reasonable way. Patrick said that if Spain attempted to put obstacles in the way of Scottish membership of the EU, there would be outrage in Spain. And there would be. But more specifically, there would be outrage of a Catalan sort.

The essence of the dispute between Catalonia and the Spanish government is that Spain insists that the Spanish constitution does not give Catalonia the right to self-determination. The Spanish constitution contains a clause saying that Spain is indivisible. Spain says it recognises that the UK constitution recognises the right of Scotland to self-determination, and so Spain has no objections. This is the argument Madrid uses to counter objections from Catalonia that Madrid undemocratically rejects the right to self-determination.

However if Madrid was seen to be punishing Scots for daring to exercise their constitutional and legal right to self-determination, they destroy their own argument against Catalonia. And the Catalans know that too. Madrid would be showing that it was after all, merely opposed to the democratic right to self-determination. Catalonia would press ahead with a referendum in the teeth of Mariano Rajoy's objections, and dare him to challenge them.

This is precisely the kind of event which the Catalans would use in order to internationalise the Catalan referendum question, and go to the European courts for a ruling. Of course there is no guarantee that Catalonia would win its case. But there's no guarantee that Madrid would win either. And Spain could potentially find itself in the humiliating position of being told by the European Court of Human Rights that it's in breach of the fundamental terms of its own EU membership. Which is not a good position to be in when your budget depends on net transfers from the EU.

So you can see why Spain is very keen not to say anything too specific, but is extremely keen on adding to the "Oh it will be cataclysmic if you vote yes" mood music.

If Scotland votes Yes in September, Spain's interests will lie in ensuring that the entire question of Scottish membership is done and dusted as quickly as possible. That way they can continue to assert to Catalonia that they do so recognise the legal right to self-determination, and to continue saying that Catalans don't have it. Meanwhile Mariano Rajoy will rest assured that funding from the Galician fishing industry will continue to fill his local party coffers.

* Yes, I know that Michael Jordan is a basketball player and not a baseball player. But I don't know the names of any baseball players because I know and care as much about American sports as BBC Scotland knows and cares about Spanish politics. There's Babe Ruth I suppose, a name which some in the Tory party were fondly hoping might become a popular nickname for Ruth Davidson, only we all started calling her the Action Krankie instead.

20 June 2014
The true story of a ginger dug

For many years in Spain, I edited and published a monthly English language features magazine. It was a great wee gig, it allowed me to be self-employed, to have no boss, and provided was a nice little income for many years. It was a job I could do from home, and it was doing the magazine that taught me how to write quickly and to meet deadlines. There's nothing like an impending print date to concentrate a writer's mind.

However, after the Spanish economy went down the toilet pan, it became harder and harder to keep the magazine going. It was free to readers, and funded exclusively by advertising, but with the problems in the Spanish economy, the magazine was no longer paying for itself and I took the decision to close it down. This happened as my partner Andy's health had started to deteriorate, and he needed me to stay at home, so I didn't return to work although I'd received a number of job offers in Spain. Financially things were tight for us, but looking after Andy was more important.

Every month, I used to publish photos from local animal rescue charities of dogs and cats which had been rescued as strays and which needed a good home. There is a huge problem with abandoned cats and dogs in Spain. In rural parts of the country it is sadly not uncommon to come across a dog which has been abandoned and left confused, sad and lonely to its own devices. And those are the lucky ones. Some in the Spanish hunting fraternity have been known to hang dogs they no longer want from trees. I informed everyone that the magazine was no longer being published, and no longer received details of poor doggies and cats who tug at the heartstrings.

Over a year later, I got up one morning and while making Andy a spot of breakfast, he told me about a vivid dream he'd had the night before. He'd dreamed that we had acquired a ginger coloured young male dog, with a rough coat, a wide head and short muzzle, and a curly tail. "It was such a vivid dream," remarked Andy, "We called the dog Ginger, and we were living in Scotland. And Scotland was independent. It was very odd."

Neither of us thought much of it, especially the independent Scotland bit, this happened a few years before the SNP won their landslide victory and the referendum became a reality. After breakfast I went and switched on the computer to check my emails. Out of the blue I'd been contacted by a local animal charity I'd not previously worked with, who had found the magazine contact details from an old copy of the magazine and hadn't realised it had ceased publication over a year before. The email contained photos and details of four dogs which had been rescued just a few days earlier.

One of the pics was of a ginger coloured dog, with a wide head and a short muzzle, he looked just like the dog Andy had described in his dream. The dog had been rescued two days before from the banks of an irrigation canal near the town of Elx, just to the south west of Alicante. He'd been dumped there a few weeks previously, according to the local residents who had been leaving food out for him.

I pulled the photo up, and called Andy over to the computer without telling him what the photo was.

"That's the dog!" he exclaimed. "How did you get that photo? Does the dog belong to someone we know and that's why I dreamed about it?"

I told him what it was, that it was sheer coincidence and the dog was newly rescued and needed a good home. At the time we had another dog, an elderly bitch called Lottie who was the love of Andy's life. She was pining for another dog we used to have, who had died a few months before.

"It's a sign," said Andy. "It's not a coincidence. We need to get that dog."

So I called up the doggy rescue people, explained that the magazine was no longer being published so unfortunately I was unable to help them with that, but that we were very interested in adopting the ginger coloured dog in the photo.

Within 24 hours, Ginger was with us, and he's been a much loved part of the family ever since. He was in shocking condition when we got him, his spine and ribs were sticking out and he was severely malnourished. He'd been badly neglected for a long time. He didn't have a name, so we called him Ginger. For the first few months we had to feed him extra and make sure he received extra care, but he's a healthy animal, and was soon bouncing about full of the joys of doggy life.

Like many rescued dogs, he has "issues". Ginger was clearly not properly socialised with other dogs when he was a puppy, and is nervous and can be aggressive around other dogs. He learned to tolerate our other dog, and never displayed aggression towards her. She died about a year later at the advanced age of 15, and since then Ginger has been noticeably more relaxed.

But he adores humans, even though some humans have clearly been cruel to him in the past, and apart from having to keep him away from other dogs, he's the easiest dog to look after that we've ever had. He's a real joy.

When Andy's health deteriorated further, it became clear that we would have to return to Scotland. Andy is English, but I needed the support from my family and friends in order to continue looking after him at home, so we came back to Glasgow instead of returning to the south of England where his sister lives. She has health problems of her own. Naturally Ginger came with us.

Ginger took very quickly to life in Scotland. He loves the grass under his paws, the smells that the wet ground holds much better than the dry dust of southern Spain, and he loves that Scotland has a dog-friendly culture. In Spain people do not generally approach strange dogs, but Scotland is full of folk who love dogs and give the local doggies treats. Ginger is in his doggy element. He loves being a Scottish boy.

One part of the Ginger Dream has already come true. We have a dug called Ginger and we live with him in Scotland. Let's make the other part of the dream come true too, so Ginger lives in an independent Scotland.

21 June 2014
Diplomatic handbagging

The British civil service, we are constantly told, is impartial and carries out the task of running the institutions and organs of the British state in a neutral, quietly efficient, and Great British Fairness sort of a way. You know, like the BBC.

But the British civil service is not so neutral after all. The British ambassador to Spain, Simon Manley, tweeted last week on the official account of the British embassy saying "Scotland is a part of a United Kingdom with a united future". He added "find out more", giving a link to the UK Treasury's paper on the independence referendum - that would be the paper whose relationship to the economic prospects of an independent Scotland are similar to Erich von Däniken's relationship to astrophysics. The paper is another of those collections of half-truths, misleading statistics, and outright myth dressed up as a serious investigation. It's the Chariot of the Treasury Gods.

Sorry, that's unfair. Erich von Däniken does actually agree that the vacuum of outer space exists, whereas the UK Treasury is hoping no one notices the vacuum between Danny Alexander's ears. And Erich does have more in the way of substantive evidence that beings from outer space have visited us than the UK Treasury does that an independent Scotland will be financially better off with UK Governments spending our resources on making London a global city. You only have to look at the drive-by Tories of the cabinet on their trips to Scotland to realise that alien pod people already walk the face of the Earth. Oh... and UK Defence Minister Philip Hammond did warn that an independent Scotland would have no means of defending itself from "threats from outer space", because we'll no longer have access to RAF jet fighters which can, apparently, shoot down a mother-ship from Alpha Centauri because the MoD possesses technology to put the fear of god into a civilisation that's thousands of years more advanced than ours, just like Neanderthals could throw rocks and fend off an invasion of tanks. Actually, this analogy is getting worse and worse the more you look at it.

But back to the undiplomatic Simon. Scotland is currently engaged in a democratic debate about our future. Simon has certainly noticed that, although the Foreign Office is clearly struggling with the "democratic" part of the statement. We have a clear case of UK diplomats seeking to influence the outcome of a democratic vote, a vote which is legal, peaceful, and entirely in accord with the constitutional arrangements of the United Kingdom.

Can you imagine the outrage that would be generated in the UK media if the British ambassador to Spain had tweeted during a General Election campaign that the United Kingdom had a Conservative future? Politicians and political commentators would be lining up and calling for him to be recalled to London so that the mandarins of the Foreign Office could whack him over the head with a diplomatic bag. But that is exactly equivalent to what Simon Manley has just done. From the UK media and the watchdogs of government standards, there's not a word.

The defence given by UK politicians on the rare occasions that they are challenged by the UK media about their campaign to recruit foreign politicians, businesses, and money to shore up their crumbling credibility in Scotland - which is to say, never - is that the UK diplomatic corps is acting in the UK national interest. This is a defence which raises some very interesting questions of its own, and if anything only increases the depth of the undemocratic mire into which the Westminster parliament is sinking.

What is the UK national interest? Who gets to define it? Perhaps I'm naive, but I'd always assumed that in a democracy, the national interest was decided democratically. The ballot box is the expression of the national will, and the national interest follows from decisions made by citizens during the ballot. The national will of the UK, or any other democracy, is what its citizens say it is, otherwise we live in an oligarchy, a dictatorship, or a clerical state. Or in Scotland as part of the UK.

We are currently in the official campaign period for the referendum. The topic of the UK's national interest with respect to Scotland's future is being actively debated and discussed by people in Scotland - by voters who are UK and EU citizens who have the legal and constitutional right to decide what their national interest is, not civil servants. And if citizens in this part of the UK decide that Scotland's national interest is best served by independence, then by definition that is also the national interest of the UK, and alternative arrangements must be made accordingly. The citizens of the UK will have spoken. It's not for Simon Manley or the civil servants of Foreign Office to pre-empt the decision and tell us otherwise, especially if they are acting on instructions from the very same elected politicians whose future is being decided by the vote.

Simon's simple minded tweet was spotted by a UK national resident in Spain, who wasn't best pleased to be told by a UK civil servant what was in his national interests. Christopher Carnie has written a letter of protest to the British embassy in Madrid. He's given permission for his letter to be republished. Here it is:

20th June 2014

Dear Ambassador,

As we enter the final phases of the referendum in Scotland, could I ask you to be strictly neutral on this issue?

I have heard that the UK Government is seeking the opinions of other governments and companies, organisations, and individuals in other countries about the possibility of Scotland becoming an independent nation. There have been reports that the UK Government is engaged in a campaign to solicit support for the anti-independence cause from abroad. I was shocked to see that yesterday you tweeted from you @ SimonManleyFCO account that "Scotland is part of a United Kingdom with a united future."

I am writing to express my unhappiness that the UK Government is seeking to influence the democratic decision of the people of Scotland in this manner. It is inappropriate for a Government to seek foreign support in order to undermine a peaceful, democratic, and legal debate amongst its own citizens.

But if Your Excellency is actively soliciting opinions on Scottish independence, I would like to state my belief that the independence of Scotland would be of immense benefit to Scotland and to the remainder of the UK.

I understand that the Foreign Office has been briefing Embassies on the independence debate. I have read a number of papers produced by the Civil Service and am dismayed that UK taxpayers' money, mine included, is being used to produce such uneven commentary (you will have read the coverage of the recent Treasury paper and its exaggerated claims of the cost of setting up Government ministries in Scotland -

claims refuted by the academic on whose work the paper was supposedly based).

I hope that you are not being briefed with this partial, biased material.

I and many Scots in Spain and Catalonia support independence and look to you to represent fairly, on behalf of all you constituency of still-British citizens, a debate that deserves clarity and depth.

Please pass this letter on to the Devolution Unit of the Foreign and Commonwealth Office.

Yours

Christopher Carnie

Christopher has also contacted the SNP's Westminster spokesman Angus Robertson to inform him of the actions of the UK Embassy in Madrid, and to urge him to ask a question in the House of Commons. Christopher's email to Angus is as follows:

Dear Mr Robertson,

As SNP Shadow Spokesperson on Foreign Affairs, you will be aware of the activities of UK Embassies abroad in promoting the "Better Together" political line.

The UK Ambassador to Spain, Simon Manley, Tweeted yesterday, 19th June at 21:04 the following message on his account @SimonManleyFCO: "Scotland is part of a United Kingdom with a united future. Find out more in @hmtreasury's latest paper #indyref"

A friend here in Spain, Pilar Aymara Fernandez, is coordinating a campaign to write to the Embassies about their biased projection of the argument. I have written to the Ambassador.

Would you consider tabling a Parliamentary Question to the FCO on the issue? For example:

To ask the Secretary of State for Foreign and Commonwealth Affairs if he has briefed UK Ambassadors to represent the debate on the Scottish Referendum fairly; and if he has briefed, instructed or otherwise required Her Majesty's Ambassadors to represent one side of the Referendum debate, to lay before Parliament these briefings; and if the actions of Her Majesty's Ambassador to Spain in tweeting, on 19th June 2014 at 21:04, a personal opinion on the Referendum were duly authorised by his Department.

In a separate email, I will attach copies of the Ambassador's tweet, and my letter to him.

Many thanks, Mr Robertson, for your help in this matter.

All the best

Christopher Carnie

Pilar Aymara Fernandez is co-ordinating a grassroots campaign, Solidarity with Scotland, to challenge the misinformation and manipulation of the UK Foreign and Commonwealth Office and its diplomatic corps. These diplomats are paid for by supporters of Scottish independence as much as anyone else, and they are obliged to represent our interests too - not the narrow party political interests of Westminster. And this is the case even when all the main UK political parties are in agreement.

If you are reading this outside the UK, or if you have friends and family outside the UK, take part in the Solidarity with Scotland campaign and make sure that Scotland's voice is heard. Scotland's national interest lies squarely in having a debate about Scotland's future without undue foreign influence manipulated by the UK government.

22 June 2014

Crass Weirdness en de beste vrienden van Davie in Europa

Some things in life are entirely predictable - like the universal stretching of the fabric of space time which is slowly pulling apart all matter and which one day, billions of years in the future, will leave only formless disjointed particles of nothingness lost in the cold dark vastness of the cosmos; and then there's BBC Scotland which manages the same job in about half an hour. There a wee sciencey joke for you Ken son, hope it cheers you up, because you must be sick about what your bosses have done with your programme.

I tuned into BBC Scotland's new Crossfire programme, the replacement for the popular Headlines programe. This is the programme that Kezia Dugdale became unavailable for at the last minute, because she's been too busy recently complaining to the

Daily Mail about people being nasty to her. The Daily Mail know a lot about being nasty to people, and so does Kezia so it's a match made in heaving - and quite a bit of retching too.

Or at least I tuned into Crossfire for about five minutes, which was more than enough. You're not going to get a proper review because listening to the show's heid pounding shoutiness was like suffering all the symptoms of a hangover, which is not really something you plan to experience on a Sunday morning unless you got rat arsed the night before. And if you were rat arsed the night before, you're not going to be getting up on a Sunday morning to have your heid nipped - unless it's by your significant other. If I had wanted to spend my Sunday in the company of shouty people yelling at one another, I'd have gone and visited my sister and her teenage offspring.

The programme seemed to consist of swapping sound bites from press releases and very little else. There was precious little in the way of insight or informed commentary. For most of the few minutes I was listening some woman, whose name I didn't catch and don't want to catch in order to spare her embarrassment, was following in the footsteps of Magrit Curran and talking a lot of mince over the top of everyone else. Though it's probably viciously sexist to point that out. The only thing anyone has learned from Bit Whore Tag Udder in this referendum campaign is that it's bullying and abuse to criticise pro-Union misinformation when it comes from women, carers, mothers, lesbians, gay men, straight men, ethnic minorities, disabled people, elderly people, English people, authors of fantasy fiction, warmongers, Westminster politicians, members of the Labour shadow cabinet, Slovenians with a persecution complex and OCD, Labour MSPs and cooncillors, members of the House of Lords, lizard space aliens, garden gnomes, and stuffed toys - that would be David Mundell.

Feeling caught in the destructive and non-illuminating crossfire of political dogwhistles, I tuned out and turned on the kettle instead. It made a reassuring whistle when it boiled and I had a nice cup of tea, unlike the Crossfire programme, which just boiled and steamed away and made a mess all over the floor of the BBC studio. The used teabag ended up in the bin, which is where Crossfire's stewed bag of vegetable matter with the taste leeched out is likely to end up very shortly too.

You've got to wonder about BBC Scotland management. Is it possible to be this incompetent by accident? Or are they doing it on purpose? It is a possibility that BBC managers are playing their part in a devilish strategy to produce such crap programmes that no one will engage with the referendum debate, but that assumes a level of guile, intelligence and cunning which there's no evidence that they possess. But it does take a very special kind of moronic incompetence to produce a radio progamme that would actually have been more listenable if it had had Kezia Dugdale in it.

Please send your questions about BBC Scotland's descent into irrelevance on a postcard to Ken MacQuarrie. You won't get an answer, but Ken's looking to add to his collection of smutty seaside innuendo. It started after a BBC staff member archly asked him if he was going to continue with the cock ups, and Ken thought it was a recommendation to look at dirty postcards.

Meanwhile in news you may have missed because the BBC's Crass Weirdness has left you bleeding from the ears, the Sunday Herald reports that Davie Cameron's Tories, lost and friendless in the European Parliament, have now formed a new grouping of MEPs together with the Flemish centre right N-VA party. Mainly because no one in Europe wants to be seen dead with the Tories either.

It's possibly cruel to point out - and naturally that means I'll be pointing out with glee - that the Tories' new pals in Europe support the independence of Flanders from Belgium. They're also pretty keen on Scottish independence too. In order to have any significant influence in the European Parliament, Davie's boys and girls now find themselves reliant upon the support of a party who cheer for Alicsammin. That's gotta hurt.

In April this year, the party's online magazine carried an article by one of its leading MEPs, Mark Demesmaeker who sits on the European Parliament's external relations committee. The article extolled the Scottish Yes campaign and praised Alicsammin's speech in Bruges. It's all in Dutch, but the article is titled YES SCOTLAND! in English, which kinda gives you a clue as to the sentiments expressed within it.

The article goes on to explain that in the view of this N-Va politician, there should be no difficulty with an independent Scotland rapidly acceding to full EU membership in its own right, and agrees with the assessment that Scotland will be able to negotiate its membership in the period between a yes vote in September, and the formal declaration of independence some 18 months later.

The Tories were hoping that Yes supporters in Scotland hate foreigners as much as they do and won't pollute their eyes with texts which are not in English. But the Nederlands-challenged can get the gist of the piece courtesy of Google Translate - which is apparently the same service the Scotsman newspaper used to mistranslate Pope Francis's comments on independence for Catalonia and Scotland.

The N-VA's online magazine also carried a recent piece by Dr Dirk Rochtus, a professor of politics and social sciences at Leuven University and a senior fellow of the Centre for European Integration based in Bonn in Germany. Dr Rochtus has a long and respected list of publications in the field of independence movements and international politics.

Dr Rochtus wrote an article looking at the issues facing an independent Scotland which seeks membership of the EU. The Dutch language article, entitled *Een onafhankelijk Schotland: automatisch EU-lid of niet?* (An independent Scotland: Automatic EU entry or not?) was published in the N-VA party magazine in January this year.

Dr Rochtus recognises that there are questions about Scottish membership, but notes that the objections raised by No campaigners in Scotland - he cites Alistair Carmichael - are politically motivated and politically based. The professor notes that they have no basis in EU law. He goes on to make a number of interesting points. Scottish membership of the EU may not be automatic - but Scottish expulsion from the EU is not automatic either, contrary to the opinions proferred by the likes of the Alistairs. In fact, the expulsion of Scotland from the EU throws up far more complex and thorny legal issues than Scotland's automatic accession to full membership. So it's not going to happen.

It's a safe bet that the opinion of a professor who specialises in the study of independence movements and who is a senior fellow with the Centre for European Integration is probably somewhat weightier than that of a solicitor in Kirkwall. Dr Rochtus appears to be of the view that any issues in the way of an independent Scotland gaining EU membership are solvable and can be surmounted.

So we have the Tories to thank for this new support for Scottish membership of the EU. If they hadn't formed an alliance in the European Parliament with the N-VA, it's likely that no one on the Yes side of the Scottish independence debate would have gone looking for the opinions of the Tories' new best pals in Europe.

But now we know. In order to secure his much wanted renegotiation of the UK's terms of membership of the EU, Davie Cameron must rely upon the support of a party that's strongly in favour of a smooth entry into the EU for an independent Scotland. That's an even bigger screw up for the No campaign than the launch of yet another PR disaster for BBC Scotland.

24 June 2014
Debating behind the bikesheds

The English lexicographer, wordsmith and scottophobe Samuel Johnson once said: "Depend upon it, sir, when a man knows he is to be hanged in a fortnight, it concentrates his mind wonderfully." Alistair Darling knows exactly what that feels like right now, although he's got a bit more than a fortnight in which to ponder his impending doom. I'm quite relieved that it's more than a fortnight away, as it gives plenty of time to learn Morse code so I can check if Alistair is frantically blinking H.E.L.P...M.E...R.O.N.A. during the debate.

Ali and Alicsammin debating is one of those things that Westminster thought wasn't supposed to happen, like the SNP winning an outright majority in an electoral system Labour and the Lib Dems had designed to ensure that never happened. But that set a pattern, and this referendum campaign has been full of things that were not supposed to happen. The referendum itself wasn't supposed to happen. Holyrood setting the terms of the vote, the timing, and the question wasn't supposed to happen. Mass popular participation in the debate and the campaign wasn't supposed to happen. Scotland responding to a barrage of scare stories and threats with laughter, mockery and ridicule wasn't supposed to happen. Yes snapping at the heels of the Bet You Don't Know What We're Called This Week campaign in the polls wasn't supposed to happen. The momentum of a Yes grassroots movement that's bigger and reaches further than any political campaign in modern Scottish history wasn't supposed to happen.

You'd think, given that there's a precedent or ten for Scottish things that Westminster thinks aren't supposed to happen actually happening, that they wouldn't try and act macho about something that they're praying won't ever happen. Alistair Darling must now rue the many days he called on Alicsammin to debate with him, all the while in the belief that Alicsammin would continue to refuse. It's like the school bully's nyaffwank wee pal suddenly discovering that the big Bullingdon bully won't be giein him haunders after all. Now the whole of the school is going to meet up behind the bikesheds at the STV studios and watch him get a wedgie with his pants on fire. It's a painful and humiliating thing when a wedge strategy goes wrong.

Alistair has a reputation as a calm and dignified statesperson. He maintains this by being remote and distant, and doesn't do combative interviews, preferring instead a nice wee chat with Jim Naughtie. The calmness of his badger fur is never ruffled. Not once during the entire campaign has he debated with or been interviewed alongside someone from the Yes camp. It's easy to look dignified when you maintain an aloof aura aw roon, and you're away in the big important parliament far away in London doing big and important things but have deigned to lower yourself to paddle in the provincial pond in order to tell Scotland how lucky we are to have people like Alistair far away.

But the debate with Alicsammin will teach Scotland the lesson Father Ted tried in vain to teach to Father Dougal. Alistair isn't far away, he's just small. And Davie Cameron is a wee dot in the field outside the caravan window, running away as fast as he can.

STV tried to force the issue with a highly reluctant No Comment campaign, which has been refusing to put up speakers for public debates on the grounds that people who are not politicians might disagree with a politician, which is clearly abusive. Eventually STV informed each side that they either put up a speaker or they'd 'empty chair' them. They should have gone with the empty chair, it would make a more positive case for the Union than Alistair has ever managed. Chairs can at least provide comfortable support, and Alistair's would be well-upholstered. Furnishings can be claimed for on expenses.

Despite the attempts to spin events as Alicsammin being "smoked out" - geddit? smoked, because Salmond sounds like salmon and no one has ever used that joke before - this is a disaster for the No Sex We're British campaign, as it's been well and truly screwed. It's understandable that Cameron didn't want to debate. He's going to lose. Badly. That said, he should still debate. He is, let us not forget, the Prime Minister of Scotland, and this country is currently engaged in a debate about whether or not we want to let him keep his job. It is after all one thing for Westminster to tell us that after independence we can't have the pound, or EU membership, or the BBC, or defence from invasion from outer space if you believe Philip Hammond the Tory defence minister, it is however the height of inanity to tell us we can't question our own Prime Minister while we're still a part of the Union.

If Cameron had debated, expectations of his performance would have been low. Low expectations like if you'd entered John Reid in a humility contest, or nominated the Collected Speeches of Johann Lamont for the Nobel prize for literature, or asked Tony Blair to apologise for Iraq. In order to have the UK media hailing his statemanlike powers and magnanimous grace, all Davie would need to do would be to come out with some meaningless PR mince about family of nations WW2 Olympic spirit Willnkate (don't mention the helicopter) Harry Potter and 307 years of everything joint except the stuff that gets you stoned. He could, if he had been smart about it, turned it into one of those Great British Dunkirk evacuation style defeats, a defeat but a glorious and heroic one. Except that glorious and heroic aren't adjectives usually associated with Davie Cameron, unless there's a "not" in the sentence, and quite often a "useless fucker" in Polish as well.

Instead we're getting the Labour party's Alistair Darling as the Tory understudy. That's really going to appeal to those wavering Labour voters isn't it. He's spent the last two years pointing out the uncertainties of independence, even though many of those uncertainties exist only inside his own head, and most of the remainder are uncertain only because the sole body which has the ability to clarify the uncertainty is the Westminster Parliament. And they're certainly not for telling. He's now exposed himself to questioning on the uncertainty of new powers for Holyrood in the event of a No vote. Or more precisely, questioning on the certainty that after a No vote Westminster will kick the entire issue into the long grass that still doesn't get you stoned. Scotland won't be very mellow about that at all. Alistair's a backbench MP for Her Maj's Opposition, he's in no position to offer any certainties, and the squabbling members of the No We Can't Agree On Anything Except We Hate Alicsammin campaign don't provide him with much comfort, no matter how well upholstered his chair. He can't even be certain about how much bog paper he's going to need after debating Alicsammin. Probably quite a lot though. But he can get it on expenses.

Samuel Johnson also said "The noblest prospect which a Scotchman ever sees, is the high road that leads him to England!" He was, let's face it, a bit of a nyaffwank. The only reason the ingrate is famous is because a Scottish guy with more writing talent than Johnson, but a rampant case of runaway cringe, preserved his witticisms for posterity. And his dictionary is pish too. It's missing the word nyaffwank* for starters. The relationship between Johnson and Boswell is a metaphor for the Union. And that's pretty nyaffwank too.

But in Alistair's case the noblest prospect he's got in store will be the road out of an STV studio, leading to a hole in the ground somewhere where he can hide under a blanket and rock back and forward, wondering why it all went so wrong.

*a flaccid and embarrassing indulgence with no satisfactory outcome which leaves you feeling short changed and annoyed

25 June 2014
Dress for yes success

Tuesday was a beautiful day, even if the weather was back to grey after a rare spot of sun. I went out socially for the first time in ages thanks to a neighbour who's a trained carer who sat with my partner allowing me to meet up with a couple of friends for lunch in a nice restaurant. A few weeks back, they gave me an iron because the old one had exploded as irons are wont to do. So I ironed a shirt and put on my best suit. A handmade three piece Savile Row suit bought in a charity shop in London nearly 25 years ago for the princely sum of a tenner. It's my lucky suit. Every time I've worn it to a job interview I've been offered the job.

I wore it to a posh do at the Irish Embassy after accepting one of those jobs - which happened to involve the occasional trip to places like the Irish Embassy where they didn't offer anyone Ferrero Rocher and I was totally gutted - but by way of compensation an even posher man from the UK Foreign and Commonwealth Office came up to me and attempted to engage me in conversation. I'm sure he fancied me, because I was still young and had hair, but he didn't look like any of the James Bonds so I wasn't really interested. In the plummiest of tones he said: "I do so love your suit. You must give me the name of your tailor!" And I said, "Aye, it wis Relief Fund for Romania." He sidled off quickly.

I used to buy all my suits in charity shops. But that was before vintage menswear retro became fashionable, prices went through the roof, and hipsters ruined what was once a cheap hobby. And made me fashionable, which was quite annoying because one of the reasons for getting into retro vintage gear in the first place was because it was deliberately unfashionable. I used to tell people I was an anarchodandyist - bringing about the downfall of capitalism by being extremely well dressed.

Some people believed that was a real political position. Which only goes to show that there's a proportion of the population who are more prone to believing things if they're said with conviction by man in an expensive looking suit - this explains a great deal about modern politics and why things need to change. The great Steve Biko, the anti-apartheid activist who was murdered by the racist South African police in 1977, knew that too. He said, "If you want to say something radical, dress conservatively." But I digress.

Anyway after a very pleasant afternoon with my friends, and without being asked for the name of my tailor by any posh Foreign Office persons, I come home to find there's been news in the independence campaign. Very good news indeed. The lucky suit's been lucky again.

The Radical Independence Campaign published the results of their mass canvassing held on 22 June. The results show why the No Hope campaign has been in full-on panic mode for the past few weeks - because they're doing private polling and canvassing too. The 978 volunteer canvassers spoke to the residents of 46 districts across Scotland, getting 8317 responses; 40% Yes, 29.5% No, 30.5% undecided. In every area canvassed, Yes was ahead of No, often by a considerable margin. In some districts, the percentage of No voters was as low as 14%.

The usual caveats and disclaimers apply. Good news always comes with small print, but it's still good news. Extremely encouraging news, and news which for once chimes in with the opinions and views of the people I actually encounter in real life. In this part of the East End of Glasgow, there are a lot of Yes supporters, a lot of don't knows, a not insignificant number of don't give a shits, but very few confirmed No voters. The Yes supporters are the ones who are excited and motivated and are going to turn up and vote. Yes supporters are the happy ones. Their excitment and motivation is proving to be contagious. It's not the virus of nationalism after all, it's the cross-fertilisation of hope, supporting Yes is infectious like laughter.

There's not much in the way of joy from the miserabilists of No. The stitching has come loose in the arse of their suit troosers. The expensively besuited Alistair Darling has spent the last six months telling anyone who would listen that he would debate Alicsammin "anytime, anyplace". He must have been wearing his lucky suit too because over the weekend Alicsammin waved the sparkly debate wand and granted his wish, with the proviso the debate was held after the Commonwealth Games have finished and there's half a chance people might watch it. You'd think Alistair would have been happy, since "in an STV studio in August" does indeed fall within the definition of "anytime, anyplace".

But it transpires that Alistair meant "anytime, anyplace" except August, because he's off looking for a tailor to repair the arse of his troosers. Oh and any day with a Y in its name is right out too. It's a religious thing, like not eating meat on Fridays or not being eaten alive by a First Minister any time at all.

However he's still willing to debate anyplace, although just not anywhere on planet Earth unless it's deep within the security bunker of a BBC studio where he's protected by 6 foot plates of Jim Naughtie. To be fair, this still leaves over 99% of the rest of the solar system, so it's not like Alistair is being unnecessarily restrictive. I should really stick in a Uranus joke here, but that would just be adding to the cruelty.

Ah but - in breaking newspincycle - it's actually Alicsammin who's the big feartie because he won't debate Alistair in July when Scotland goes on holiday. And it's all the fault of that nasty STV which is in cahoots with Alicsammin, and probably allows him to broadcast his mind control waves over their transmitters. Someone of Alistair's stature can't possibly appear on a minor regional TV channel. He hasn't run away to hide at all, oh no. He's just an ageing silent movie star who thinks it's the pictures that have got too small. The suits of Better Together are lying face down in the swimming pool with knives in their backs. I'm ready for my close up Mr Naughtie.

But rather than descend further into the madness which is the No Clue campaign, I'll just rehash a Martini advert jingle. It's in keeping with the lounge lizard suit vibe.

Anytime anyplace anywhere
BT's speaker is an empty chair
Not the grey one
the scared one
Feartie Ali.

So bring on the empty chair. The case for the Union is brought to you by a vacant space. Tells us all we need to know, doesn't it.

Perhaps I need to wear that suit more often. After all, Yes is the elegant equation in this debate. Dress for Yes Success.

We're here, we're queer, we're voting yes

Stu Campbell, who runs the Wings Over Scotland website, has recently come under sustained abuse by Unionists. He's been accused of just about everything with the possible exception of being personally responsible for the killing fields of Cambodia - although it's probably only a matter of time before a swivel eyed No supporter on Twitter makes the claim that Wings Over Scotland is published from Phnom Phen.

A persistent claim is that Wings Over Scotland is homophobic, misogynistic and transphobic. It's a shameless attempt to deter ordinary Scots from engaging with the arguments and information published on the site. I have never read any articles on Wings Over Scotland that I have considered homophobic. Wings Over Scotland and the other pro independence news sites provide information in a clear and straightforward manner which is accessible to all and inclusive of all.

Just today Stu received another tweet from a Unionist describing him as a "homophobic c**t". Stu Campbell may be many things, but he's not homophobic. I've had a number of personal contacts with him, and I know from personal experience that he has demonstrated nothing but respect for my partner and me as gay men, and for our status as a married couple. The same experience has been repeated countless times with all the many and diverse people I've been privileged to meet and get to know as a part of this remarkable mass movement. Acceptance and love. The love of Scotland is a many gendered thing.

Stu is not versed in the arcane language of the organised LGBT movement, but there is no reason he should be. Lack of awareness is not abuse. Accusing an individual of abuse in attempt to deflect from unrelated arguments - that's abuse. And worse, it's abuse which diminishes and damages the struggle against real homophobia and real social exclusion. Those who make such accusations should hold their heads in shame.

Sorry readers, but this is not going to be a happy post. It's an angry one. It's the height of hypocrisy for the No campaign to make accusations of homophobia. Scotland is a nation. It is a modern European nation like any other. It contains a minority who have homophobic attitudes. Those who possess such attitudes are represented on both sides of the independence debate - although they are without a shadow of doubt louder and more prominent on the No side. Yet these No campaigners are the people who'd have us believe that the traditional Scottish sentiment "A man's a man for aw that" is a statement in support of transphobia and 19th century gender roles and who are trying to make us fear than an independent Scotland would be less progressive than Russia in its treatment of its lesbian and gay minority. That's abuse. That's cheapening the struggle I've spent my adult life involved in.

Certainly there are homophobes amongst Yes campaigners, but homophobia is more of a problem for the No campaign. People who are on the same side of an independence debate as the Orange Order, UKIP, the Tories, the fascists of Britain First, and the Daily Fucking Mail have no business taking the gay rights moral high ground with anyone. Remember that Labour hacks, next time you pen an article for that right wing rag or take to Twitter decrying the abuse you claim to suffer.

Labour's LGBT claque does not speak for me, it does not speak for the majority of lesbian, gay, bisexual or transsexual people in this country. They speak for their own ghettoised style of politics. Real Scottish lesbian and gay people are here, we're queer, and we're Scottish independence supporters too. We're not going to live in a ghetto in an independent Scotland. We're going to be mainstream, out in the open, and participating fully.

I'm a late middle aged man who's recently made the shocking realisation that I'm eligible for a Saga holiday offer. I made the realisation that I was gay a long time before, during the 1970s. I came out in the early 1980s when the Aids crisis was in full blown media hysteria and newspapers regularly engaged in witchhunts against gay people, when people were still sacked from their jobs for being a queer. We were public enemy number 1. Coming out, I got beaten up for my pains, I was estranged from certain family members for many years. I was no longer welcome in the home I was born in.

I've experienced homophobia - real homophobia and not the homophobia of the trivial Twitter complaint variety "Oooooh s/he's said something nasty about me." I didn't bother myself when people called me a poof or a pervert, I had far more serious abuse to deal with - the abuse which prevented lesbians and gay men living the life we had a right to live. The abuse that left real bruises, not metaphorical ones.

I was never a prominent campaigner. I didn't join political pressure groups and sit on committees or seek positions of influence. But I was there. Not mincing but marching. Not complaining about abuse in the pages of the Daily Mail, but doing something about it. I was there in Parliament Square on the evening of 21 February 1994 when the Westminster Parliament rejected proposals to equalise the age of consent for gay men with that of everyone else. I was there during the protests that ensued when the crowd realised that our Parliamentarians had chosen to maintain legal discrimination against us. I was there to witness a group of angry gay men trying to storm a Westminster Palace which had locked its doors against equality.

I was there at the beginning when parental rights where a major issue for lesbian and gay people. And at a time when the Daily Mail and the gutter press insisted we had no right to have children, that we were a threat to the well being of young people, I started a family with lesbian friends. We didn't ask any straight person's permission. We didn't appeal to authority for help. We just did it. We were amongst the first generation of lesbians and gay men to do so. We established that it was possible. We proved that it was good. We opened the doors to parenthood for the generations of lesbians and gay men who followed.

I didn't have kids to prove a political point, that would have been crass and shallow. I had kids for the same reasons anyone has kids. But we were fully aware of the political significance of the simple act of conception. My children have brought my family immense joy and pride, they are happy, well balanced, doing well in life, they grew up surrounded by love. I am zealous in my protection of my daughters.

I will not be lectured to by the Labour party about homophobia or LGBT issues. I am sickened and revolted by the modern attempts of Labour to assert that it was and is the leading organisation in the societal struggle against discrimination. Because the Labour party was as complicit as the other mainstream parties in maintaining and fostering homophobia.

My partner suffers from a terminal illness. I spend my days caring for him. Yet when he dies I will not inherit his pension rights, because the Labour party decided when it introduced civil partnerships that pension rights would not be backdated. We've been a couple for decades, but in the eyes of the law our relationship dates only from our civil partnership ceremony a few years after the law was changed in 2004. I face an uncertain financial future due to the Labour party. That's real homophobia. That's discrimination and abuse which is far worse than being called rude names on Twitter. And it's the Labour party which is responsible for it.

I am of the gay generation which defined homophobia. I'm of the gay generation which taught the likes of the LGBT claque in the modern Labour party what homophobia is, how to identify it, how to challenge it, and how to overcome it. So I'll not be having them telling me what is or is not homophobic. I'll be telling them. And I am telling them that Stu Campbell and the readers and followers of Wings Over Scotland are not homophobes. Neither are they hypocrites - that would be the No campaigners making accusations of homophobia in a transparent attempt to create fear, doubt and uncertainty.

No is the campaign of fear and looking over your shoulder to the past. The Yes campaign is the Scotland of equality and inclusion, it seeks to give ordinary Scottish people the tools they need to determine their own future on their own terms. The gay rights movement sought the empancipation of gay people, it fought for equality and inclusion, to give ordinary lesbian and gay people the tools they need to determine their own future on their own terms. Gay rights and Scotland's rights are part of the same struggle.

Yes is the future, it's multicoloured, multiethnic, it's straight, bi and queer. It's Scotland in all her glory. We're here, we're queer, we're voting yes.

26 June 2014
Invective: Terms and conditions

I've got an invective policy on this blog. There are some topics and individuals upon which the only tongue lashings are the threads tying down a sharp tongue. That doesn't mean I'm not burning with smart arsed and bitchy put downs against [inaudible mumble] and their [inaudible mumble] which furgodssake [inaudibly mumbled]. But I keep schtum anyway, even when it's [inaudible mumble] John Mason. Is that hypocritical of me? Quite possibly. I don't care. I'm human, I contain contradictions. We all do. That's what makes us human.

I will not criticise any individual, organisation, or campaigning group actively seeking a Yes vote in September. No one told me not to. I've got protection from undue influence - through the magic of scissors and PVA glue I transformed my lovely free expensively produced UKOK bookletty thingy into a lovely hat which protects the sensitive regions of the neo-cortex from SNP mind control rays. It works better than tinfoil, though it's certainly less stylish.

But the fact I'm not going to criticise or mock them doesn't mean I agree with everything every other Yes group or campaigner says or does, nor does it mean I agree with their strategies or tactics. This is a grassroots movement. That's the opposite of a manicured lawn, which is a monoculture of manufactured sameness. A mass movement is a big breathing living mass of organic nature, a forest or a field of wild flowers. That's the whole point of being a mass grassroot movement. It's not a controlled domesticated thing. It contains contradictions and incompatibilities. And that's precisely how it should be.

All of us come to this debate with our own histories, our own stories, our own perspectives. We've got our own expectations, and our own priorities about the things we want to achieve and how to achieve them. The only thing we have in common is the agreement that Scotland requires the full powers of self-government in order to tackle them effectively. I don't criticise other Yes supporters, even those with whom I have fundamental political disagreements, because I refuse to be distracted from the prize of a Yes vote in September.

I'm not saying others should follow my example. That's entirely up to other people. Like I said, we each come to this debate with our own experiences, our own perspectives, and our own priorities. What I see as my priority is not necessarily what others see as theirs. This is a mass grassroots movement, there is no party line - but I would ask people to reflect upon the fact that there are now just 83 days to go until the most important vote in Scottish history, and perhaps to consider the need for a bit of self-discipline.

There is a good argument to be made that it's arrogant to tell a person that they must delay or downplay their own important issues in the cause of another campaign. It's an argument I've used myself often enough in the past - see what I mean about hypocrisy and contradictions? I remember many years ago an unreconstructed socialist telling me that all that "homosexual stuff" was a dangerous distraction from the real prize of building socialism in Britain. Only once that had been achieved would the workers' collectives arrive at a true and just dispensation for the good little gay people who'd kept their mouths shut for the cause. But it's not for him or anyone else to tell me what my political priorities ought to be. The political is personal and I'm not about to put off making much needed changes in my own life in the vague hope that one day paradise will arrive and someone else will do it for me. I'm going to do it myself. Now.

In fact it's just like Labour's solidarity argument - Scotland must put off tackling her own problems with poverty and social exclusion until the bright dawn comes and we get a UK Labour government which is actually a Labour government as opposed to the Labour goverments we actually get. Only Labour's paradise never comes. This is something else we need to do for ourselves too, and why we need to vote Yes.

Political campaigns are like good comedy, except politicians aren't funny on purpose. But the secret is still in the timing. There's a time to pick a fight, and there's a time to put that fight off for another day. Right now, those who are blocking progress towards tackling the many social and political issues Scotland faces are not other Yes campaigners - no matter how distasteful or reprehensible you may find them, their views or their tactics. It's those who want us to vote

No who are the immediate obstacle to progress. It's the No campaign which seeks to deny us, all of us with our various opinions priorities and perspectives, from taking control of the tools Scotland requires to begin to work on the problems Scotland faces. And when Yes supporters attack each other, we do the No campaign's job for them.

As we approach 18 September, and the possibility of a Yes vote becomes real, there is a greater tendency to jump the gun and start fighting the fights we can only fight in an independent Scotland. Right now we're 83 days away from the referendum, hoping that Yes supporters do not criticise other Yes supporters is not the same as asking women or gay people or black people not to tackle pressing issues of sexism, homophobia or racism until the glorious day sometime in a vague and undetermined future when the revolution arrives and all these things will be sorted for us. There's an expiry date on the referendum special offer, and it's one that's not far off. On 19 September, everything changes. And after that date, we will still have our own priorities - but with a Yes vote we'll have the tools we need to tackle them ourselves.

This is not a student debating competition. There's a far bigger prize. Keep your eye on it and don't be distracted. Keep calm, keep focussed. Direct your ire carefully. Prioritise it. And we will win.

28 June 2014
Running to Brussels in Y-fronts

You know the telly is really bad when you're upset that they've taken off Bargain Hunt. I hate football, dear gods I hate it so much. And don't start me on tennis, sexual grunts with spaghetti driers on sticks and not a celebrity masterchef in sight. And we've still got loads to look forward to, like the bleedin Commonwealth Games and the Ryder Cup, which is apparently to do with hitting a small ball with a long stick which is rubbish for drying spaghetti, and horses are not involved at all.

They're only bloody games, people. That means it's not real. It's just a game, the clue's right there in the name. Game. It's playing. Kicking and batting baws and running and jumping about a bit.

Why are they running a marathon anyway? It's 26 miles for godssake. Can they not get a bus? That's why buses were invented, so people didn't have to run 26 miles. Let's make up something pointless and call it a competition and get it plastered all over the telly. Only they've taken off Pointless too. The basterts.

And you're taking off my soap operas for this, you TV scheduling testostemaroids. Invented things should come with invented stabbings, bitchery, the occasional murder and burying the body under the patio, long story lines about on-off-on-off again romances, and oooh-what-total-bastards, thank you very much. But the best on offer is some overpaid eejit biting some other overpaid drama queen on a fitba pitch because he was annoyed that he wasn't getting his turn to kick the baw. He should go buy his own ball if it means that much to him, it's not like he can't afford it. It was funny how he made like he'd injured his teeth though. That was inventive invention. It was even more inventive that no one seemed to think he should have been huckled off by the polis immediately. Why are they indulging the overpaid egoist with an anger management problem? He's not a genius, he's not a god. He's just a spoiled wee thug with better than average eye to foot coordination.

Sport is what weans do only with more expensive equipment and much bigger egos. Why is this taking up three quarters of the news? Shoot me. Shoot me now. I'm a freak, a mutant, born without the sports appreciation gene. I'm sportophobic. That probably means I'm abusing Magrit Curran, because women play sports too.

Sportophobia has led me to the realisation that Unionist politicians are in fact attempting to channel the spirits of 1970s PE teachers. They weren't very bright either and as a class they likewise contain a higher than average proportion of spoiled wee thugs with anger management problems. But we have to see them once a week when they visit on a power trip for a spot of attempted ritual humiliation, and the demand that we run around the playing field in our underwear. A teacher did once order me to do that, on one of the many many occasions it had quite slipped my mind, no honestly the dog ate the post it note on the fridge, that I had PE that day. "Right boy! Take off your trousers and shirt and do 20 laps of the field," he ordered. I'd seen him do this with other boys in the class before, and couldn't understand why they complied with the command. Why be complicit in your own humiliation? It made no sense.

"Oh that's *so* not going to happen," I told him, "If you want humiliation rituals you can do it in your own time." He went bright red and then went ape-shit, but to be fair that was sorta the point of saying it to him. Playing mind games with PE teachers was the only sport I really enjoyed and I was laughing because I'd won. In retrospect, he was probably secretly into getting spanked by a dominatrix and I'd struck a nerve that was rawer than his backside. But that didn't cross my mind at the time. I was a bitch, but an innocent one, at least at the time. I got the belt, but it was worth it. I didn't run round the playing field in my underwear or do PE that day. Nor indeed for the rest of my school career.

You can't humiliate people who are laughing back at you. No one can wipe the smile off your face when you can see what's funny. That was the only lesson I ever learned in PE, but it was a good one. Unionist politicians are funny and make me laugh. "Oh that's *so* not going to happen," is the best response to them as well.

The only appreciable difference between the humiliation rituals of 1970s PE teachers and Unionist politicians is that Unionist politicians can't give us the belt, or even lines or detention, they have to make do with warnings that we'll be unprotected against threats from outer space, or that they'll have to impose border controls. That's rubbish sadomasochism that is. And not a gimp suit in sight, just plenty of gimps in suits.

Unionist politicians see Scotland as a venue for acting out their power fantasies, but it just leaves them looking like they're running round the playing field in their Y-fronts. Do they really believe we're small children who can be intimidated by ridiculous stories bereft of logic or reason? Apparently they do. Let's be having those suit troosers then, Eds Miliband and Balls. Let's see the colour of your Y-fronts. I'm guessing brown.

The UK isn't exactly flavour of the month with other EU countries, a fact which Ed Miliband is hoping is news of the "except for viewers in Scotland" sort. The UK, you know, the one that punches above its weight and has massive influence in Europe, just got outvoted 27-2. That's even rubbisher than the square of the rubbishness of the Spanish and English world cup squads combined. The only cheerleader Davie could muster was Viktor Orban the far right Hungarian that no one else wants anything to do with. In 2013 the European Parliament endorsed a report criticising the dangerously undemocratic way in which Orban was centralising power and control into his own hands, and stated that his changes to the Hungarian constitution were in conflict with the fundamental principles of EU treaties. So you can see why Orban wasn't keen to support an EU President who was chosen by a majority of EU parliamentarians. There's massive UK influence for you. What was that about knowing people by the company they keep Davie?

After Davie's wee stropette with the presidency vote, few EU members are predisposed to doing the UK too many favours just now. Meanwhile Westminster wants to renegotiate the terms of its own membership of the EU, causing immense problems both at an EU level and at the level of domestic politics within many other EU members - which have their own EU issues. And if Westminster doesn't get its own way it will hold a referendum on leaving.

These pissed off EU countries are the same countries which Westminster assures us will rush to support the view of the Westminster government that it and it alone inherits EU membership upon Scottish independence, and will concur that a Scotland which is quite keen to remain an EU member is a naughty child who must wait at the back of the EU queue in its Y-fronts.

The UK obtained its much prized Schengen opt out because the UK is situated on some islands, and because its only land border is with a smaller EU country the bulk of whose contacts with other EU nations transits via the UK. It's much simpler for us just to control a few seaports and airports ourselves, said the UK government during Schengen negotiations. Ireland said they'd like to join Schengen, but since the UK wasn't going to it really didn't make any economic or political sense for them to join either. You know what that Westminster is like, added Ireland with resignation. And the other EU countries said, OK fair enough then, Westminster causes enough grief as it is, and oh look at the time, isn't Bargain Hunt on telly? Let's go home for lunch.

Now Ed Miliband is saying that the UK, or more precisely the England-Wales-Northern Ireland component of the former UK, will maintain its opt out on Schengen while erecting border controls with its neighbour to the north. Because we'll have become foreigners, and foreigners are bad. Foreigners attract other foreigners, and the newly foreign Scottish foreigners will let loads of other foreigners in who will immediately want to go south of the border because they don't like Scottish foreigners either. At least I think that's the logic. It's hard to tell with Westminster PE teachers. They're not really renowned for joined up thinking.

Because it certainly can't be because Scotland might adopt an immigration policy that was different from the one Ed wants. The Republic of Ireland already does that, they have their own immigration policy which does not require prior approval from the UK Home Office. Oddly there's no passport controls between the UK and Ireland, what with them being a part of a Common Travel Area. And it can't be the foreigner thing either in Ireland's case, what with the 1949 Ireland Act passed by Westminster deeming that Irish citizens are not foreigners, and the Republic of Ireland is not a foreign country, for the purposes of UK laws.

So that only leaves "we're just spiteful gimps in suits" as the reason for the Scottish border controls, which doesn't sound like an attractive reason for voting No in September. Expensive things border controls, all just for the sake of an infantile strop. And all the cost on their side - like Scotland needs to bother protecting the border when they're doing such a sterling job of it. But sterling is something else the border will be porous to as well.

The threat has no substance. It's a wee fantasy the Eds want to scare us with. They want us to take off our trousers and run at their command. But let's indulge the Eds in their little power trip fantasy. What happens next? The northern neighbour will, upon being cut off from the rest of the UK and Ireland by red tape passport controls and a fit of Westminster pique, go "ach fuck it, let's join Schengen and then we can go to Benidorm without a passport", thus removing from the rUK the sole reason it got an opt out from Schengen in the first place, because all of a sudden they've got a land border with a Schengen member after all. One they could so easily have avoided creating. And Ed proposes to create this 100 mile long rod for his own back at the same time that Westminster wants to renegotiate the UK's EU obligations and opt outs with Brussels. Meanwhile the other EU countries are going "Oh look we've got shiny new ways to put pressures on Westminster that we couldn't use before." Way to go to strengthening your negotiating position with Angela and François, Ed. He'd be as well flying his Y-fronts from the flag pole in surrender. Let's hope they're still white.

I've got way more self respect. I'm not going to be humiliated by a wee gimp in a suit. He'll be the one that's humiliated and running to Brussels in his Y-fronts when we ignore his petulant threats and vote Yes in September.

And there will still be no border controls.

July 2014

1 July 2014
Monkey poo and panda poems

Jim Murphy has got first dibs on the monkey with the red rosette, which gives him and his Labour colleagues sole monkey poo throwing rights in the referendum. For the duration, they're turning a blind eye to monkey poo throwing from the other Unionist parties, like the Orange Order. But Jim is very upset that this referendum has unleashed troops of unelected who have discovered how to throw poo without him giving the orders. That's worse than proper professional monkey poo throwing, it's unauthorised monkey poo throwing - and to make things worse it's by amateurs who've got a good aim. He's even more upset that it seems to be panda poo and much of it is directed at him.

According to la Murph's latest retaliatory, or possibly pre-emptive but we've given up counting, poo throw, evil pando poo throwing nationalists are bullying the poor defenceless shrinking violet that is the BBC.

Jim is a rare and delicate flower who gives a drag act suffering a paranoid acid flashback a run for its money in the hysterical overreaction stakes - only without the double entendres, the humour, the glam, or indeed the drug fuelled reveries. Flowers like Jim can only flourish in a carefully cultivated ecosystem which discourages third party competition. Thankfully he is well fertilised with his feet firmly planted in a big pile of rancid monkey poo. Professional monkey poo throwers are so organised, makes you proud to be British doesn't it? Great British poo is the best poo in the world, they said so on the BBC, and they're unbiased.

Because he's bagsied poo throwing rights, Jim struggles with the demo part of democracy. The little people should not be allowed to organise themselves and protest in Jim's world. Proper protests can only be those which are organised and led by people who spent a decade in student politics and getting censured for "intolerant and dictatorial" methods, before going straight to being a Labour MP and becoming a member of Tony Blair's government. They're the only people who've earned the right to throw monkey poo. People like Jim, in fact. The rest of us do our poo throwing all wrong, and there's a very easy test of what's right and wrong in political poo throwing. It's whether or not any of it lands on Jim or his pals.

In a state where the two main parties are indistinguishable in their important policies, poo throwing is all that remains. For decades, UK politics have consisted of little else. It's dreary, depressing and decreasingly relevant to the real lives of real people. The poo throwing is stage managed, and isn't even entertaining any more. But Jim trained specially as a poo thrower, it's what he does. Only now him and his pals in the Unionist Wing of a decreasingly united Labour party find that it doesn't work against a mass movement consisting of a diversity as diverse as Scotland itself. They're no longer throwing poo at a party, they're throwing poo at a people.

Jim has been joined in his poo throwing efforts by that doughty campaigner for social inclusion and equality, except if you're on benefits, Kathy Wiles, the Labour prospective parliamentary candidate for Angus. Kathy charmingly launched a very big jobbie of her own, which sailed all the way across Godwin's Law and out of contention - which is also a fair description of the trajectory of Kathy's career in politics. In a not over the top way at all, she didn't liken a pic of some weans at the BBC demo to the Hitler Youth, it was just a juxtaposition. Because comparing folk to Nazis is something only Yes voters do. Oh look, a flying poo.

The big problem Jim and Kathy face however is that the non-professional political amateurs aren't really interested in political monkey poo throwing. It's not that the amateurs of Yes never indulge in a spot of poo throwing of their own, it's just that being amateurs they do it in their spare time, and so expect their poo throwing to provide at least a modicum of entertainment value. For Jim it's a soulless and joyless career. And there he is, out-pooed and out-politicked by a bunch of amateurs.

However Yes supporters are not involved in this debate in order to play Jim's favourite professionalised sport, dominated as it is by over-indulged and spoiled egos who confuse their earnings with their worth and talent. Yes supporters are far more interested in politics as an organic and natural fertiliser which can produce a crop of enthusiastic, engaged and interested voters debating the future possibilities this land presents. Throwing poo at that sort of movement only makes it grow more. It makes more people take notice, and wonder things like how can a peaceful protest featuring weans reading poems and panda power possibly count as bullying a big national broadcaster that puts single mothers in jail for not paying the licence fee?

After all, it must have been a quiet and problem free protest, there wasn't any rioting on the BBC news. Because the BBC is unbiased isn't it - a sentence which can by now only be uttered in a Scottish accent if the intonation marks it for sarcasm. And there's this politician saying the BBC is being bullied because people who aren't licenced poo throwers have the audacity to point out that the greatest national broadcaster in the wurruld, or the wuld if you're a BBC presenter, is in fact a bit shite.

And then they think, och that's Jim Murphy throwing red rosette monkey poo again. Poor quality low grade stuff that. Panda poo makes your garden grow better. It's the bamboo diet. It might even grow a garden where poo throwing is once again an art form and not a political career. That's a choice Jim isn't inclined to give us, because for Jim the whole point of poo throwing is to smooth a nice career path that ends with a cosy seat in the House of Lords Hospice for Intolerant Dictatorial Poo Throwers. And in the process of that chain of thought another undecided has switched to Yes, another No has become undecided. That's the problem when you combine monkey poo with political spin, it's very likely to come back at you and hit you in the face.

Meanwhile more and more Labour supporters and members make the journey to Yes. The fearmongering and the demonisation is no longer aimed at dissuading the unconverted from engaging with Yes. It's now aimed at No supporters, it's the corralling of the wagons in the hope that their remaining support won't evaporate like the 20% plus lead in the polls did.

But even they are beginning to ask themselves, if the great British state can be bullied and threatened and brought to its knees by a panda with a poem, it's not going to be much use when faced with a real bully - like an international corporation that's not keen on paying taxes, or a bank that's too big to fail. So what then, exactly, is the point of keeping it? And then they decide to investigate panda poems instead of monkey poo.

2 July 2014
¡Viva la evolución!

Jack McConnell wants us to vote No in order to preserve "Home Rule". That would be the home rule that doesn't give you control over your own home, the home rule that lumbers you with a Trident lodger you can't evict even though it spews radioactive waste all over your Firth of Clyde patio and pisses plutonium particles in your petunia bed. You still get sent to bed while the grown ups from the EU come to visit, you're certainly not allowed out on the international stage yourself - they're keeping your passport.

Scotland still won't get enough home rule to prevent one fifth of its citizens from living in relative poverty. Supervision isn't cheap you know, someone's got to pay. But we have to keep the rich sweet. London needs to be a global city or there's no home rule for you, and London needs a shiny new train set so the big boys will come to play. You pay trains, they play trains. That's home rule.

Jack is in favour of the home rule that tells you you don't control your home's finances, but you can live on some pocket money while the grown ups in Westminster make all big decisions for you and control all the pursestrings. They'll decide how much pocket money you'll get. You don't rule the earnings of your own labour, Labour does.

You're allowed to decide what wallpaper you want for your bedroom, but Westminster will keep its paws firmly on the TV remote control. You're not grown up enough to home rule the telly. And no, you can't get one for your bedroom. You might break it. You're too wee, and you're not responsible enough, not like the grown ups who jealously guard all the power and lecture you on democratic representation from the House of Lords.

They might consent to giving you a loan of a little bit of power. But if you don't behave, the big boys and girls can take away your home rule privileges whenever they see fit. That's why they call it devolution, because they see it as the opposite of evolution. Or at least a 19th century understanding of evolution, because that's about as modern as Westminster science gets.

Westminster sees devolution as a reversal of the onward march to ever more intelligent and civilised life, an unfortunate kink in the chain of being which ends with them and their godlike power. It's evolution in reverse. In the minds of the Westminster parties, it's a process which can only start with cavemen and work its way back to primordial slime. But that's happening to them anyway, they descended into sleaze a very long time ago. If Westminster loses any more of its authority they're afraid they'll devolve so much they'll no longer be capable of tying their own shoe laces. It is a justified fear.

Devolution is a hiccup in the path to progress of an ever more perfect Westminster. They're still a long way short of that and getting further from it with every passing day without any assistance from Scotland, so you can understand why they're not so keen to give any of their authority away to uppity Caledonians with the notion that they can do the job better by themselves. Face it, it would be harder to do any worse, we're talking about a low bar here.

The United Kingdom is one of the least equal countries in the developed world, the inequalities are only getting wider. Low paid jobs on short contracts have become the norm. People in full time paid work still qualify for benefits. Our governments subsidise employers to create jobs which can't pay a living wage. Trickle down economics, the only trickle is the sweat on the brow of the woman faced with a choice of feeding her kids or switching off the heating in a cold November. And Labour politicians tell us that people need to be motivated to find work by stripping them of what dignity they have left.

The UK is the most centralised state in Europe. Scotland has greater control over her own affairs than other parts of the UK, but devolution gives Holyrood fewer tax raising powers than the average municipality in other countries. Scotland has no control over its own resources, and is the only oil producing country in the world without an oil fund - except Iraq. We get 30 minutes of Jackie Bird, stories about cattle that fell in the watter and had to get shot and a whole load of stuff about people playing games, like Jim Murphy the professional monkey poo thrower. It's what passes for news in devoland. There's lots of fitba at the end too for sports fans. Catalonia has a 24 hour news channel and five TV channels of its own. And the Trident lodger is staying put.

The UK has put all its economic eggs into the basket of the global finance centre of London. All else in the UK exists only to serve the goal of global player worldstage strutting. Devolution won't change any of that.

So Jack McConnell and Jim Murphy had a great idea. Let's call it home rule instead. Let's resucitate an old slogan from the dusty shelves of history, because everyone who knew what it meant is deid. Then Jack and Jim can tell us what it means. It's One Nation Labour's new trick, reviving slogans from the 19th century. That's progressive politics Labour style. Scotland can swap its sovereignty for a snappy Victorian soundbite.

But we already know what Jack McConnell's home rule means, it's teenage life with a tagging order. There may be a parole hearing, sometime after the next General Election, and they'll decide whether to allow you a little bit more freedom. But nae promises. Only the Yes campaign is expected to provide certainties. Scotland is on probation until we stop thinking about absconding from the sludge that successive UK governments have created.

It's for the people of Scotland to decide what we want out of this Union or whether we want out of it. Jack and Jim want us not to think about it, until they can tell us what to think. Further devolution is a conversation we need to have with the whole of the UK, say Jack and Jim. That's why you can't have a vote on it. But the real reason is that they don't want us to state what we want to say before the conversation starts. Then they'd be obliged, and that would never do. You can't be having power coming from the people. That's not the devolved way.

We've been here before. Not once. Not even twice. We've seen this continually over the past 40 years as our faith in the willingness of Westminster parties to devolve has devolved even quicker. We were promised something better in 1979 and got Maggie Thatcher and 18 years of pain. Labour promised a parliament with real tax raising powers so Scotland would never again be dependent on the whims of Westminster. We got a parlie but the tax raising powers were designed to be unusable, and have remained unused. Which proves they're working. Just not for Scotland. Scotland gets pocket money instead. And a civic civil nationalism that devolution didn't kill stone dead.

We were promised more powers with Calman, but discovered that a Calman was the name of a fish dish that was gutted, filleted, and had its bones and flesh consumed in Commons committees. Scotland got left with a greased soaked newspaper.

Now we're told they'll devolve home rule, which is suitably vague and encompasses everything that it might be fondly imagined to be from Unionists who believe in federalism fairies, to those who want to kill nationalism stone dead. Even Michael Forsyth, once Tory handbagger in chief in Scotland, is keen to offer us new toys. Small toys, not a train set. Perhaps a Kinder surprise egg's worth of devolution. He's changed his tune. But we're assured the conversion is sincere, if unexplained.

It's too little too late. Scotland's faith in Westminster's ability to deliver has devolved into a pool of raw materials awaiting the spark of a Yes vote for it to spring into life.

And something is stirring in the Scottish soup. The amino acids of activism are forming protein chains of ideas. Links are forming, bonds being created. Self sustaining actions and reactions are taking place.

People are thinking things they never thought before. Seeing things in new ways. Things like - this isn't about Alicsammin at all. It's about me. It's about my family. It's about my friends.

We're too evolved for devolution. We can walk upright. We can think for ourselves. We can evict the Trident lodger, get the TV remote control and decide for ourselves what sort of country we want to live in.

Scotland's political life is evolving into sentience. People are having intelligent conversations about possibilities and the kind of Scotland that could evolve into being. They've already realised that Scotland doesn't have to live in the slime. It can be a fairer place, a more just place. It can be a place of dignity, where mothers' brows only sweat with worry because weans are weans and dae schtupit things. But their tea is always on the table, and the hoose is always warm on a cold winter's night. That's the kind of country that Scotland can only evolve into with a Yes vote in September.

¡Viva la evolución escocesa!

3 July 2014
The SLAB sleb that's missing

There's new game in the referendum campaign, spot the missing celebrity, the name that's missing from the List of No Fame. So where is HE then? You know, him, the Great Unmentionable One. Care must be taken not to utter his name because if you say it three times in a row he'll come back to haunt you.

The No campaign are extremely fond of their celebrity endorsements. We've heard from just about everyone, from Janette Krankie and John Barrowman, thon Canadian actor who does a convincing Scottish accent if you don't have a Scottish accent yourself, via JK Rowling and Bowie, and passing through every UK politician you've ever heard of and hundreds that you've not, to Obama and - allegedly - the Pope. The only global celebrities they've not dragged out so far are the Dalai Lama, and He Who Must Not Be Mentioned.

It's pretty obvious why Secretary of State for Scotland Alistair Karma Kill wouldn't be keen on the spiritual leader of Tibetan

Buddhism, what with having such a Buddhist-unfriendly name. But there's also the wee question of the Dalai Lama being the leader of an independence campaign of his own. So they're trying to get Sting instead, next time he pops up out of a tantric yoga lotus position.

But no one's asking Don't Mention His Name, the PM who came between Major and Broon, both of whom have already put in an appearance - or in Gordie's case launched and relaunched more often than an obsessive entrant in Britain's Got Talent who never gets past the selection round due to the jeers of the audience. He can try again in Edinburgh next month in front of a specially selected audience of fans.

The One Who Is So Messianic Even Murdoch Asks Him To Intercede With God is way more famous on the international stage than Gord, who is widely regarded as an embarrassment that it's best to draw a veil over. Gord's former boss is bigger than Big Sean, who has only made movies. The Light of the Middle East (that's phosphorus bombs for you) has had movies made about him - admittedly not movies that portray him in a sympathetic light, but then he's not a sympathetic character and you can't have everything even if you are Alistair Campbell. He is no mere mortal, he hath ascended into a being who moves in atmospheres so rarified that there is little oxygen - which may explain why the conscience centres of his brain have shrivelled and died as his bank balance has ballooned.

Unlike the PM who came before him, the Famous One is Scottish, as we are so often reminded with glee by commentators in the UK media. His Scottishness constitutes proof that Scotland shouldn't complain about not getting the governments we want. Was it not you-know-who who headed the government that introduced devolution? And Labour keeps telling us they're the party of devolution, and not the party who conceded devolution reluctantly and half-heartedly after Scotland had spent a decade and a half demanding it. So you'd think that Alistair Darling would be keen to enlist the support of his old boss to reaffirm the devo credo.

But scarcely a word has passed his lips on the topic of the land of his birth. No one has solicited his opinion or his blessing. No one wants his opinion because his blessing is toxic.

So they settled on Jim Murphy instead, who had only a minor role to play in warmongering. He'll make do with a coach and a small entourage of ordinary person stand-ins for press photography purposes, who've all promised not to go tweeting photies of the Hitler Youth in return for being considered as the new Labour candidate for Angus.

The other Alistair did express an interest in divine intervention from El Capo de Tutti Careerists. He went a lot further and prophesied the Second Coming of the New Labour Messiah. Back in May 2012 he assured Andrew Marr that [fill in name here] would form part of a "call to arms" to resist independence. Which was possibly an unfortunate turn of phrase to use seeing as how the individual in question is most famous for his dodgy call to arms over weapons of mass destruction that turned out not to exist, plunged the Middle East into chaos, and setting off a chain of events that have so far caused the deaths of over 500,000 human beings. He's since spent his energies enriching himself by speaking up on behalf of downtrodden innocent dictatorships, when he's not been fending off allegations that he's a war criminal.

However Alistair assured us that his former boss and ideological master was going to play a big role in the No campaign. "He's got a lot to contribute and I hope he'll contribute more in the future," Alistair added. And if you listened very carefully you could hear the sound of 100,000 Iraqi ghosts crying.

Yet by the following December, the Godlike One had still not contributed despite Alistair's fond wish. While in Edinburgh that month he was asked by a reporter from the Scotsman whether he'd participate in Scotland's debate. He replied: "I'm very happy to play a part in it but it's up to those who are going to organise the campaign."

So where is he then? Has Alistair been too busy to ask him? Has the Ego On Expenses been too busy? Perhaps someone ought to ask Alistair if ever anyone manages to pin him down anywhere anytime long enough to have a debate.

But it would seem that the Labour party is not keen on the intervention of their Special One. Dragging That One out might remind us that we were wrong when we thought it was impossible to hate a politician more than your average Scot hated Maggie Thatcher. You can say what you like about Attila the Handbag, and gods know I have, but she was an evil Tory bastert who made no bones about being an evil Tory bastert. In the long dark night of the soul that lasted from 1979 until 1997, you knew you would wake up in the grey dull morning to evil Tory basterts. You knew what you were dealing with, and the cynicism and contempt of Thatcher bred cynicism and contempt in equal measure. Labour was supposed to be the cure.

Resuscitating the biggest sleb SLAB's got might remind us that Alistair Darling, Gordon Brown, Jims Reid and Murphy, the Sainted Wee Dougie, George Robertson, George Foulkes, Eds Miliband and Balls and the other big beasts of Labour were every bit as bestial as the man they don't want us to remember. They were up to their necks in the New Labour nightmare too. They enthusiastically took their cue from the man who burst the bubble of hope, and flushed public trust down a privatised toilet. We might start to ask questions about their complicity, and reflect that they're asking us to trust them again. We might remember the jaunty campaign song in 97.

Things can only get better together. Sounds a whole lot more hollow this time round, doesn't it.

3 July 2014
Blithering idiocies and the maturity of children

How do you respond to blithering idiocy without descending into idiocy yourself? It's a difficult question, and one which is regularly posed to independence supporters. Anger at the shit-stirring proclivities of mainstream journalists itself becomes murphed into the 'abuse' of poor Unionist commentators who have a god-given right to spew lying bile in a crude and transparent attempt to mislead and misdirect, and it becomes a tale of evil bullying nationalists and not a tale of a journalist who traduces his profession.

Tom Brown is described by the Record as a "legendary political commentator". Judging by a jaw-dropping piece he's published for the paper this week, that would be legendary in the sense of mythical monsters. Tom's article was replete with myths and monsters, disguised as a serious intervention in the referendum debate. It was a string of insults dressed up as facts. Baseless fears masquerading as evidence. It was infantile crap even by the standards of a publication which specialises in infantilism.

There are four people in this world I love more than anyone else. My partner, my daughters, and my mother. Of the four only my mother is Scottish - and she's largely Irish by descent. The others are English, London born, London bred, London raised. My daughters were born to English mothers in England. My daughters have two mothers and two fathers. I'm the only Scot. They've lived in London all their lives. They still live there, the Sarf London Innit joy of my existence. They are my children, the flesh of my flesh, the light of my soul. My love for them is unconditional. Tom wants us to believe that love is determined by passports. And this is the man who thinks independence supporters are narrow minded and short sighted.

Tom wants my daughters and me to believe that if Scotland becomes independent my English loved ones and I will become foreigners to one another, that my parents will be blocked by barriers of nationality from the love of their granddaughters. We will be estranged, our relationship tense and fractured. Unconditional love replaced by a stamp in a booklet at a border crossing that only exists in his mind, in the fevered frantic spin in defence of an indefensible political system.

How dare you Tom Brown. You will not tell me or anyone else what our feelings will be towards our English relatives. Do you seriously believe that my children will become alien to me? That I will no longer love them just the same? That's some nerve you've got there. Your fears Tom, are you own, do not project them onto me. Do not project them onto my daughters. Do not project them onto my parents. If you genuinely fear that you will no longer love your own grandchildren just the same after Scottish independence, then you are in desperate and urgent need of family therapy and counselling. Because Tom, you are the one with the problem and it is a specific problem peculiar to you, not to a nation.

By a strange coincidence, just this morning I got a letter from my elder daughter. She's a talented photographer and I'd nagged her for a while about sending me some copies of her photos so I can get them framed, and displayed proudly on the wall. We don't get to see one another as often as we used to since my partner's health declined. They can't stay here as my partner is too frail to cope with visitors coming to stay for a few days - and the truth is I want to protect my children from witnessing the decline of a man they have always looked to as their other Daddy. That's a real barrier to our relationship, a real obstacle in the way. But it changes nothing about our feelings for one another. Love conquers all. Tom Brown doesn't know what love is if he doesn't know that.

Just a few days ago, my elder daughter and I had been chatting on the phone about the scaremongering in the referendum campaign and how Scots were being told that we'd be estranged and alienated from our loved ones in England. She laughed. She thought it funny. She thought it funnier when I remarked that she was already alien to me because she's a girl in her late teens, and the workings of the teenage female mind are profoundly alien to crabbit auld gits like me. So she finally sent me the photos of her and her sister I'd been reminding her to send for months, and at the bottom was a PS in the handwriting of my younger daughter: "You'll never be foreign to us. xx"

I'm even more crabbit after reading Tom Brown's offensive tirade. Tom tells us that it's insulting to his grandchildren in England that they will have to apply for Scottish citizenship. The only insults here are the insults Tom throws at those of us who are far more mature and adult than he is - people like my teenage English daughter and her 11 year old sister.

Grow up Tom. When an 11 year old has more maturity than you, you've lost the argument, you've lost moral authority, you have lost any respect you once claimed to have as a "legendary political commentator".

7 July 2014
The alienation of an alien nation

So we've had Danny Alexander making up statistics about start up costs and his arithmetical nervous breakdown being taken apart by the very man who supplied the raw data to begin with. The Foreign and Commonwealth Office has been running Liz's state coach and horses through the civil service neutrality guidelines and using British diplomatic staff to drum up support for No. We've had the running sore of the CBI and its yes-no-yes-no-yes we're a no saga and the highly dubious manner in which its registration was handled and a supposedly apolitical business organisation that is in fact highly politicised. And over the weekend the director of a leading pro-devolution body, Reform Scotland - a group which, let us remember, is in favour of retaining the Union - strongly criticised the UK government for its misleading and inaccurate statistics on Scotland's potential oil revenues, and said that the true picture meant Scotland could more than pay its own way and have plenty of cash left over for better health or education services.

And what's the lead story on the BBC Scotland news? Alicsammin sent the fishing industry a letter pointing out that some of their fears were ridiculous scaremongering a la David Mundell, and the fishy man thinks it is intimidatory to point out that a stupid scare story is in fact a stupid scare story. Bullying nationalists and cod stories!

If Alicsammin was indeed trying to silence the shy wallflowers of the fishing fleet, he's clearly not very good at intimidation techniques, because fishy man is all over the BBC like a drunk pub goer with a whole fish supper on his shoulder telling everyone how hard done by he is. Perhaps that will be the next anti-independence spin from John Boothman - independence is a bad idea because the Scottish Government is rubbish at Labour and Tory intimidation techniques and suborning the civil service.

As the independence campaign has progressed, I've found myself increasingly detached from the UK media and its Scottish branch offices. I'm not alone in this alien nation. The media reports on a country I don't know, a referendum I'm not participating in, a campaign that's not the campaign I take a small part in. We're the people they don't want to become foreigners but we're already foreign to them.

Who are they talking to? It's not ordinary Scottish people. We're being talked at, talked down to, told that the important issues are not those that we might find important. It's an experience of alienation that's being repeated across the country. The media is doing itself no favours, especially as many of us were already pretty alienated to begin with.

Alienation is the first step to independence. When you're alienated, you're already independent, you just haven't realised it yet. It's a very short step from alienation to becoming a new nation, and we have the UK media to thank for it. More and more the little people, the pixies and brownies and elfs of Scotland, are realising that we are already independent of the trolls and ogres and the big scary monsters. And we don't want to live with fairy stories any more, we want documentaries and dramas that relate to the lives we really live.

When I was young there was no equality for people like me. Gay men were second class citizens in the eyes of the law. Lesbians didn't exist at all, ignored and marginalised out of existence.

You can respond in a number of ways to this, you can accept it, return to silence, be quiet, remain invisible. Or you can ignore the ignorance right back, you can refuse to accept it. You can refuse to accept the role that's been determined for you. And you can shout it from the rooftops. So we lived our lives as though we were already equal, and by living as though we were already equal, we became equal. Liberation starts in the head. Liberate your own head and heart, the rest will follow.

There was no same sex marriage so we got married anyway, in a humanist ceremony in the early 90s which had no legal recognition. But legal recognition is secondary, the most important recognition is the recognition you grant yourself. In our eyes, and in the eyes of our family and friends, we were already married. When civil partnerships became legal, it was only the law catching up with the equality we'd already established in our own lives and our own hearts.

Scottish independence starts in your own head. All across Scotland, women and men are making their own private declarations of Arbroath, their declarations of Galloway, declarations of West Lothian, of Glasgow, of Aberdeen, Inverness, and Orkney. People are thinking independently, freeing themselves from a Westminster trackway that doesn't reach their homes, a high speed railway to nowhere we know. They're ignoring a media that doesn't tell stories they recognise, and are creating new means of communication, new networks, new connections. Scotland is becoming independent in hearts and minds. Shout it from the rooftops, tell everyone you know.

I don't want to talk about BBC business correspondent Robert Peston and his "all you need to know about independence". I know what independence means without the BBC telling me, and I suspect I know far better than Robert Peston what I need to know - so do you, so does everyone who actually lives in this country. What we need to know is what sort of country we can make this into. We can do better than what's on offer. We can be better, because we are better already.

The UK media's priorities are not mine, their interests are not mine. I don't want to talk about Westminster's welfare. I want to talk about dignity. I don't want to talk about interest rates. I want to talk about fairness and equality. I don't want to talk about currency unions. I want to talk about land reform. I want a land whose own voices are heard.

Independence of the mind means we no longer need to focus on the stories and spin the media tells us is the story. We can write stories of our own, we can begin to imagine the kind of country that Scotland could be, that Scotland should be, that Scotland will be. A country whose citizens think independently.

Westminster and the UK media want us to focus on the process, not the state of being. It's like going on a trip around the world, new experiences open up before you, possibilities undreamt, opening your eyes to the great diversity and the dances of life and becoming a part of it. You have all this to look forward to, new ways, new sights, new sounds and new directions that you choose for youself. It's the trip of a lifetime. But the UK media only wants us to talk about the potential for hassles in the queue at the airport, anything to stop us getting on a independent plane that soars away from Westminster's narrow expectations.

When you decide you're voting yes, you have freed yourself from the shackles of a future that's determined for you by people whose interests are not your own. You've realised that there are different paths to tread, different destinations to strive for. You're independent already, and you already live in a Scotland that Westminster cannot deliver. Live independently in your own head, and you're already a citizen of a new Scotland.

A yes vote in September just makes the law catch up with the reality we've already created. Independence has already been declared.

Think independently, vote yes.

8 July 2014
What John McTernan did on his holidays

John McTernan, in case you're lucky enough never to have heard of him, which makes this your unlucky day, was once employed as Tony Blair's spin doctor. He then went off to Australia to perform the same job for Julia Gillard, before her own party got so fed up with her and John's spin, smear, and slurring that they stabbed her in the back and removed her from office - putting John out of a job was just a fortunate by-product. John left Australia leaving lots of enemies behind, and now he's back in Scotland pissing rank urine all over the independence debate.

John's just gone on his holidays, and last week he used his column in the Scotsman to tell us all about his wee trip to Catalonia. A weekend in Barcelona has made him an expert in Catalan politics, and now he wants to tell us why the Catalans are really not keen on this independence malarky after all. Because John knows best, just like he knows that the Iraq War really was a good idea, he knows that Tony Blair is honest, upright and true, and he knows that he represents all that the Labour party really stands for. That last one being the only one that's objectively true - and if that doesn't make you realise just how low Labour has fallen, nothing else is going to.

I can't help but wondering why John McTernan goes abroad. He could just install a sunbed in a Better Together office and achieve the same effect. Or maybe he didn't go abroad, he went on a virtual reality tour of Barcelona while plugged into a No Thanks holographic projector, which carefully filtered out anything that might contradict

John's - can someone please tell me a polite word for delusional - take on the prospects for independence in Catalonia. Nope, I'm still stuck on delusional.

For anyone who has actually spent any time in Catalonia, some of his impressions just don't ring true at all. For example he said the signs in the airport were only in Spanish and Catalan, seemingly oblivious to the fact that they're in English as well. He also said that his halting Spanish was met with replies in Catalan. But Catalans are well aware that when they are presented with a foreign touristy person with a limited grasp of Spanish that the person is unlikely to speak Catalan either. Friendly and polite foreign touristy persons in this situation are met with kindness and replies in Spanish, and if you're a very friendly and very polite foreign touristy person they even will attempt some limited English. Use just a couple of words in Catalan, and you'll be invited home to meet the family for a wee copa or three. That's Catalan for a swally.

Which means there are only four possible explanations for John's report that he was answered in Catalan. 1. His limited fame as a No campaigner and apologist for warmongers had spread before him, and the Catalans just wanted to piss him off. Or 2. he's just rude and arrogant and they responded in Catalan precisely because they knew he wouldn't understand and they wanted to piss him off. Or 3. they were in fact replying in Spanish but their Catalan accents hopelessly confused John and his limited Spanish because he wasn't really paying attention so they ended up wanting to piss him off . Or 4. They were replying to him in Catalan accented English, and when they realised he still couldn't understand them they decided he was an eejit they wanted to piss off.

We've already seen that John isn't good at recognising English even when it's written down for him, so my money's on four. This may or may not be related to the listening skills he acquired while working as Tony Blair's spin doctor. Your guess is as good as mine. Mind you, *si fos jo a Catalunya, Joan, et respondría al Català també - i el parlo molt mal - no mes per tal de molestar-te.*

He couldn't resist a wee pop at his own culture though, being a ProudScot™, and made a disparaging remark contrasting the real language of Catalan with "synthetic Scots". Synthetic Scots? That's a wee jibe at attempts to create a variety of Scots that suitable for official use, a Scots which is urgently needed to ensure that the language stays alive. The Scots he contrasts with the Catalan he sees on the airport signs as he's fumbling through his Spanish phrase book and not noticing signage in English.

But John doesn't believe in looking beyond the surface of things. He's all about the image and the spin. John's interest in words begins and ends with constructing a sentence which is not technically untrue even though it's fiction. That's the easiest linguistic trick of all. That's the low rent end of the wordsmith's trade. And that's where John belongs. Oh the things we could say about you John, no word of a lie.

Which makes you wonder, where exactly does John think that the standard Catalan suitable for official use comes from? The language goddess created it by the miraculous transformation of a Spanish phrase book? Is that what makes Catalan a proper language but Scots is not? Was Catalan waved into existence by mysterious and unseen forces beyond the ken of humanity? We already know it was beyond the ken of John.

Modern standard Catalan was created in the 19th century on the basis of Catalan orthography during the Golden Age of Catalan literature in the Middle Ages. It's a form of Catalan that was self-consciously purged of Castilianisms and loanwords from Spanish. Spellings were standardised and the new written language consciously sought to distinguish itself from its close relatives. New vocabulary was created in order to make it fit for use as the language of a Catalan state. Catalan people did this quite consciously, and in the act of creating a national language they reaffirmed that Catalonia is a nation. Since all the other institutions of Catalan nationhood had been abolished by the centralising Spanish state, Catalans invested their nationhood in their language in a way that Scots didn't have to.

Linguistic misconceptions aside, the main impression John took from his holidays was the notion that Catalans are going off the idea of independence. It's a form of wishful thinking exactly the same as his wishful thinking that few in Scotland are seriously attracted to the idea of independence either. And it's equally wide of the mark.

John believes that Spain's economic crisis is making the Catalans think again about independence. He couldn't be more wrong if he'd tried. The Spanish economic crisis is the driving force of the Catalan independence movement. It's the years of mismanagement, corruption, self-interest and lack of accountability from Madrid which has turned many Catalans who were previously lukewarm about the idea of a Catalan state into strong supporters of independence. It's what's happened in Scotland too.

John thinks that Scotland and Catalonia are better together with the people who caused the problems in the first place, the people who brought ruin, who destroyed the economy, destroyed hope of a better future, and who still sit in power collecting brown envelopes and fattening their bank accounts. But John talked at some Proud Catalans™ on his holidays, and he knows better.

The most recent opinion poll in Catalonia, taken at the end of June - when John was trying to negotiate his way through Barcelona airport - showed that 50.9% plan to vote yes if an independence referendum is held in November this year, as planned by the Catalan Parliament. Only 30.1% plan to vote no, the remaining 19% are don't knows. If don't knows are removed, this would produce a result of 62.8% in favour of independence. So aye John, the Catalans are really going off the idea ...

Some of us don't just speak halting Spanish John, we speak it pretty well, and we speak Catalan too. And when you talk to proud Catalans you find that they're overwhelmingly in favour of independence. Funny how our media publishes such one sided accounts of Catalan affairs as well as Scottish ones. You'd almost imagine they were trying to put us off the idea of independence.

Visca Catalunya, visca Escòcia, visca la independència.

10 July 2014

Martin Kettle's pandanoculars

You have to love the Guardian's Martin Kettle, this week he's desperately seeking an intellectual case for Scotland to remain within the Union, and all the while he examines Scotland from afar through

Paul Kavanagh

the wrong end of ink covered binoculars that leave him panda eyed. If Tian Tian isn't pregnant after all, we could probably hire Martin to stand in as third panda. It would at least allow him to make a relevant contribution to Scottish discussions. Zoo visitors would even be prepared to look indulgently on Martin's habit of ramming a bamboo shoot up his backside and calling it an insight. Aww ther a cute wee Guardian columnist, bless, inty lovely. Oh look, ther a monkey in a rid rosette throwin poo.

You can, if you put your mind to it, rustle up a suitably intellectual sounding justification for pretty much any proposition you care to mention. All it takes is some impressive sounding words, a liberal sprinkle of quotations, and a selectiveness with facts that makes a vegan with a wheat allergy seem like an unfussy dinner guest. This is why there are people in this world who sincerely believe that Native Americans are descended from the tribes of Israel who got lost on a package holiday to Miami, that the standing stones of Calanais were built by aliens as a landing strip (but without a Sunday service, of course), or even that Scotland 2014 is a programme worth watching. Well OK, maybe not that last one. No one with any understanding of Scotland believes that, not even Sarah Smith. Martin probably does though, and that explains why he is desperately trying to rustle up an intellectual case for the extraordinary proposition that a country shouldn't govern itself and electing its own government is an extraordinary state of affairs. He does this by rebutting the arguments of a Scottish independence campaign which is even more phantom than a panda pregnancy and exists solely in the hormonal flushes of a senile UK establishment.

You can only maintain your intellectual pretence when your audience is in possession of even fewer facts than you are. What you can't do is to put lipstick on a pig and pretend it's a panda, with or without the benefit of inky binoculars, because the dedicated panda watchers of the referendum campaign will still spot the difference. Martin's big problem is that referendum panda watching is now a mass participatory sport in Scotland, and even small children can tell the difference, leading commentators like Martin and Labour party candidates to mutter about Alicsammin der Pandaführer.

Martin argues that Scotland is a partner in the Union and has not been singled out for special mistreatment by Westminster. And this last bit would be true. Wales, Northern Ireland and the English regions have equally suffered from Westminster's focus on developing London as a global centre of finance. But that is not the same as Scotland remaining a partner in the Union. Scotland along with all other parts of the UK have declined from being partners in this Union to being colonies of the financial industries of the City of London. Our resources are used to build infrastructure in London, our brightest children attracted to the opportunities the city presents - because there are no such opportunities for them at home in Scotland, or in Wales, or in Manchester or Liverpool. Scotland, Wales, Northern Ireland and the English regions are all equally internal UK colonies who exist to service and further the development of the Global City.

If Martin really wanted some solid evidence that Scotland is not a partner in this Union, he only needs to look at the state-sponsored hoo-ha with which Westminster has surrounded the issue of a currency union. If we were truly a partner in the eyes of Westminster, a currency union would not even be subject to discussion - it would be seen as a perfectly logical and rational means of preserving and fostering cooperation between two neighbouring nations which have strong economic, personal and cultural links. Instead we have the bitter refusal to acknowledge that Scotland has played any role at all in "Westminster's pound".

If Scotland was truly a partner in the eyes of Martin and his Westminster chums, there would be no dispute that Scottish independence means the end of the Union of 1707, instead there is the insistance that Scotland was dissolved and abolished and Westminster not Holyrood represents the sole continuing state. That's not partnership, that's possession.

Back in the 1970s, the Marxist writer and thinker Michael Hechter published a highly influential book - at least it was influential on the Scottish left - called Internal Colonialism - in which he argued that the "Celtic peripheries" of the UK were internal colonies of the British state. At the time it was argued that Hechter's analysis was mistaken, a Scotland which still preserved much of its traditional industry and was one of the centres of the UK economy could scarcely be said to be a colony. But then Thatcher happened. Scotland's traditional heavy industry was decimated, along with that in the rest of the "British periphery" - in the English regions as much as Scotland or Wales. With the UK's postwar failure to maintain itself as an industrial and military superpower, the new goal was for the UK to strut the world stage as a financial superpower. The regions and nations of the rest of the UK are the new colonies, serving the goal of maintaining London's position as a leading centre of the financial industry, sources of revenues and labour to further those needs. That's about as close to colonialism as you can get without actually being a colony. 40 years later the core of Hechter's analysis has come true. But Scotland can choose another path, a path Martin can't see, blinded by his pandanoculars.

There are only two exceptionalisms in the Scottish case for independence. The first is that the Scottish independence campaign is the only one in the history of the United Kingdom and its many colonial possessions where the party of UK government has been less fertile than a panda. Out-fucked by a panda, there's an epitaph for the Union. The second is that unlike the rest of the UK, there is something Scotland can do to address the lamentable state of self serving affairs which passes for governance in the UK. The UK constitution exceptionally recognises the right of Scotland to self determination, and Scotland's exceptionalism is the claim that Scotland can be a normal country like any other. Scotland's exceptionalism is the exceptional ability to deliver Westminster a Glesca kiss and escape its strangling embrace.

It's not really that exceptional in the cosmic scheme of things, but we can see why it's got Martin worried. We have the exceptional ability to burst the bubble of the London commentariat. And we're doing it for Wales, Northern Ireland and the English regions almost as much as we're doing it for ourselves.

The real exceptionalism is Martin's and his exceptional panda eyes. Vote Yes so Scotland can be a normal country.

15 July 2014

Not falling out with family

So have you fallen out with any family members yet? Over the referendum that is, not because your brother in law didn't return your cordless electric drill. I couldn't tell you if I've fallen out with any family members over the referendum, although mocking words have certainly been said, largely by me if I'm honest. But then that's normal under any set of circumstances in our family and at any given time there will always be some of us not talking to the rest of us except via UN Blue Helmet wearing peacekeepers carrying coded messages. And more often than not, yours truly is the one with the Blue Helmet, which ought to give you some idea of just how prone we are to falling out. And you thought I was bitchy?

So given our familial propensity for having big fall outs, my granny was a woman who lived to be 100 and nursed a number of grudges for about 99 of those years, I'm feeling a bit left out, because according to the newspapers Scottish families are estranged and at odds over the referendum and we're close to civil war. At least according to Madeleine Bunting who's on leave from the Guardian to write a book about the relationship between Scotland and England. Maddie thinks we're on the verge of irreconcilability and she's a top Guardian commentator who studied at Oxford and comes here on her holidays and everything, so she's clearly an expert on the dynamics of interpersonal relationships in Scottish families.

Mind you I can't help but wondering why it is that commentators from the metronomenklatura have suddenly discovered that Scotland is a land riven with schism and social division, constantly on the edge of open warfare. But my more cynical half suspects that they might just be reacting against a debate that they feel excluded from and powerless to influence. Which is actually quite a good summation of how the average inhabitant of Scotland has felt about UK politics for the past 40 years and explains why we're having this debate now. After all, if you continually exclude a group from a conversation, you can't complain when they go off and talk amongst themselves like the people of Scotland are doing just now. But Maddie thinks this is dangerous, as Scottish punters aren't licenced properly and don't have degrees from Oxford. She's touring Scotland looking for division and fall outs which the rest of us aren't seeing.

So where's the great Scottish stairheid rammy then? Magrit Curran's probably away for her holidays, but that doesn't explain the general absence of stairheidrammage. This is an essential precursor to any irreconcilability, because unlike the cultural norms to which Maddie may be accustomed, in some parts you cannot have an irreconcilable falling out with someone without first telling everyone you know, plus their relatives, just how much of an utter utter bastard the person is that you're no longer talking to. Otherwise what is the point of falling out?

As everyone in Glasgow knows, a verbal disagreement doesn't count as a falling out unless A) there are actual threats of violence which might actually come to pass, as opposed to suggestions that there may be malkydom in the near future or imprecations to get it up ye, and / or B) one party gets the other party's mother involved. And it's only really serious when B happens.

My sister, who's a confirmed No voter - and I can say this safe in the knowledge that she doesn't read this blog and she's not going to clype me to our maw - told me she didn't want us to fall out over the referendum. I was a bit surprised, not because she's a No voter, the fact she is a No voter is the opposite of surprising. And it's not surprising that she's quite keen to tell everyone about it either. There's no sign of shy no voter with her, nor with most of the relatively small number of people I know who are certain to vote no. They're pretty loud about it on the whole.

I was surprised that she thought I might believe I was able to change her mind, because she's never listened to anything I've said for the past 50 years and there's no reason she's about to start now. But also I was surprised because she knows as well as I do that we have a million and one things to fall out over first before we get around to falling out over anything remotely approaching the independence referendum. However she's now quite convinced that she must protect her virgin like innocent nawness from the deprecations of bullying Yes voters who might tell her some facts. She's not keen on facts, like the fact that in our family she is in a small minority in her banged on nawness. I blame people like Madeleine Bunting.

However not for the first time in her life, my sister hasn't been thinking things through, because as far as the referendum and my No voting sister go, I'm onto a winner either way - as I previously explained to another No voting relative. Either Yes will win and I get to be a smug git, or No will win and then when we get screwed over by Westminster - as we invariably will - I'll get to say "See I told you so" for the rest of her life, and get to be a smug git. So I'm not about to fall out with my sister any time soon, there's far too much smugging gitness to look forward to.

But what the media campaign of "bullying Yes supporters" aims to achieve is to make Scots afraid of "the other", only the "other" is ourselves and our own families and friends. It feeds on the ancient stereotype of Scots beloved of some outside Scotland that as a nation we are argumentative - which is probably true - but also that we are incapable of handling disagreements and are prone to irrational violence. Scots are supposedly too politically immature. It's a form of anti-Scottish racism, a type of Cringe. Political discussions must be left to those who are suitably qualified, like those with a degree in Politics Philosophy and Economics from Oxford University, staff writers on the Guardian, and elected politicians. The rest of us shouldn't discuss politics because we might break something.

But the reverse is true. Scottish families fall out all the time and then we kiss and make up because family and friends are too important. Disputatious people are good at disputes, we have had years of practice in dealing with them and resolving them, and this referendum is no different.

The only difference is that for the first time in decades Scots have found differences of opinion about politics, when for the past 40 years there has been little disagreement amongst the Scottish public about the nature of politics. Politicians could all be summed up in one statement just about everyone could agree on: "They're aw shite, aren't they." Only now there are many of us who think there's something we can do about the shiteness of our political classes. We can do a better job ourselves, and with a Yes vote we can get a written constitution which ensures that politicians are properly accountable.

I won't be falling out with anyone over this referendum. That doesn't mean I won't be disagreeing or putting my case across. And I'll still be disagreeing with my sister, and may very well fall out with her about things unrelated to the referendum, because I have no intention of changing the habits of a lifetime. But as far as the referendum goes I'll be concentrating my efforts on those who do actually listen to other people's points of view.

The Scottish public are considerably more mature and grown up than the Westminster elite and their media hangers on give us credit for. The truth is, they're the ones who behave like spoiled and greedy children who have temper tantrums when they don't get their own way, and in September Scotland can put them on the naughty step for good. My sister will get over it.

16 July 2014
Juncker's hammer blow

On Tuesday the UK media and the No campaign got all excited when EU Commission President Jean Claude Juncker said that he was not in favour of enlargement of the EU for the next five years or so. Suddenly they've got a new blow for Alicsammin from the man who just the other week said that he would accept the result of the Scottish referendum whichever way it went. It was a hammer blow for Alicsammin's EU hopes, said Wee Dougie Alexander, fresh from polishing his halo and not falling out with his sister. Scotland would have to join the queue behind Moldova and not gain entry for a decade.

Everyone in Europe hates us, the French think more highly of Turkey's prospects of EU membership, Scottish Unionists chorused smugly, in a demonstration that they've really not quite got the hang of this smugness business. But acting smug after your country receives an apparent kick in the nads and a message of rejection is the new definition of ProudScot in the lexicon of Unionese.

It was all very convenient on a day where the other referendum related news was the strengthening of the hand of the Eurosceptic faction in the cabinet after Davie Cameron's reshuffle. The Tories are now increasingly dominated by politicians who want the UK to withdraw from the EU, but failing that want the UK to opt out of the European Court of Human Rights. This demand is likely to form a centre piece of the Tories' package of EU renegotiations, but it's a demand which runs directly counter to the foundation treaties of the EU and equally likely to prove incompatible with continuing UK membership. The chances of the Tories managing to negotiate a new settlement that their more swivel eyed wing finds acceptable got more remote yesterday, and with moves towards Euroscepticism boosting the Tories in polling south of the border, the prospect of a UK exit from the EU looms ever closer.

There was another wee development in the appointment of the Eurosceptic Philip Hammond as the new foreign secretary. Together with the appointment of some no-mark no one has ever heard of as the new UK EU Commissioner, the UK media has interpreted the reshuffle as a two fingered salute to Brussels from Westminster. The UK home teams may have been utterly rubbish in the World Cup, but that won't stop Westminster from demonstrating that they're still the top Euro hooligans. Cameron's reshuffle sent the EU the message: "We're the Westminster boot boys, everybody hates us and we don't care."

Hammond was the top Tory widely rumoured to have been behind the anonymous admission of a "senior Conservative cabinet minister" to the Guardian that "of course" a currency union between Scotland and the rest of the UK would be negotiated. As foreign secretary, Hammond will play a key role in any future negotiations between a Yes voting Scotland and the Government of the rUK. So there's interesting.

But within a couple of hours Juncker's office issued a statement saying that he wasn't referring to Scotland at all, adding that Scotland was an internal matter. So it was a hammer blow for Alicsammin in the same way that Wyle. E Coyote's Acme rocketsled hammer is a blow for Roadrunner. It launched onto the airwaves and in a graceful arc swung back round and squashed Blair McDougall's tuba. Juncker's clarification not only confirmed that he wasn't referring to Scotland at all, it also confirmed that in his eyes the issue of Scottish membership doesn't count as an EU enlargement and is quite a different kettle of eurofish from the accession to the EU of external candidate countries. Scotland becoming a member of the EU in her own right is no more enlargement than dividing a large room into two rooms counts as building an extension to your house.

The No campaign are still desperate for you to believe that Scotland becoming independent means we are automatically outside the EU and would have to reapply for membership from outside the EU like Serbia or Turkey. This is a lie. I'd like to be kind and say it was a bit of a misunderstanding, or maybe a misreading or a genuine failure of comprehension. But it's not. It's a lie. Many in the No campaign sincerely and genuinely believe the claims of Unionist politicians, but those who head the campaign are still telling a porkie pie, and not even a Melton Mowbray one whose contents are guaranteed by a European protected designation of origin, it's an entirely ficticious pork pie. They know they're not telling you the truth.

What the Unionists want you to believe is an implication which they derive from a fact. The fact is that an independent Scotland will not have signed the EU accession treaties, the implication is then that Scotland cannot be a member of the EU and must therefore be automatically excluded.

But that's not the logical consequence of Scottish independence at all. EU law recognises only one procedure for a country or territory to leave the EU, it's covered by Article 50 of the EU Treaties. Leaving the EU can never be automatic, because EU law grants rights and imposes obligations on individuals as well as on member states. These rights and obligations must be carefully disentangled before leaving the EU. An EU exit must be negotiated, and negotiations can only commence when the government of the territory, country or state which seeks an exit makes a formal request to Brussels. Scotland has no intention of doing that. Scotland's independence is, as Juncker repeated yesterday, an internal matter. Leaving the EU doesn't enter into it.

Scotland is not going to leave the EU as a result of voting Yes in September, we are not voting to leave the EU, and we cannot be expelled from the EU by voting for independence. It's against EU law. Juncker's comments tacitly confirmed this. It's an internal matter, he said, and the implication of his remarks are that Scotland's independence is qualitatively different from the application of an external candidate state.

That means that after a Yes vote, Scotland will still be a part of the EU, in the first instance because immediately after a Yes vote Scotland will still be a part of the UK, and the UK is - for now - an EU member. A yes vote means that the Scottish Government will have the mandate to negotiate Scotland's independence from Westminster, and it means the end of the political union between Scotland and the rest of the UK, but as far as the EU as a whole is concerned, this is a matter for Scotland and the rest of the UK to sort out. Yesterday Juncker repeated that he will respect the result of the vote and the subsequent negotiations.

At the same time as Holyrood negotiates Scottish independence with Westminster, negotiations will also start between Holyrood, Westminster and Brussels regarding the status of Scotland and the rest of the UK with respect to the EU. This will happen while Scotland is still a part of the UK, and therefore still a part of the EU as a part of the UK.

Scotland cannot be automatically expelled from the EU, it's against EU law and in breach of more articles of the EU Treaties than the strategists of the No campaign have ever told lies about. If negotiations on Scottish membership are not complete by the time that Scotland becomes formally independent, transitional arrangements will be made in order to ensure that Scotland remains within the EU while negotiations are completed and the single market is not broken. Scotland will be negotiating her own membership of the EU from within the EU, and will accede to full EU membership in her own right from within the EU.

So Juncker's intervention yesterday was indeed a hammer blow. It was a hammer blow to Unionist scaremongering. Blair McDougal's tuba will never sound the same again.

20 July 2014

The purpose of the heart

We're told the independence campaign is a battle between head and heart, at least a lot of folk in the papers and on telly seem to think so. Usually, it has to be said, it's those of a Nawish persuasion who see themselves on a self appointed mission to blind the bravehearts with a facsimile of logic. Yes supporters counter with logic of their own, and before you know it the debate has descended into an exchange of sterile spreadsheets and legal papers rolling back and forwards in front of the glassy eyes of a population who've lost interest and have gone off to have a laugh at Rory the Tory's - did you know he's Scottish? - attempt to build a big pile of stones on the Border as a symbol of unity. Even though I'm a supporter of independence, I'd be quite happy to donate a big heavy rock to Rory's wee project, just as soon as I get the Freepost address.

But madcap rockery schemes aside, for people who are not versed in EU law or the intricacies of currency unions, which is to say just about everyone, the usual media driven debates have as much meaning and significance as an argument over the carrying capacity of a pinhead of dancing angels. They're not going to help you make your mind up how to vote in September. Logic is a useful tool, but unless it's grounded in a recognisable reality and people without degrees in constitutional law or currency regulation can follow the links, the chain of logic leads straight to the door of an angel disco whose bouncers refuse you entrance.

A chain of logic is only as good as its weakest link, and the No campaign's links rusted through long before an anti-independence argument was suspended from it like a shiny disco ball. This weekend the European Commission president Jean Claude Juncker yanked on Westminster's eurochain and their glittery disco ball of lies came crashing down onto the angelic dancefloor. Which was a lot more entertaining than Strictly.

In case you missed it, Scots are the special ones, according to the EU. José Mourinho eat yer heart out. Speaking to the Scotland on

Sunday newspaper, officials from Juncker's office have confirmed that an independent Scotland's application for EU membership would not be put at the bottom on the pile below Serbia, Moldova and Turkey. Juncker's office have said that Scotland would be a "special and separate case" and would not have to go through an application process which is designed to ensure that new member states are in compliance with a raft of EU legislation and provisions which Scotland has been in full compliance with for the past 40 years. Juncker's spokesperson went even further, adding that the EC president was "sympathetic" to Scottish membership. It's payback time for Davie Cameron's opposition to Juncker's presidency.

This is what Yes supporters have been arguing for quite some time. There's a point to an EU application process, and the point is to ensure that new member states are in compliance with the foundation treaties of the EU and conditions of membership. Scotland's already doing all that. We are in full compliance with EU rules and have already passed our EU driving test. Scotland has been successfully motoring down the euroroutes for decades. We don't need to sit the test again just because we've ditched Westminster's gas guzzling rust bucket for a compact and more environmentally friendly model, and it ought to be fully established by now - at least to everyone outside the Unionist parties and their pals in the media - that it is against EU law to expel Scotland for having an independence vote. On the shiny disco ball in Yes Scotland's dance, open to all, Scotland will be applying for EU membership in its own right from within the EU. The No campaign's threats of vetos or delays are irrelevant.

The No campaign has a big problem, as there is little in the way of emotional support for the Westminster system in Scotland. Those aspects of "Britishness" which appeal to most in Scotland are cultural and personal, and include Ireland and the Irish as much as England or Wales. For Scotland, support for the Union has always been conditional, it depends upon the Union being seen to be better than the alternative. It's difficult to make a positive case for a Union which can't offer its citizens anything better than workfare and wonga loans, so the Unionists must base their emotional appeal upon fear. Fear can be generated by bombarding the voters with "facts" and chains of logic whose weak links are buried under a mountain of irrelevancies and appeals to authorities which on closer inspection turn out not to be so authoritative after all.

Although political campaigns claim to be based on logic and reason, humans are not logical beings and our actions are not driven by logic. We are intensely emotional beings who are capable of logic. That's not the same as being logical. The purpose of human logic is not to determine our goals. Logic serves to determine the course, not the destination. The destination is where the heart lies. As Hugh MacDiarmid pointed out in the poem Twilight, one of the heart's main functions is to power the brain. Do what your heart tells you, then everything else becomes a practical problem. Practical problems have practical solutions, and that's the point where logic comes into it.

The Unionist argument has it the wrong way round, it seeks to confuse and frighten the brain into ignoring the heart. But a No vote based on fear is not a vote for the Union. It's a vote for independence, just not yet. The Union died the day that the No campaign decided to base its strategy on scaring Scotland into submission.

The Yes campaign has it the right way round. It seeks to assuage fears by showing that there are practical solutions to the practical problems thrown up by the challenge of independence. That's why even many No supporters acknowledge that the Yes campaign is better presented and more effective.

So listen to your heart, use all your senses. What does Scotland feel like? What is the taste of Union, is it bitter or is it sweet? Whose music is discordant, whose is melodic? Your heart isn't wrong. Once you've listened to the beat of your heart, you know what your emotions tell you, then and only then can you engage your powers of logic in order to work out how to get from where we are now to where your heart tells you you want to be. Many Scots like the idea of independence, it feels right, it tastes good, it sings to them in catchy tunes, but they're still confused and bewildered by the barrage of misinformation emanating from the No campaign and its supporters.

The key to independence lies in the heart. The logic of the brain tells us how to unlock the door and overcome the barriers. So when you engage in conversation with your undecided family and friends about the independence debate, start with the feeling, and once you've established the fears and uncertainties, then you bring logic into it. Logic allows you to identify practical solutions to the problems of fear and make them practically vanish.

The purpose of the heart is to power the brain.

22 July 2014
The one who cannot be mentioned

The One Who Cannot Be Mentioned has mentioned the independence referendum. It's not that I don't want Tony Blair to come back, I do, preferably in handcuffs. But he's come back minus the handcuffs and he's backing a No vote, like anyone is surprised. Giving a lecture for some think tank in an expensive hotel in London, his speech expressed his fears about what his own party might do, not his fears about what the Tories might do. In Tony's universe, you must not base your politics on how you want the world to be, Tony thinks that's delusional. If Keir Hardie and Robert Cunningham Graham had believed that, they'd never have founded the Scottish Labour party in the first place.

For Tony politics is about managing the expectations of the voters downwards. And in this he richly succeeded, our expectations get lower and lower with every passing vote. But mainly it's about making money and creating the conditions where a small number are able to get extremely rich. Individuals enriching themselves form Tony's definition of 'wealth creators', a definition that would apply just as well to a common or garden thief. But Tony won't be standing trial for his crimes. He's a respected elder statesman. Respected by those who matter that is, that wouldn't be you or me.

The man who brought us the dodgy dossier and the delusional weapons of mass destruction in Iraq is warning us against the delusion that there is any alternative to neo-conservative economics and a professionalised political class with a career plan that ends with a seat in the Lords and a clutch of directorships, stopping off for the occasional foreign war en route.

Despite the best efforts of the No campaign to pretend that Tony Blair never happened and doesn't exist, he's now opened his lying gob on the topic of the land of his birth. But it was only so Tony the Middle East Peace Envoy didn't have to answer questions about why he was giving a speech for a think tank in a posh hotel in London and wasn't in Gaza negotiating an end to rocket fire blowing up hospitals. Though the answer to that one is easy - the catering in London hotels is better. And so is Tone's pay. Besides, Gaza may be the only place on Earth where Tony is more reviled than he is in Scotland and the rest of the UK, although not by much.

But you've got to hand it to the auld warmonger. He achieved something that was previously thought impossible. He broke the laws of nature as well as the laws of war. For years most of Scotland did not believe it was humanly possible to loath a politician more than we loathed Margaret Thatcher, until Tony Blair proved us wrong. So he gets kudos for that, if nothing else.

With Thatcher you got what it said on the proverbial tin, a headlong rush into the cold embrace of the worst of capitalism, an unseemly eagerness to go to war, selfish greed rebranded as a virtue, and lack of compassion as something to aspire to. Tony gave us all that too, but with added hypocrisy, and the last vestiges of hope that Labour would lead us out of the nightmare were crushed under the weight of a pile of broken bodies in Baghdad. No wonder Thatcher once described him as her greatest legacy.

Tony took our dreams and trashed them. Those carefully nurtured small flames that we'd kept alive in our souls throughout the long dark night of the Thatcher years were snuffed out. We'd kept the faith. We'd believed. We'd trusted. Things were going to get better, the day would come when Labour's feeble fifty were feeble no more. Justice would walk the Earth again. But the light at the end of the tunnel turned out to be the last random firings of the neurones before brain death set in, the body of Labour shut down for good and began to rot from the head down. With Tony the Hope Killer, Scotland finally completed its transition into a land where cynicism was the last refuge of dignity.

Now the missiles rain down on Gaza while tanned Tony preaches before an audience of sycophants, politely applauding while he smiles with his tombstone teeth and tells them what they want to hear. The politics of privatisers and PFI contracts is the only way, Tony's third way. ASBOs for the poor, but personal enrichment for those who're guilty of the greatest acts of anti-social behaviour. Shatter a window and you'll get tagged, shatter the dreams of a nation and you'll get a seat in the Lords.

Tony shaped the Labour party we have today. Together with Gordie Broon, his partner in warcrimes, they took our hopes and aspirations and used them to power their own careers. They gave us a Labour party that has no answers, that can only offer more of the same, a slow decline into the impoverishment of the soul. Labour gave us the British Parliamentary road to socialism that started in the lofty aspirations of Hardie and Cunninghame Graham and ended with a missile on the road to Basra and the screams of an Iraqi child.

I'm tired of being cynical. I'm tired of wrapping myself in a coccoon of callouses and keeping my dreams in cold storage while money grabbing pharisees preach the inevitability of poverty for the masses. A Yes vote gives us a chance to hope again, to take back our dignity and rescue it from Tony's lies and the Labour party he mutated into a sick version of himself. There is another way, a better way. A way that doesn't have Tony in it. No wonder he's opposed to it.

If Scotland becomes independent, Tony Blair will become a citizen of Scotland. He was born in Scotland, his right to a Scottish passport is absolute and he will become a Scottish citizen automatically even if he does not bother himself with applying for a Scottish passport. The Scottishness of Blair is no cause for mourning or regret, because it means that if the war-mongering bastard ever sets foot north of the Border he can be arrested and put on trial for his crimes against humanity, for taking us to war on the basis of lies - and as a Scottish citizen facing Scottish justice he won't be able to count on the protection and assistance of the Westminster authorities or the diplomatic corps of the Foreign Office. So that's something to hope for then.

Vote Yes and we can bring Blair to account. That's something worth hoping for.

23 July 2014
Kailyaird kitsch on acid

It's the Glasgow Commonwealth Games, whoop de bloody doo. Many of the residents here in the East End of Glasgow have been left feeling like someone's holding a party and a lavish banquet in our living room, only we've been confined to the spare bedroom with the dug for the duration of the proceedings with a packet of crisps and an auld telly whose channel is stuck on Dougie Donnelly. Naw, ye cannae get oot intae the lobby, away pish in a bucket. The neighbours have organised a "we're trapped" party.

My hoose is going to be cut off because of the Games. The main road will be blocked off so that there can be a cycle race, even though the main road provides the only access for our wee area to the rest of the world. The cooncil haven't seen fit to inform everyone officially - some neighbours got a letter, but there was none at this house or several others locally - despite the fact that this area is home to many elderly people who depend upon visits from care assistants. Just how are the care assistants expected to get in and out? What happens if a doctor needs to be called? Your guess is as good as mine. I'm just relieved that my other half, who suffers from vascular dementia, is currently in hospital, otherwise I'd be worried sick. Seemingly the care needs of Glasgow's elderly and vulnerable people is not as important as a few people running and jumping about a bit. But never mind, Gordon Matheson can get to be on the telly and that makes it all worthwhile.

Being a sportophobe, who would attend therapy sessions to get over my irrational revulsion for all things involving semmits and running shorts only I can't get oot the hoose for folk in semmits and running shorts, my natural instinct is always to regard sporting events with a bemused condescension. Sport is as relevant as tiddly winks, and less productive than macramé, yet millions of people invest it with an immense significance. Sport is just video games for people who don't know how to switch on an Xbox. It's a pastime, an amusement, a means of passing the time. So is sex, and sex is much more fun. Achieves the same thing too - you jiggle things about a bit, get hot and sweaty and lose calories, only with sex if you do it properly you get an orgasm out of it too. I know what sort of pole vaulting I prefer.

But I am unable to regard the Commonwealth Games with the usual detached bemusement, since I can't get out of my fecking house to be detachedly bemused anywhere. Not even at therapy sessions for sportophobes. Instead I need to content myself with being detachedly bemused at whatever clown thought dressing up weans as Tunnocks teacakes was a good idea for the opening ceremony. Possibly the set designer for BBC2's Scotland 2014. Maybe it was an artistic comment on the childhood obesity crisis from the same folk that thought blowing up the Red Road flats was a statement about urban renewal.

There are all sorts of pastimes, but only a minority get the glory and the TV airtime. I play with model trains and trams, but I don't expect the bloody main road to be closed off just so someone can demonstrate their new scale model layout of Brechin train station circa 1950. And it's even got working buses, which is more than you can say for the main road by my house during the Commonwealth Games. But some pastimes get a lot more attention than others, and those would be the butch male pastimes as opposed to the more female pursuits or geeky male pastimes. It's patriarchal oppression you know. Is the Judean People's Liberation Front represented at the Games? Or did those splitters in the Popular Front get the place instead?

Why are there no Commonwealth Games for women and geeks - or that minority group that just about everyone overlooks, geeky women. There's a gold medal for fencing furfexake, how many fencers have you ever met? I did once know a guy with a samurai sword, but he got arrested for drug dealing and the polis confiscated it. That's the closest to fencing you'll get in this part of the world - apart from the neighbour who got creosote all over the back garden. There are no medals for creosoting, and the neighbour wouldn't win one even if there were. There are no medals for knitting or extreme ironing either. No really, extreme ironing is a thing, and if it was a Commonwealth sport I might not moan about the Games being on ... Well, OK, that's a lie, I probably would. I reckon I could win gold medals for Scotland for camp bitchery, gay humour, and working up a full steam of righteous indignation. And also probably for telling gay jokes about car parks, but that might not go down too well with Gordon Matheson. Unlike his pal in the car park.

During the Winter Olympics at Sochi, there were calls for an international boycot of the games because of the appallingly homophobic laws and practices of the Russian state. Yet these Commonwealth Games will welcome nations which make Moscow seem like an Amsterdam leather bar in terms of its acceptance of LGBT people. In Scotland, the openly gay man writing this blog can poke gay fun at the openly gay man who is the leader of Glasgow city cooncil. In many Commonwealth nations both Gordon and I would be in jail. In no less than 42 of the 71 countries and territories which will participate in the Commonwealth Games, it is illegal to be gay. In Uganda it is an offence punishable by up to three years in prison for any person who discovers that someone else is gay and doesn't report it to the police within 24 hours. All of you reading this blog would face up to three years in a Ugandan prison for not dobbing me into the polis within 24 hours of reading this. And I don't sell drugs or possess a samurai sword.

Mind you, John Barrowman should definitely be in the jail, but that's got nothing to do with him being gay and everything to do with crimes against fashion and good taste. That suit he was wearing during the opening ceremony should have come with a warning for epilepsy sufferers.

I'll stop with the gay politics, because we're not supposed to be using the Games to make political points. Nor apparently, points about good taste or artistic expression, and definitely not independence related points. The RAF doing a flyover trailing red white and blue smoke over Celtic park can't possibly be read as a symbol of ownership or anything. Anyway, it's only evil nationalists who could dream of politicising the Commonwealth Games, but despite the angst in the UK media, no one booed the English team, which was possibly a first in the history of Celtic Park.

The opening ceremony is still going on, but I'm going to end my review here - before I go blind with the bland multihued Rod Stewartness of it all. It's like Brigadoon on acid, kailyard kitsch on smack, thus handily combining the two cultural stereotypes for which

Scotland is best known - at least in the UK media. And this in a city which has world class designers, they must all have been away for the Fair.

As opening ceremonies go, it was pretty naff. It didn't get the billions thrown at the London Olympics and we got an exercise in colourful cringe for ProudScots™. But what did you expect? It's a ceremony that's trying to achieve two contradictory aims - on the one hand its obstensible purpose is to celebrate the city of Glasgow and the country of Scotland, but on the other the City Faithers don't want to celebrate too much in case we get ideas above our station. So the independence debate is carefully danced around by brightly clothed volunteers wielding dinner chairs - nope, no idea what that was about either. The Games are the Basil Fawlty Don't Mention the Indy Debate sketch in the middle of the referendum show. What they give us is the best of both Unionist worlds, John Barrowman in a lurid suit, and Susan Boyle crooning. It's the best we can aspire to - under the Union at any rate. A wee pat on the heid from the big boys for trying, but you're still a bit rubbish. Some people are more comfortable when no one notices them, that's Scotland's place in the Union.

Just about every symbol that represents Scottishness or Britishness can be seen as political during the referendum debate. But we're not supposed to be mentioning the politics of the Games in case some Scottish person running away really quickly and getting a medal for it makes the rest of us realise that we can run away from Westminster and win a major prize too. Better than a gold painted medal anyway.

Running away from Westminster is one sport even this sportophobe will enthusiastically participate in. I'm looking forward to the event on 18th September.

Scotland's going to win its self determination - that's worth more than gold.

25 July 2014
Smoke and mirrors

Scottish colours are political, British colours in the exact same context are not political, it's official - or more accurately, officious. The private company organising the opening ceremony had planned that when the Red Arrows did their flyover, they should trail blue and white smoke - the colours of the Scottish saltire - seeing as how the Commonwealth Games are being held in Scotland. Despite the best efforts of a very shouty Gordon Matheson to assert otherwise, Glasgow is most definitely a Scottish city. I'm sure I'd have noticed if it wasn't, and my geography is pretty good - I can get zero points on Pointless geography questions even when the answer isn't Central African Republic.

Anyway, the request for Caledonian contrails went to the MoD, and got a Naw from the Tory Defence secretary Michael Fallon. Mikey was rehearsing for all the Naws Scotland is going to get from Westminster if we're daft enough to vote Naw in September. Mikey is now being bigged up by the Daily Mail as the man who faced down the evil Alicsammin and his dastardly political plot to get the Red Arrows to display the colours of the Scottish flag.

It has been pointed out that the RAF has previously blown smoke in shades other than red white and blue. The Red Arrows did a red and white display for the Maltese, and even made a lovely St George's Cross for the English fitba team - and in 1999 they trailed blue and white smoke over Edinburgh to celebrate the opening of the Scottish Parliament.

But Michael insisted that Saltire smoke wasn't going to happen, and demanded that the smoke trails were red white and blue. So we got the RAF flying over Celtic Park trailing red white and blue smoke while someone in the stadium sang God Save the Queen and that isn't remotely political at all, and isn't going to piss off any Celtic fans who're still uncertain how they're going to vote. Aye, *that* Celtic Park. This may or may not be connected to the fact that Michael Fallon is himself a ProudScot™, born in Perth in 1952 into an upper middle class family of Tory voters. Like many ProudScots™ of that ilk he went south in order to get a political career because no one in the land of his birth wants to vote for him.

So instead of a streitched oot Saltire, we got long lines of red white and blue in the sky instead, which by a pleasing coincidence recreated the design of the Luxembourg flag. This was Westminster's way of trying to sook up to Jean Claude Juncker the EC Prez after Cameron pissed him off by trying to block his election. Because the Luxembourg flag consists of horizontal stripes in red white and blue. Knowing that is the kind of thing you get zero points in Pointless for, as is knowing that Luxembourgy things are actually called Luxembourgeois. Michael Fallon is pretty pointless too, and receives zero votes in Scotland, and he was probably hoping we'd think the RAF fly past was Lothianbourgeois.

The Red Arrows could in theory create a Union flag, but only at the risk of multiple mid-air collisions and this is generally held not to be such a good idea. They just do a red white and blue tricolour, so not the Irish one then, and everyone pretends not to notice it looks more like the French flag than the British one. Vive la Auld Alliance. Mind you, the smoke trails looked purple from my windae, and gradually merged into a charming shade of lavender, so maybe they were celebrating Gay Pride a week late.

Despite the fact that the Scottish Government's presence in the affair was about the same as the Tory party's presence in the East End of Glasgow, this hasn't stopped the UK media presenting this non-issue as a major blow for Alicsammin. They needed something to beat the independence campaign over the head with, since the crowd at Celtic Park had greeted the English team with cheers, thus failing to demonstrate the anti-English hatred which is supposedly consuming Scotland just now. So in the absence of anything as substantial as a tweet slagging off JK Rowling sent from a non-Scottish nutcase in Blackpool to use as a demonstration of Scottish unreasonableness, we get this non-story instead.

The No campaign is up to its usual tricks again - blaming its opponents for its own crimes. Just as the constant barrage of condescension, insults, abuse, and patronising dismissal directed at Scotland in the UK media isn't remotely anti-Scottish racism at all, but Tweets from random nutjobs are evidence of systemic anti-English hatred. Likewise the Yes campaign isn't supposed to politicise the Commonwealth Games, but Britishness is not political, so we can be deluged with Unionist symbols and that's got nothing to do with the referendum campaign. The people handing out flags with Union flags on one side and Saltires on the other outside the venue weren't making a political point at all, even if those flags have only previously been seen at Unionfests. Apparently the flags are being handed out by the Help for Heroes charity, although since they're being handed out for free it's not a fund raising campaign - which would be understandable. Instead this is costing the charity money, and it's highly debatable just how exactly handing out Union Saltires to crowds at the Commonwealth Games does in fact benefit ex-servicepeople. I do not know for certain whether it was Help for Heroes, but as a former worker in the voluntary sector this activity seems to me to cross the legal line preventing charitable groups from participating in political activities. Oh but I forgot, promoting Britishness during the Scottish referendum campaign isn't political at all. It's only promoting Scottishness in Scotland that's political.

But all of this misses the real point. The real point is that a major Scottish event which shows the city of Glasgow and the country of Scotland off to the world can be hijacked by a Tory in London that no one here has ever heard of - except for his maw and da - who wants to use it to make a political point in order to tell us that his politics aren't political at all. And Unionist politicisation gets transformed into an attack on Alicsammin who is accused of politicising the event. That's Unionist smoke and mirrors and Scotland is put back into its wee red white and blue box.

We'll still get grandstanding patronising politicians in an independent Scotland. We'll still witness political hypocrisy and crass stupidity. The difference will be that they'll be politicians that Scotland has elected, and politicians that we can then remove from office - and unlike Michael Fallon's other Scots Tory pals like Michael Forsyth, they won't have a House of Lords to be bumped up to. Until then, we'll continue to be treated like surly teenagers by a Westminster Parliament and and UK media, and not allowed even to decide on the entertainment for our own party. This must be more of that Home Rule that we're promised, the kind that doesn't allow us to home rule our own TV viewing.

Vote Yes, so Scotland can be a grown up country.

Windae polls and weegie-weighting

It's been a hectic day. The other half is still in hospital. Today the nurse on the rehab ward phoned to say his health has taken a bit of a turn for the worse, and he's been moved back to the acute ward in the Royal. We're still waiting for the test results, hopefully it's just a wee infection and isn't too serious, but it's put back the likely date that he'll be back home. Which is a bummer. But after visiting him I felt a bit better. He's comfortable, and resting.

My parents decided to take advantage of the sunny weather to have a family barbecue. So naturally it rained. They say you can choose your friends, but not your family. Which is only partially true. You can choose not to talk to certain family members, which is how me and my gran quite successfully arranged things until she popped her clogs a few years ago. We cordially loathed one another. Guess who I got the bitch gene from eh? However these days we are all, more or less, on speaking terms with one another, so a sizeable chunk of my extended family got together for burnt sausages and half cooked chicken in the rain.

The dug and me were only there a wee while before I left to visit the hospital, but it was enough time to speak with my maw and collate a wee poll of family referendum voting intentions. It's not like it's a representative sample or anything, but it was interesting to work out how many of us are likely to vote Yes. Few of us are SNP supporters, we're overwhelmingly Labour voters, although we also tend to despair of the current incarnation of Labour. In terms of occupation and income we have a wide spread, and in terms of religion we split like most Glasgow families these days - a minority which is Catholic, a minority which is Protestant, and a majority which couldn't care less. We even cross the great team divide, and include both Celtic and Rangers fans amongst our number. And a Clyde fan, but he keeps quiet about that.

Like a lot of Yes voters, I worry that I live in a wee bubble of Yesness, so the fact that a large majority of my friends are Yes supporters I tend to put down to a form of confirmation bias - you tend make friends with people who you agree with - you can't say the same with family. I'm only counting friends I made outwith the Yes campaign for the purposes of gauging my friends' responses to the independence campaign. I've made a lot of new friends as a result of this campaign, but of course they're Yes voters already. But even so, you still ask yourself whether the fact you seem to have so many Yes supporting friends is a sort of self-selecting thing.

I did a wee poll of my other half's care assistants. Not yer actual poll, but they're all very friendly and chatty women, and of course the referendum comes up in conversation. It's not like I've been pumping them for information or anything. They're all working class, and hard working, women from the East End of Glasgow - and out of his regular care assistants, only one was a No (she's on a different shift now, so we don't see her). All the rest, the six whose intentions I know, are strongly Yes. So much for women being reluctant Yes voters. But then you wonder if perhaps it's maybe a demographic thing, or maybe you've just by chance got the six Yes supporting care workers.

It's interesting that it's Yes supporters who seem most prone to confirmation bias, or being accused of confirmation bias. You'd think it ought to be the other way about. It should be No supporters. They're the ones who have the media backing, which makes them think there's a whole lot more Nawness going on than there really is. But it's the fact that the media is almost uniformly opposed to independence that makes Yes supporters doubt the evidence of their own eyes and ears.

So back to the great family referendum vote. Not counting the weans who are too young to vote, the results from my extended family who were present today are: 7 definitely or probably No; 4 won't say or don't know; and ... drumroll ... 18 Yes or leaning strongly to Yes. Which gives 62.0% Yes, 24.1% No, don't know or won't say 13.8%.

Because this is my family and I know them better than YouGov, we can apply our own Weegieweighting to the don't knows and won't says. One of them is almost certain to vote Yes - according to my maw - but he's not talking to me about it because we always fall out about politics. Another won't say is probably going to vote No but doesn't want to discuss it because she knows that she'll be out-argued. The aunt with Alzheimers will most likely forget to vote, and my Yes voting uncle said if he thinks she's going to vote No he won't remind her. We have no idea about the final niece because she wasn't there today and neither my maw or me have seen her for a few months. That gives us 19 Yes and 8 No and we'll ignore the other two. So that's 70.4% Yes, 29.6% No. Everyone plans to vote, except the aunt with Alzheimers who keeps having to be reminded that there's going to be a vote.

All the relatives in England are in favour of Yes. They've not been included in the figures because they don't get a vote. And so are all the actual English people my family members have married and the English kids we've produced. Our English relatives don't seem to notice much in the way of anti-English racism. Not even the really posh one who teaches in a posh private school.

Have you been noticing more Yes signs in windows and on cars recently? Or is it just me? I walk the dug to the hospital where the other half is, or was until today. Over the past week I've noticed a new Yes poster just about every day. On the way home on the bus from the Royal Infirmary this evening, I spotted 6 houses along Alexandra Parade and the beginning of Cumbernauld Road with Yes signs in their windows - and I was only looking out one side of the bus. I've added my windows to the total. There are already a couple of others in local streets. I'm also seeing more and more cars with Yes stickers.

There's not a single No sign anywhere, despite the fact that the Labour party recently dropped off a pile of Labour's own No Thanks papers which had a cut out No Thanks on the back cover with an invititation to stick it in your window. Not a single person has taken up the offer. The only No posters I've seen - apart from the commercial advertising - are the wee Naw stickers that appeared on all the lampposts along Alexandra Parade after the Orange Walk.

So screw the opinion polls. Weegie polling tells me there's going to be a Yes.

28 July 2014

No bad

Despite claims from the Naw camp that it's in the bag for the Union, I'm not thinking about what I'll do with myself if there's a No vote. In no small part because it's not in the bag for the Union at all - for reasons which were explained in the previous blog post.

I don't believe it's in the bag for Yes either, which is not a bad thing - the worst thing any campaigner can do just now is to take a result for granted. But the Yes campaign is only just getting into gear. We haven't really started yet. It's all going to come down to the final straight, and that's where Yes has the people on the ground.

The more senior members of the No campaign don't believe they can take a No for granted either - they just want the rest of us to think that. It's a tactic aimed at preventing a late surge for Yes like the late surge in support for the SNP which swept them to an absolute majority in the Scottish elections of 2011. By shouting from the rooftops of Pacific Quay that the Yes campaign has already lost, they seek to deter undecideds and weak No's from moving over to a Yes vote and to pre-empt the Yes campaign's grassroots strength.

From its launch the No campaign was founded in projection. One of the key components of negative campaigning is to accuse your opponents of your own sins. The instances of that from the No campaign are too numerous to detail. Their claim that the vote is already in the bag is another example. It's an expression of their fear that Yes has already won. Because even though not a single vote has yet been cast, the No campaign has already lost in just about every other respect. They've lost any residual respect that Scotland had for Westminster. They've lost the power to mobilise - that must be a bitter pill for Labour, the self-described people's party, to swallow. Labour called a campaign and the people didn't come. Just look at the disparity between the enormous grassroots movement of the Yes campaign, an organic sprouting of enthusiasm, of positivity, of hope, and the studio and newspaper column campaign of No. Increasingly the No campaign is only talking to itself about a Scotland that no longer exists or never existed. The audience isn't listening, they're either cynical and disengaged, or engaging with the ideas of Yes.

Irrespective of how the vote in September goes, the Union is already dead. The independence campaign has forced Westminster to reveal just how they really view Scotland, the UK's recalcitrant northern province. We're a land which they don't want to become foreign, but with every statement they make they reveal that Scotland is already foreign to them and always has been. The Scottish view of the Union - an equal partnership of kingdoms - is not Westminster's view. Scotland compares itself with Denmark or Finland, other small northern European countries. Westminster compares Scotland with Yorkshire. Scotland's view is a foreign view, one to be slapped down, patronised and dismissed.

Scotland has watched and learned. What we've learned will not be unlearned.

We're told to be proud that a Parliament has the almighty arrogance to abrogate to itself the right to determine our personal identities. We've learned we should be proud that one of the world's richest countries cannot ensure its citizens have the means to feed themselves, to heat their homes, or to work for a dignified wage. We are asked to be proud of foodbanks defended by nuclear missiles. We have the best zero hours contracts and should take pride in benefits sanctions which punch above their weight. We're asked to be proud of a country with structural inequalities, a widening chasm between the rich and poor, and to be proud of the fact we have no means to remedy the situation but to throw ourselves upon the mercy of the farsighted political masters who have brought this sorry state about.

We've learned that the Unionist ProudScots™ are proud of a regional identity. For them Scottishness can only flourish when it is subordinate to a British identity. So they keep making a point of telling us how proud and patriotic they are. They're proud of a shrivelled Scottish fruit on a sickly British tree, the ethnic kail in a Great British vegetable patch overrun by slugs. Proud Scots suffer the pride of over-compensation, the pride of the emotionally insecure. But when you're secure in your identity you don't need to tell people how proud you are of it. You just live it instead. When you act on your identity, there is no need to proclaim it because it's self-evident.

Affirmations of identity are the obituary notices of the living, they're monuments to an identity that is not lived except in the imagination. Rory the Tory (who's Scottish you know) is building a big chambered cairn on the border as an affirmation of Scottishness as Britishness. A chambered cairn is a Neolithic grave, so he's building a tomb as a monument to ProudScot identity in the Union. It's more appropriate than Rory ever realised.

I'm not proud to be Scottish any more than I am proud to be left handed, or proud to be gay, or proud to be Glaswegian. I just am all those things and I act accordingly. The Proud Scots TM of the No campaign miss the identity point. When you are secure and confident in your identity your identity does not define you - you define your identity. And you define it by your deeds and your choices and how you live your life. Scottishness is what we make it, not what we are told it has to be. Identity is a living thing, not a faded photo of an ancestor in tartan. So let's live Scottishness, not commemorate or celebrate it in a stone age grave.

I want to live Scottishness by helping to build a country which is inclusive and diverse, where politicians are held to account under a written constitution. I want to live Scottishness by having the choice to vote for a Scottish Labour party that is actually a Scottish Labour party. I want to live Scottishness by helping to build a country which can provide a dignified life for all its citizens. I want to live Scottishness with a political system that takes equality, justice and fairness as its starting point. I want to live Scottishness by getting rid of the obscenity of nuclear weapons of mass destruction. I want to live Scottishness with a media which truly reflects the diversity of opinions and views and experiences in this country. I want to live a Scottishness that does no harm.

I don't want to be a Proud Scot, I want to live in a land where I can say "Scotland? It's no bad."

29 July 2014
The crumbling wall

Many years ago when I was a student, I taught English in Finland for the summer. I travelled there by train via the Netherlands, Germany, Denmark and Sweden, taking advantage of the student Eurorail ticket. Backpackertastic. For about £100 you had the freedom of European trains for the whole summer, or at least you had the freedom of the western European rail network - most of Eastern Europe was still cut off behind the Iron Curtain and travelling there required visas in advance.

On the way home from Finland I had the opportunity to travel to Berlin, but didn't go. Instead, being 18 and daft and hormonal, I went to Amsterdam for men and drugs. And I'd be lying if I said I didn't have a whale of a time. I must have done, because memories of that trip are hazy and patchy. But I never made it to Berlin to see the Berlin Wall and to witness a city divided in two by opposing ideologies. It will still be there next year, I told myself. Berlin had been divided all my life. Geopolitics could wait. There was debauchery to be had.

Back in the 1980s Europe was divided into two. The Berlin Wall with its concrete barrier, the 100 metre wide death strip, the barbed wire and the few heavily controlled checkpoints was a symbol of that division. It was going to be there forever. But in the space of a few short years at the end of the 80s, the Communist bloc of Eastern Europe collapsed, the Wall came down, and the Soviet Union dissolved into its constituent republics. The Wall is gone, and its passing is not mourned. But back in 1981 no one expected that the Wall would be consigned to history before the end of the decade and that Europe would change irrevocably.

Another Berlin Wall came down in the 1990s. Social attitudes towards gay people underwent a rapid shift. The barriers of homophobia collapsed. Homosexuality was illegal in Scotland until 1981 - although there was an unwritten rule that no prosecutions would be brought in Scotland for acts which were legal in England and Wales where homosexuality had been decriminalised in 1967. But by the 1990s public opinion had undergone a sea change. Today, although homophobia lingers, it no longer has the backing of law or widespread social support. Public attitudes have changed irrevocably. Back in 1981 I never thought that would ever happen.

Westminster is not the Warsaw Pact, it is not institutionalised homophobia, but like both it was until recently seen as a permanent fixture. Unchanging, unaltered, it ruled our lives from birth, it determined the choices that we could make, and would continue to do so long after each of us have gone the way of the Wall. At least, so we thought, before the referendum campaign. Irrespective of how the vote goes in September, Westminster rule is no longer seen as unchanging and unchangeable. The old certainties are dead and will not be mourned. Scotland has changed irrevocably.

While on my European train trips all those years ago, I was reading a book called The Shape of Futures Past by Chris Morgan. The book looked at past predictions of the future, and compared them with the reality of the 1980s. It was an examination of literary and scientific futures - the future as depicted in fiction, or the predictions of think tanks and scientific organisations, not the futures predicted by fortune tellers or Tarot card readers.

The most striking thing about these predictions was not how amusingly inaccurate they were - illustrated with quaint drawings of traffic jams of biplanes in the skies above London - it was what they got wrong. None of them predicted the rapid social changes in attitude and outlook that would occur during the 20th century. The city gent stuck in his private biplane was on his way home to a little woman making his dinner in a kitchen filled with gadgetry. Everyone was white and middle class, the men wore suits and the women frocks. No one predicted the rise of feminism, the success of anti-racism, or the annihilation of homophobia as a "respectable prejudice". And doubtless none of them would have predicted that Scotland would regain her confidence and would chap on the door of independence.

Alistair Carmichael didn't see it coming. He is currently stuck in a biplane in a Westminster traffic jam, trapped in a past future that will not come to pass, as the realisation dawns on him that the little Scottish wummin might not be at home to make his tea. She's out campaigning for independence. Alistair thinks that the reason so many in Scotland support a vote for Yes is because Westminster has been hollowed out in Scotland by "nationalists". But Alistair is living in a fantasy as unrealistic as the steam powered spaceships of Victorian science fiction writers.

Alistair got part of his diagnosis correct. Westminster rule has indeed been hollowed out in Scotland, but it hasn't been hollowed out by the "nationalists". Westminster did it to itself when it embarked on the privatisation of the nationalised companies and institutions that maintained a sense of Britishness. British Coal, British Rail, British Steel and the rest - they've all gone the way of the Berlin Wall. The safety net of the Welfare State now has more holes than net. The proud boast of the British state that it provided care for citizens from the cradle to the grave has become a bitter pill on the half-empty shelves of a foodbank.

Westminster has a plan for the future that's already out of date. Their solution is to tweak devolution, to make more of a show of British presence in its northern province. More bunting and parades, more benefits cuts for the poor and tax breaks for the rich. And there will be attempts to ensure that Scotland can never again scare the bejeezus out of Westminster like we're scaring them right now. Nick Clegg is calling for the UK government's role to be "enhanced" in Scotland - forgetting that it was an unchecked UK government that Scotland didn't vote for which produced the demand for devolution in the first place, and which is fuelling the independence debate now.

No one can predict the future accurately. So it becomes a question of faith and of trust. Do you trust Alistair and his pals to represent your best interests? Do you have faith that Alistair and his pals know what your best interests are? Look at the hollowed out rule of Westminster, and you'll know what the answer is.

Another brick crumbles and the Westminster Wall weakens a little more. It will fall by September.

30 July 2014
Unchaining the heart

There's a common Unionist argument, most often espoused by those who fondly believe they're supporting a progressive politics, that Scotland is not any more left wing than the rest of the UK. We've even got our very own Jibberjabber the Hutt, UKIP MEP for not doing anything at all except mouthing off, so we are clearly borderline fascists. It is peculiar that these self-described progressives appear to take a certain pride in the fact that Scotland has an elected UKIP politician, but that's really a matter for those progressives and their therapist.

Even with independence, we are told, Scotland will still be run for the benefit of the rich and the well-connected. "They" will still be in charge. It will be every bit as shite living in a country run for the benefit of the bosses in the financial sector in Edinburgh as in a country run for the benefit of the bosses in the financial sector in London.

So vote No, and let's just sit here in the shite and not bother trying to get out of it. It's Great British Shite that you can rely on, it's certain shite, not like the hypothetical shite of the nationalists. And at least we will have working class people in Liverpool and Newcastle as company in our misery, and then we can all have a jolly working class time of it being salt of the British earth types even though there's a terrible smell. There may be some rocks we can all go and crawl under, but be quick, they'll be privatised soon. There is no alternative, there is no escape. It's solidarity as a suicide pact.

At its core, this argument wants us to believe that there is a better chance of a UK government espousing and implementing a set of progressive political policies than there is of a Scottish government doing so. And by progressive I mean genuinely left wing as opposed to the Labour leadership's definition of "progressive". Labour's definition of progressive is "whatever happens to be Labour policy this week and assists in the progress of a Labour MP's career". Or in the case of Johann Lamont, "wanting to have a debate about whatever policy Labour would perhaps like to introduce at some point in the future after a newly appointed commission has reported back, if that's alright with Eds Miliband and Balls".

So we are invited to reject an independent Scotland because it might possibly be shite in order to remain with the certainty of UK shite. It's not exactly the strongest argument in the No Thanks Little Red White and Blue Book of reasons not to be cheerful. The fact it's trotted out at all, and with mind numbing regularity in the comments section of the more, ahem, liberal periodicals, is because the rest of their arguments are pretty crappy too.

And that's the big flaw in this Unionist argument. What happens in an independent Scotland is as yet hypothetical, but we can actually see how the UK parties act.

Over large swathes of Scotland, the Conservatives effectively ceased to exist in the 1980s and 90s. Labour was the Westminster party supposedly capable of mobilising the populace to campaign for the Union. The referendum campaign has left Labour exposed and naked, its progressive union jack knickers have snapped their elastic and flap around their ankles.

The British Labour party began life as the political organisation of a grassroots labour and trades union movement, it was the Parliamentary manifestation of hopes and dreams of a better life. It was the head of a socialist heart. That's why Labour still proudly claims to be the People's Party. But over the years the Parliamentary party took over the movement, and the head began to direct the heart. Now British Labour has become the Party of Managing the People's Expectations. It's an instrument of rule, and no longer a grassroots movement. It's a party which is prepared to accept unemployment and benefits cuts in order to brown nose the financial sector of the City of London. The certainty of shite, that's the UK's political and economic system - jobbieness and joblessness.

Labour is no longer the People's Party, it no longer expresses the heart. Labour sold its soul and disconnected itself from the beating heart of hope. 18 years of Tory rule was followed by 13 years of Labour majorities, and nothing much changed as Tony Blair smiled his dead eyed smile. The heart was sold off in privatisations, blown apart in illegal wars, bled dry by troughers and politicians whose main concern is securing themselves a profitable portfolio of directorships and a made up pretendy title in the Lords.

For years the heart was quiet and muffled, pulsing slowly despite the weight of cynicism and alienation that threatened to crush all life and hope. The heart was imprisoned in PFI contracts, tied up in an ATOS interview. The heart was a small voice lost beneath the bluster of the politicians justifying war in Iraq. The heart marched in protests that went ignored. The heart was a flash of sunlight glimpsed beyond the grey clouds of crushed expectations. But the heart still beat, in late night conversations, in plans put on hold, in dreams unrealised.

But then the referendum happened, and the heart discovered a connection to a new artery of aspiration. Cautiously, tentatively, the blood vessels flush out the old cynicism, they clear the fatty blockages of careerists and miserabilists. There is no guarantee of success, there is no cast iron certainty - but hope is in movement again. There is a place to go, and it's a space we can make for ourselves. Hope is alive again.

The heart beat is getting louder, it grows stronger every day. You hear it in the conversation between two women on the bus who wonder whether independence means their grandchildren can stay in Scotland. You feel it in the hope that fills the air of the public meeting. You see it in the Yes signs that sprout on windows like bluebells after the long cold winter. Hope will triumph over cynicism. The multicoloured diversity of yes will defeat the bleak grey monochrome of miserabilism.

Can you feel the heartbeat, can you feel the hope? The heart is pulsing to the beat of a different drum, a Scottish bodhran beating a new tune. There is another way, it sings. It's the song that choruses a tune of accountability, of keeping politicians close by so their arses are within reach of our feet. It's a reel that tells of a written constitution that spells out the rules for one and all and reels in those who seek only their own profit. It's the Scottish air that sets the air free. No one knows how the song ends - but it's a song we write for ourselves. And we will write our own destiny.

Scotland's heart is unchained. It can't be chained again.

31 July 2014
Back to the future with Marty Kettle

The Guardian's Martin Kettle has been making use of his steam powered time machine Delorean to voyage into the future and has written an article for the paper looking back at the independence referendum from the vantage point of 2024, using a route planner that Nick Clegg sketched on the back of a Lib Dem election pledge. Marty was hoping that this would help him find the plot that he lost when the referendum was announced, as previous attempts to locate it had depended on using the same dowsing rod that Iain Gray had employed when he was searching for a Labour majority in the 2011 Scottish elections.

Marty's time machine tells him that the independence referendum is all a dreadful waste of time, and for some inexplicable reason that Scottish independence is going to spark off a civil war in Ireland - possibly because Gerry Adams will be outraged that he can no longer watch River City on the BBC.

The article was allegedly intended as a light hearted humorous look at a subject which Marty finds both deeply unfunny and intensely perplexing. These articles exist solely in order to give Unionists the opportunity to tsk that independence supporters have no sense of humour, because making jokes about bomb blasts in Belfast is just a bit of fun when Westminster supporters do it. If a Yes supporter was to do the same, it would be evidence of the atavistic nationalism that Marty only espouses when it's called British. Because then it doesn't count as nationalism.

Like most UK media commentators whose umbilical cords are firmly attached to the belly of the Westminster beast, Marty can't conceptualise political debates which take place in areas where Jim Murphy's bus tour can't reach. So instead he prefers to blame it on atavistic English hating nationalism, a concept which he can get his head around better than the shocking truth that as far as Scotland is concerned Marty and his opinions are about as informed and informative as a Glesca bus timetable during the Commonwealth Games. That's his real difficulty - he's faced with a political discourse in which he is irrelevant, so at least you'd think he'd now appreciate what Scotland has experienced in UK politics for the past 40 years. Sadly not.

Marty's a fully paid up member of George Robertson's Cataclysm Club, and his wee prediction checked all the Unionist dire consequence tick boxes with the exception of the plagues of frogs and locusts, and the invasion of lizard aliens from outer space. Which is a bummer because I was quite looking forward to the lizard aliens, they're far more fashionable than the genocidal robots from the Andromeda Galaxy who're set to take over an independent Catalonia.

According to Marty, 2014 is the "last golden summer of the UK". So enjoy those ATOS disability interviews and Danny Alexander admitting he was wrong about the Bedroom Tax while it all lasts then. But the only gold in the UK these days is creamed off by bankers in bonuses, the rest of us are left with the radioactive heavy metals that are the decay products of a Trident warhead and a media without a clue.

About the only thing Marty wrote that wasn't utterly risible was his premise that Yes will win in September. We've come a long way from 2011, when the Unionist parties were claiming that an 80% majority was in the bag and Scottish nationalism would be killed stone dead - again. However at last the penny is beginning to drop that Scotland can no longer be taken for granted. We're being noticed and told we're loved by people who never noticed us before. They're still praying for a No vote so they can get back to ignoring us. Little people aren't qualified to decide what's best for themselves. Only people who ignore little people can do that.

Marty and the rest of the UK media are never going to understand the independence debate, because understanding it would mean grasping a true appreciation of the bankruptcy of the political system that they have hitched themselves to. And they have no idea how it should be fixed. They don't want to fix it. It already works just fine - at least for the only people who count. That would be those who are in it, and people like Marty whose careers depend on reporting them and presenting their views to the rest of us.

Scottish independence is about recognising that the Westminster system of politics is irretrievably knackered. It is not capable of reforming itself. No further evidence is needed than the continuing existence of an unelected second chamber. When it was enjoying its record breaking three consecutive majority governments, Labour abolished the right of heriditary peers - or at least most of them - to sit in the Lords and influence our legislation, but they replaced it with the only system that could be worse. Instead of the lottery of aristrocratic birth, peers are now entirely appointed by politicians who increased the power of their own patronage.

The result is that UK politicians are the least accountable in any democracy. To cite my favourite example of odiousness, during the

1997 General Election Michael Forsyth led the Tory party in Scotland to a wipeout at the polls. Politicians like to tell us that they must listen to the message sent to them by the voters, and in 1997 Scotland sent Michael Forsyth a message. We told him that we didn't want him, we didn't want his policies, and we didn't want his party. Every single Scottish Conservative MP lost their seat, and the party has apparently abandoned any hope of ever recovering. Short of sending him to the bottom of a coalmine in Sverdlovsk, this is the strongest message an electorate can send to a politician in a democratic system. And the message was "Away you tae fuck." But what happened? Mikey got a seat in the Lords and he's still casting his baleful influence over our legislation and our lives.

But lack of accountability also means that political manifestos have become even less fact based than the proverbial Glesca bus timetable during the Commonwealth Games. They mean little or nothing. So we get a series of political parties making promises they have little intention of keeping, and there's nothing we can do about it. Vote one lot out and the next lot will take over and do exactly the same. The only difference is the PR. The Magic Roundabout of Westminster, it's the only ride in the Magic Kingdom amusement park where the little people aren't admitted. We press our noses against the fence while Marty drops nuggets of wisdom for us to digest gracefully.

The independence debate has upturned the old certainties. Now it's Marty who's pressing his nose against the fence, complaining that a debate is taking place that he's not a part of. The single biggest prize we can achieve with independence is a written constitution that spells out the checks and balances required to keep our politicians accountable, and which will put a spanner in the works of the Magic Roundabout.

And then perhaps we might even achieve a media which understands the country it's reporting on. But it won't be one involving Marty.

August 2014

2 August 2014
The rain in Carntyne

I'm walking home from the hospital in the rain along Edinburgh Road in Carntyne. Grey, overcast, a storm ahead and with no way to prevent my partner's decline, nothing to stop it happening. Human beings are weak and we are small, we are powerless and at the mercy of the elements, the forces of nature, the cycle of life and death.

He's not getting any better, he's not going to get better. The words go round and round as if repetition makes them easier to accept. The end is not imminent, it's not today or tomorrow, and we will bring him home - but vascular dementia is terminal, and terminal illnesses terminate. Every day that passes brings the final day closer, the last bridge to cross, the last chapter of the story is being written, and today I realised I am already mourning for a life that is draining away like the water that splashes on the roadway.

They say that the secret of wisdom is to learn the difference between the things you can change, and the things you can't, and what you can't change you must accept, however painful. And this is one of those things that cannot be changed. Sometimes it hurts so bad, it sears the soul and scorches the spirit. Yet you must accept it like the Carntyne rain. Every day another little bit of the life we have together dies. and there's nothing I can do to stop it, no dam that can hold back the stormy waters of grief. A black hole of uncertainty looms beyond the fear. I keep walking in the Carntyne rain and tears mingle with the sky and the clouds, going home to an empty heart. This is what hopelessness feels like.

I would do anything to change things, to make him whole, to stop this happening, to restore the man I love. The English man who taught me how to love and who freed my heart from the prison of cynicism. I'd sell my soul to Satan. Worse, I'd even vote No. But there's nothing that can change it, no cure, no remedy. All there is is heartbreak and acceptance, resignation - but no regrets for a life well lived. And so I know I will keep walking through the cleansing rain, carrying a bundle of precious memories that nurture and sustain - his gift to me.

In the cloudy sky above the East End, moisture condenses around a particle of dust liberated long ago from a distant hearth where people loved and laughed and told stories around the fireplace. It gains mass and a droplet is born. The droplet falls through the air, slowly at first, then gaining speed it sets itself on the trajectory that defines the life of a raindrop. It dances in the breeze, it curls and twists and falls. It splashes on my head, drips down my neck. You are alive, it writes in cold rainwater along my spine. You feel. You have become aware. Feel the things you can change and change them, the raindrop says.

The rain washes off the Naw stickers that appeared on the lampposts after the Orange Walk. The Carntyne rain on the British parade.

And then I grow angry. Angry at those who tell us there is no other way, who insist that we cannot change things that can be changed. Angry at those who choose hopelessness, who coccoon themselves in the comfort of cynicism and think that it makes them wise. The wisdom of the fools who don't know the difference between the things we can't change and the things we can. The fools who protect themselves with an ersatz umbrella of bunting and parades and the PR smiles of a Prime Minister who isn't paid to care, the narrow horizons of those whose only aspiration is to feel superior to those who have less than themselves. The chained souls who believe their foolishness is wisdom.

But some things can be changed. We can weave words and cast spells, we can work magic with words which evaporate the cynicism.

There is a better way, the rain says. The druids and druidesses of Scotland are changing the world with their message of Yes, conjouring up a Scottish rain of words to wash away the dust of three hundred years that lodges in our eyes and blinds us to our own potential. The magic incantation of Yes, the glamour that reaches deep into the soul and powers the heart and feeds the brain. I feel at one with myself and with the rain. And I know that life is good and precious. Too precious to waste on the false gods and fake authority of a Parliament far away.

Yes, says the rain, as it casts out the hopelessness like a demon expelled. Crushing the cringe and washing it away down the stanks along the Edinburgh Road. It cleanses and it makes us whole. And the rain says - choose to live your life, choose to make a splash, choose to water the soft grass on the roadside verge where the flowers blossom in the summer. Choose to drink the sweet water of choice. Choose to fill the rivers that flow to the sea and begin the cycle of life.

I stand in the rain by the side of the road. Yes is a life well lived. Yes is a life without regrets for what might have been. You don't regret the things you've done, you only regret what you could have done but didn't do. Live without regret, take your destiny into your own hands and own it. Define yourself or be defined. I stand by the side of the road and listen to the rain. The skies over Carntyne weep with joy for hopes that can be made real.

Yes means taking your fate into your own hands. It means recognising the things you can change, and taking action to change them. Take the power and own it. Take a leap of faith in yourself.

Yes means being alive and powerful like the rain in Carntyne.

3 August
Thank you

I'd just like to thank everyone for their kind words and comments on yesterday's blog post. I was deeply touched seeing the support and love which was so freely and generously offered. I visited Andy at the hospital today intending to tell him, but he was sleeping so I didn't stay long. He's suffering from another infection and they've put him on oxygen to help him breathe.

He's not quite at death's door. The inevitable is not imminent, but it is soon. He's very weak and frail now. His dementia is continuing its unstoppable progression, and sadly it seems to be progressing more rapidly than we had hoped. When he was diagnosed the doctor said that half the patients who receive a diagnosis of vascular dementia survive longer than five years after they start to show symptoms. So you hope that your loved one will be amongst that 50% and not the 50% who don't survive five years. Andy has been showing symptoms for two to three years now, and sadly it looks like he's going to be amongst the 50% who don't make it five years. But where there is life there is hope, and we can only hope that his condition stabilises. He's in good hands, and the staff at Lightburn Hospital are very caring and supportive.

Most of the time I cope, but sometimes the enormity of what is happening falls on you like the Carntyne rain - and you are suddenly overcome by it all. That's what happened yesterday, and I got a bit emotional about it. After writing yesterday's post I wasn't at all sure whether to publish it, but I am glad I did. Your words have helped more than you can imagine. And it helped me to get my feelings out. You can't bottle these things up inside. Thank you all for listening.

An old friend of Andy's is coming from London tomorrow to see him and I hope that will perk him up a bit. I need to take a bit of time for myself and Andy now, to try and get back on an even emotional keel, so won't be posting anything else for a couple of days. I plan to write a piece following the 'Great Darling Arse on a Plate Debate' so will try and publish a new piece on Wednesday.

The Dug, you'll be pleased to know, is as happy as ever. He's snoring on the sofa without a care in the world.

5 August 2014
The great maltesers debate

Here we go then, the great debate, the dug's been walked and I'm sitting in front of the telly with a mug of tea and a box - yes an entire box - of Maltesers. But Emmerdale is still on so I've been amusing myself with anagrams. The ancients thought that anagrams and other forms of word play revealed deep essential truths, but then they also thought that you could predict the future by disemboweling a chicken. So what did they know.

Mind you you can fairly predict that the chicken's going to get plucked, stuffed and cooked and I'm hoping that's going to be Alistair's fate in the debate. Anyway, with the chickenesque caveats in mind, did you know that Alistair Darling is an anagram of 'tired liar salad' - which is spookily appropriate and probably a reasonable description of his strategy for the debate. Meanwhile Alex Salmond is an anagram of 'man-sex doll', which is kind of unsettling and may distract me from my maltesers. But Alex Salmond is also an anagram of 'no lax damsel' which is a wee bit more reassuring. And Scottish independence is an anagram of 'I spend on decent ethics', which is nice to know.

But back to the main event - that would be the box of maltesers. I'm playing non-alcoholic drug free Darling Debate Bingo and will reward myself with a chocolatey treat every time Alistair says "proud", "best of both worlds", "volatile", "look...", "currency union", "no going back", or "risks". I've got a back up packet of fruit pastels. The bevvy bingo version isn't possible because I'd be rat arsed before getting this blog post finished.

The start of the programme gives a new Ipsos Mori poll showing 40% Yes, 54% No. Yes is 4% up on the previous poll by IPSOS Mori. No doubt this poll will be disemboweled like a sacrificial chicken over on Scot Goes Pop. I think IPSOS Mori is one of the polling companies which traditionally shows a lower vote share for Yes, so a 4% increase is a Good Sign. And no chickens were injured either.

Alicsammin's speaking now, wondering why some folk might still doubt that Scotland could be a successful independent country. It's because they're sacrificial chickens, if you ask me. He's asking why in such a prosperous country there are so many families who are forced to rely on foodbanks, meanwhile just down the road from the STV studios there's a stockpile of nukes that's costing us billions.

Darling's turn now: Proud! He's proud! Ooh a malteser. The maltesers are coming thick and fast now. Risks, no going back and he's scarcely finished his first sentence. See, those of you having a wee swally are hauf cut already. Other than that it was pretty content free. And he did the waggy finger. You get a bonus malteser for the waggy finger. Another "look.." another malteser.

By the time the debate finished there were no maltesers left and I was halfway through the fruit pastiles. It was a bit of a disappointment really, too much ding dong and not enough engagement. The best result of the evening was all the chocolate. I don't think anyone is going to change their mind as a result of watching this evening's proceedings. Yes supporters will still be Yes, No supporters will still be No, and undecideds will still be wondering what the hell's going on and what bastard was it that finished all the maltesers.

Darling was awful, negative, shouty, and completely lacking in any kind of empathy. It was like your dad telling you you've already spent your pocket money. He had nothing positive to say, and couldn't even bring himself to agree with the proposition that Scotland could be a successful independent country because, gulp, that would mean being seen to agree with a Tory. I was right about the tiring liar salad though. It had been widely predicted that he would batter on about the currency, and that's precisely what he did. It was his big idea after all, he lifted it from the Quebec referendum playbook.

Alicsammin was subdued, like he's afraid of passion. He seemed to be going for statesmanlike and dignified, but that's not going to change the minds of those who've already decided they dislike him. They just read that as smug. You don't win brownie points with people who already dislike you, you must start off by accepting that anything you do is only going to antagonise them. So instead you demolish their faith in your opponent. They'll still hate you, but getting people to like you is not the point. They'll have lost respect for your opponent. Statesmanlike and dignified doesn't cut it, you can get that in Madame Toussauds. You need evisceration of lying basterts and going for the jugular. Think chicken, it's all in the entrails.

He should have dealt with the currency union question better. Because the real point for me is - given that a currency union is in the best interests of both Scotland and the rest of the UK - why should the people of Scotland continue to give their backing to a political system which will wilfully damage Scotland and the rest of the UK out of spite. We're being asked to reward spitefulness.

But for the most part the currency question is technocratic pseudowaffle. It's one of those practical problems to which there is a practical solution. And there are several solutions, ranging all the way from a formal currency union to sticking the UK national debt up George Osborne's arse and setting up a new Scottish currency, and all points in between. My personal favourite is the sticking it up George Osborne's arse option, mainly because I'd like to see the look on his face. You can probably tell I'm not primarily motivated by economic arguments there.

I don't feel that independence was brought any nearer by tonight's performance, but on the other hand I'm not too devastated either. Alicsammin made some good points, and there were a few welcome sparks on display, but they got drowned out in the shoutiness of Alistair and the boring technocratese. It was all a bit sterile and heartless. Frankly, it was too fuckin middle class. I want more heart, I want passion. And above all I want vision. Vision is precisely what the No campaign doesn't have, and precisely what Alicsammin is good at articulating. That's the advantage that each of us who support a yes vote must press home. Everything else is so much waffle. It's the vision thing. Articulate your vision of the Scotland that's poised to be born.

That's what's going to win this for Yes - a positive vision of what Scotland can be. We got a wee bit of that towards the end, but it was still too restrained. Perhaps the most successful ploy of Project Fear has been to make us afraid of our own passion, our own emotion. We're winning the argument of the head, is their proud Scot boast. The heart doesn't matter to them, and they want to win a No vote in a Scotland whose heart and head are divided. And this from the people who say they want no borders - they seek to create borders within our souls. Psychologists call it cognitive dissonance.

So here's my vision, I want a Scotland of heart, of passion, of dignity and justice. A Scotland which rejects weapons of mass destruction, foreign wars, which does no harm in the world and which doesn't just speak of peace and compassion - but acts on it. I want a Scotland which is governed for the benefit of all, not for the few who are wealthy and connected. I want a Scotland which sees its priority as tackling poverty, inequality and social exclusion where it is recognised that the market doesn't always know best and the profit motive is not the only motive to prize. A land where we don't put a price on dignity. And these things are achievable with independence.

According to the post-match dissection on STV, Yes gained 2% as a result of the debate, No was static. So perhaps the wee flash of the vision thing was working. We need more of it. More heart, fewer statistics, and we will win.

6 August 2014
The Jeremy Clarkson of the independence debate

So that was the great debate then. The media has, entirely predictably, already decided that Alistair's tiring liar salad has won it for the Union, and the Yes campaign can pack up and go home because it's another blow for Alicsammin. Which is a variant on what they were saying last week, and the week before that. Alicsammin's never been known to do anything except being blown - in fact according to the UK media he gets blown more often than a sexaholic with a lifetime membership of a swingers' club. Nae wonder he's always accused of looking smug. So it's hard to judge the reality from the media reports. But allegedly it was all about bleedin currency unions and feck all else.

It's worth repeating even if a callous the size of Ben Nevis develops on the foreheads we batter off the brick wall of UK media reportage, but the currency union issue is a not a fundamental or basic issue. It's a practicality not a principle.

I have actually given serious and considered thought to the whole currency union thang. I have read economics papers, and this is an imposition to be deeply resented because they are word porridges of jargonese - about something that's bloody boring and with far less literary flavour than the instructions on the back of a packet of Scotts porridge oats. The mechanics of money just don't row my boat. I'm missing out on the capitalism gene, or maybe I'm just not a shallow materialistic git and understand that value and worth aren't the same as a pricetag. But for whatever reason, economics bores the airse aff me. And I'm sure that I'm not alone there. It makes us normal.

Anyway, like the majority in this country I'm not daft, at least most of the time. I possess a good Scottish education. I can even count without using my fingers and do long division in my head because I was born before calculators were invented. Those of us possessed of this skill are far more mathematically qualified than George Osborne or Danny Alexander. Although to be fair, Danny does know how to multiply by twelve.

So following profound cogitation upon the pros and cons of a formal sterling zone, a new Scottish currency, using the pound without a formal currency union, and the assorted other options, I've come to the conclusion - and I mean this in a considered, caring and loving way -that I really, deeply, truly don't give a flying fuck about a currency union.

Seriously, who gives a shit apart from former Chancellors of the Exchequer. It's a practical problem to which a practical solution will be found, and the only reason we keep hearing about it is because it's the central plank of the No campaign. It's the only plank they've got other than the short thick ones who get elected. And the only reason ordinary punters give a shit is because Alistair and his pals in the papers tell us that it's Pure Dead Important. It is to them - because it's their only plank. That doesn't mean it needs to be important to the rest of us.

Ireland continued to use sterling for six years after independence in 1922. Then they introduced a currency pegged to sterling. Sterling notes continued to circulate freely in Ireland for the next seventy years. Life went on and the sky did not fall in. Did the average person spending their pounds/punts in Ireland notice or care that the country went from using sterling to pegging its own currency to the pound? Nope, they just kept on using the same money. All they noticed was the pretty new designs on the Irish coinage and banknotes which circulated alongside the British money they were long familiar with. Wee Celtic animals, I seem to remember. A lot nicer to look at than a Windsor.

To the average punter like you or me it makes no difference at all what mechanism is used to keep the pound - currency union or unilaterally using the pound or whatever - we just keep on being skint or splurging out on the latest bargains as usual. Our wages and pensions are paid, our bank accounts retain the same amounts. And that's all we need to know or care about. Scotland will continue to use the pound, everything else is boring mechanics. I don't care if a car has a wangle flange accumulator spork in its engine or a differential drive shaft makeup bag, as long as it takes me from A to B it does all that is required of it and my interest begins and ends there. The currency union argument is the Jeremy Clarkson of the independence debate.

At this point, if you're channelling Alistair Darling - which is a deeply unsettling experience - you'll be going look look look, you'll have no lender of last resort, and you'll probably be wagging a finger accusingly. But that only means that Scottish banks won't be able to engage in high risk casino banking and the Scottish government will have to regulate them more tightly to ensure that they behave themselves and don't run up huge debts. This is a bad thing? It is if you're Alistair Darling or Fred the Shred. But allowing folk like Fred to determine our economic policies is why we've got all this austerity crap to begin with.

I'd quite like to see the banking sector kept on a short leash. It's highly volatile you know. Meanwhile it's worth remembering that a national government is only responsible for the debts accrued by a bank within national territory. Scotland would only have to bail out a failed bank for its Scottish debts, not its global debts.

Cooperation is required between Holyrood and Westminster in order for a formal currency union to work, it's one of the few areas where close cooperation is required after independence. So naturally Westminster is refusing to cooperate as a threat and is exaggerating the importance of the currency issue out of all importance to its true worth. They seek to downplay the damage a refusal would wreak to the rest of the UK while over-egging the damage it would do to Scotland. They want us to fixate on their pricetag but not to consider the true worth of their argument. Do you want to vote for people who threaten to rip you off and who are willing to damage you and themselves in order to punish you? Seems like poor value for your vote. Westminster are the dodgy mechanics who sook their teeth and say "Oooh, it's gaunnie cost ye."

Would Scotland be bound to follow Westminster's economic policies? Not really. There would have to be agreement on borrowing, but it takes two to agree remember. Westminster will no longer be able to unilaterally impose. This is a vast improvement on the current situation, and the Scottish government would have greatly increased freedom to make the best financial and economic decisions for Scotland. We would not be ruled by the UK Treasury, whatever nonsense that No campaigners spout.

And then there's the indebted elephant in the room. That would be the UK Treasury and the £1.4 trillion of UK national debt. The pound is a UK asset, it belongs to Scotland as much as the rest of the UK. And let's have nane o this crap about it being the property of the UK and we're leaving the UK. Right now, right here, we are the UK. And when Scotland becomes independent we will take our share of what is ours from the UK. Nae assets, nae debt.

The UK Treasury has already assured the money markets that it will retain responsiblity for the UK national debt, and there are no lenders anywhere who possess an IOU saying "I owe you squillions of quid, xx Scotland". Scotland has precisely zero legal liability, and anyone who tells you we have a moral duty to take our share of the debt or we will be punished by the markets is talking pish. Bankers don't do morality, that lesson should be clear to one and all by now. What Westminster wants is for Scotland to undertake to pay a share of the UK national debt to the rUK Treasury, not to the international money markets. And that's a very big bargaining chip in Scotland's hands. It's not one that the Scottish Government chooses to highlight, because they don't want to spook the markets. Funny thing rapacious capitalism. It savages humanity but is itself more easily startled than a new born fawn. It's a Bambi I'd cheerfully strangle.

All the banks are interested in is ability to pay. They are not going to punish Scotland for not taking on a debt for which we have no legal liability, in fact there is a good argument that they would punish us for taking on a share of the debt - what sort of creditor undertakes to repay debts which are not theirs legally? That's a creditor that a lender might be concerned about. How can they be certain we'll pay the debt we have to them if we have a history of taking on the repayment of debts that we don't have a legal obligation to pay? So it cuts both ways.

This conveniently distracts us from the million and one other areas in which Westminster cooperation will not be required after independence. All those other planks that Westminster is short of. We will not have to ask Westminster's permission to get rid of Trident or the House of Lords. We will not have to ask Westminster's permission to abolish the cruel and capricious system of benefit sanctions introduced by Ian Duncan Smith. We will not require Westminster's cooperation in order to reindustrialise the Scottish economy. We will not require Westminster's permission to introduce land reform. We can do all these things for ourselves, and do them far better than Westminster ever has, currency union, no currency union, or whatever.

Currency union? Meh. Who cares, it's a practical problem to which a practical solution will be found by our highly paid elected representatives. That's why we pay them. Meanwhile there are far more important issues which really are deserving of our attention - like the scandal of foodbanks and fuel poverty, protecting our NHS, and getting rid of the obscenity of nuclear weapons.

7 August 2014
Vote Nob Orders for nobs

While most of the media keeps up the currency naw naw naw nyah nyah nyah, there's been a wee spot of love bombing plaintively pledging its troth. Scotland got a luvvie letterette today. Now we can feel dead important because two hundred celebs have taken a few seconds out of their busy schedules and faaaaabulous lives to put their names to a paragraph long letter that someone else wrote for them. It's just heartlifting to see such commitment. How can anyone possibly complain about the need for foodbanks when we've got such immense compassion to nourish our anonymous little souls. Simon Cowell has noticed us, how many beans is that worth?

Mind you, the paean of love to Scotland might have been a teeny bit more convincing if David Starkey didn't figure amongst the list of signatories. Davie, for those of you lucky enough never to have encountered his oeuvre, described Scotland as a 'feeble little country' and Rabbie Burns as 'a deeply boring provincial poet'. Admittedly I didn't recognise a lot of the names, not moving in slebby circles. There was someone revelling in the name Jock Stirrup, which I had thought was a groin support for equestrian types until I looked him up on Wikipedia. Apparently he used to be a heid bummer in the RAF. And for some of the names which were recognisable it would probably have been better if they hadn't been recognisable at all. Like David Starkey.

Scotland has no currency, no money, it's a huge financial risk (because of course, we're a basket case), it's cursed with resources it can't possibly manage by itself and which generate huge amounts of paperwork, and is totally dependent upon the goodwill and largesse of the kind hearted Westminster Parlie. But they love us because we make them feel better about themselves, we've got gorgeous scenery, and we provide a tartan splash of colour that helps British nationalism pretend it's not a form of nationalism at all.

Still, it was awfie nice of the two hundred slebs. It would maybe have been nicer if they'd signed an open letter to the Westminster Parliament telling them that they're a bunch of unaccountable wasters whose self-interest and short-termism have turned the entire UK into internal colonies of the financial sector in the City of London, but it's likely that our elected and unelected unrepresentatives would have slung them a deifie. Which is more or less what the average voter in Scotland will do on hearing a plea from Simon Cowell. The referendum now gives the rest of us a chance to vote Simon off, who's going to resist the chance to do that? You're not going to bootcamp Simon, you're getting the boot.

The letter - well, I say letter, a paragraph doesn't count as a letter. It's more of a postcard - asks Scotland "not to leave this shared country of ours" and asks us to remember "the bonds of citizenship". And there's the problem right there. This is not a shared country, and I don't mean that Scotland is a different country from England - a self-evident truism which only needs to be explained to some of the more obtuse below the line commentators in publications like the Guardian. The UK is not a shared country, it's not a sharing country. In the UK a small number enjoy access to wealth and privilege at the expense of the majority. That's not sharing, it's dispossession. For the majority of its citizens the UK is not a nation, it's a state of alienation.

Bonds of citizenship sound lovely and cosy too. Like fur lined handcuffs. The bonding only goes one way. Non-slebby types, those of us who are not rich or well connected, are bound to put up with whatever crap, whatever political wheeze, that gets thrown at us. And there's bugger all we can do about it. Where were the bonds of citizenship when a diabetic ex-serviceman had his benefits sanctioned and died due to lack of food and a fridge that no longer kept his insulin usable. There's not much in the way of bonds of citizenship for the mother who walked seven miles to a foodbank so she could feed her weans. That's not a bond, that's bondage.

It's all very well to ask others to keep sharing when you're one of the ones on the receiving end of the largesse. The two hundred slebs don't put forward any political solutions to the ever widening social and economic chasms which disfigure the entire UK. Instead they're making a call for inaction to the only people who are proposing to do something about this lamentable state of affairs. It's like Labour's suicide pact, sorry - Labour's plea for workers' solidarity - only with BAFTA nominations. Stay with us Scotland, so we can emote about you. Vote Nob Orders for nobs.

The luvvie love bomb was organised by Dan Snow, whose faither in law is Gerald Grosvenor the Duke of Westminster. The Grosvenor family own the 100,000 acre Reay Forest estate in Sutherland. 100,000 acres is a lot of land, it works out at over 156 square miles, almost the same size as West Lothian. And it's all owned by Dan's da-in-law. Of course the gross imbalance in Scottish land ownership isn't Dan's responsibility, but maybe if Dan Dan the History Man had a wee look at the history of his faither in law's holiday home he might be a bit more understanding of the reasons why so many in Scotland think we'd be better off governing ourselves.

The Reay Forest estate, and other enormous Highland estates like it, are often what luvvie types think of when they think of Scotland, a vast tract of picturesque wilderness without any people in it. It used to have people in it, but the Dukes of Sutherland, whose family the Grosvenors bought the estate from in 1904, had handily cleared away the unsightly and distinctly unpicturesque Gaelic speaking peasantry. The area around the Reay Forest estate was cleared in the early 1800s. The people ended up on the emigrant ships, or moved to the growing slums around the foundaries and mines where today their descendants walk miles to find a food bank, or face eviction because they can't pay the bedroom tax. In this best of both worlds, this perfect union, poverty and dispossession is the only constant. We're told this is the best we can aspire to in this rich land.

And that Dan, is why so many of us are voting Yes. We want out of this cycle of despair, we're tired of being cynical, we've lived long enough with alienation. But although we are alienated from the Westminster Parliament, we are not alienated from each other. We're cynical about the motives of the powerful and connected, we're not cynical about our hopes and aspirations for dignity, equality, and justice. But we've learned that things will only change if we change them ourselves.

So don't send us a wee postcard begging us not to do it because some comfortable and connected people might suffer a pang of personal regret. Do something useful, Dan, do something unselfish. Support us.

And tell your faither in law we want our land back.

8 August 2014

The things we've learned

The independence referendum has been a learning experience for Scotland. Irrespective of how the vote goes in September - and I remain convinced that it will be a Yes - this country has improved and matured because of a campaign which has engaged this country's populace with politics in a way that has never been seen before. The grassroots Yes campaign has produced a singularly remarkable achievement - it's taught a nation of hard-bitten cynics how to hope again.

Scotland has learned some other lessons too, lessons which are not so pleasant. Even though the media in this country started out in this campaign from a very low baseline of credibility and public trust, it has managed to plummet even further. No one can seriously argue any more that Scotland has a representative media. Our newspapers and broadcasters do not reflect the breadth of this country's views and experiences, with a handful of honorable exceptions they do not speak for us. They speak for a minority which is privileged and connected, they speak down to us, not from amongst us. When only one Sunday newspaper supports a constitutional position preferred by more than 40% of the population, you have a problem.

A free, balanced, and representative media is not an optional extra in a democracy. It's not a nice wee addition to provide a bit of entertaining diversion. Without a free, balanced, and above all representative media, there is no real democracy. Citzens in a democratic country need access to all relevant information in order to make an informed decision at the ballot box. But Scotland's media is like a sex information leaflet from a fundamentalist chastity group - just say no is the only message. It doesn't want to inform you that there are other options for avoiding unwanted pregnancy or unwanted Conservative governments. And it certainly doesn't want to tell you that informed sexual independence can be fulfilling and leads to emotional maturity. It speaks only of risks, not fulfilment. And it certainly won't help you reach any climaxes. Instead we're told the safe option is to remain in the trough of despondency, despair, and hopelessness. Scotland can't possibly choose her own partners or set the terms of her relationships. 307 years and never been kissed.

The other big lesson we have learned is what our place is in this most perfect of unions. For three hundred years Scotland had laboured under the misapprehension that we were equal partners in this most perfect Union, that Scotland was a valued and respected participant.

We were told that we could be British without compromising our Scottishness. But we've learned that in the eyes of our political masters we are nothing. We are owed nothing. We contribute nothing. And we should be grateful for nothing. We have nothing and we are worth nothing, and if we are so foolish as to imagine that we might be intelligent enough and capable enough and mature enough to reach our own climax then we will be less than nothing.

We are a basket case apparently. The currency union is waved around to distract us from the reasons they cite for its refusal. It's too risky. Scotland is too uncertain. Scotland's economy is fragile and weak and too trivial to have any account. The Proud Scots of Parliament revel in the misery of our weakness and dependency like masochists being beaten by a dominatrix in a Union flag corset, triumphantly moaning with pleasure with every lash of the whip. It's the only way to get off in the Union.

And the media doesn't ask the questions this poses. Masochism is all very well in the confines of a night club or the privacy of a bedroom, but it's no way to run a country. Scotland has been in this union for over 300 years yet now we discover from the mouths of our rulers that it has left us too weak and frail to look after ourselves. Are they not the ones who are responsible for this lamentable state of affairs?

The state of Scotland as told to us by our Westminster Parliament after 300 years of what is claimed as a successful union is perplexing, a mystery which begs to be demystified. After all, taking a country in a geopolitically tranquil part of the world, with high standards of education, which is blessed with an embarrassing wealth of natural resources and a surplus of energy like few other countries possess, which is famed for the inventiveness and abilities of its people, and turning it into an economic basket case which has no other hope but to throw itself upon the tender mercies of a generous Westminster, a land where Home Rule can't even extend as far as allowing us control of the TV remote - that takes a very special kind of incompetence. A malign incompetence that verges on the criminal.

What are these Proud Scots proposing to do about it? When and how will those responsible be held to account? But the media is off on a Plan B Hunt to please the dominatrix with the whip, and all the Parliamentary Proud Scots propose is to moan more with pleasure. Oooooh.... plan B....

None stop to ask why there should be any need for a plan B or why the rest of the UK is justified in its refusal to accept plan A. Why is it that this northern partner, this North Britain, this belt which holds up the trousers of Union, is such a poor risk for the rest of the UK? But answering that question means exposing the illogicality of the premise. It means exposing the lie that Scotland is poor. We are not poor. We are being impoverished. It's not the same thing.

We are being asked to vote No based upon an argument which is at its very core self-contradictory. The supposed poverty and incapability of Scotland is given as the reason to remain under the control of those who hoover up capital to create poverty for the rest of us, and who shackle us in a political system which offers no remedy.

Once being Scottish meant being born cynical, and growing increasingly more cynical as we got older. The Proud Scots, the cannae Scots. Not any more. We've learned how to hope and we like it. We stopped looking at the powerful and looked at ourselves instead. And what we see is potential. We get a good feeling. It's new. It's the breath of life rustling through the dry leaves of books we never read before. New ideas buzz and blast, lightbulbs of inspiration pop on and flash like beacons in the long dark night. It's good to be here and now. We've learned how to light up the darkness of the souls of cynics, and that's knowledge that can never be taken from us.

10 August 2014

The crumbling castle of can't

Go home Yes supporters. Let's stick our heads under the duvet and give up. It's all over, we've lost, we've been trounced and humiliated and everybody hates us ... Meanwhile in other news from the same dystopian universe, immigrants give you cancer, benefits claimants are dishonest cheating wastrels to a man and woman, Boris Johnson and Nigel Farage are the voices of common sense, and Scotland only wants independence because we hate the English. Welcome to Ukmedialand.

A recent opinion poll has been published that seemingly shows a fractional increase in the gap between Yes and No, and it's proof positive that the only person in Scotland who is going to vote Yes is the guy with the blue painted face and the jimmy wig whose photie is always used to illustrate articles on independence. But we must not take that too seriously, the photo that is, the poll is deadly serious - no, honest. We're just being prissy and humourless to complain. In the words of Alistair Darling - Don't you know what a joke is? We do Alistair. And it's you and your entire campaign. The punchline comes on the 18th of September.

The UK parties are lining up to set their face against any grown up cooperation with the rUK's northern neighbour. Ed Miliband has pledged Labour will commit suicide in Scotland in the event of a Yes vote, by insisting that the party's manifesto will contain a promise to veto any currency union with an independent Scotland. If there is a Yes vote, Labour's MPs will face the Scottish electorate with a promise to screw over their own voters. Mind you, that's not really new is it? Labour MP Jimmy Hood has already stood up in the Commons to assure his not so honourable friends that even if it was conclusively proven that Scotland would be better off with independence, he'd still vote No. The needs of the People's Party come before the needs of the People.

But we can now see that the No campaign boils down to a single simple argument. Vote No, because Westminster is vindictive and short-termist. They promise to screw us over if we dare to challenge them, even if that means doing damage to themselves. That's the definition of malignity. And the lies continue - telling Scotland it "can't have" the pound, when they know that the argument is about the precise mechanism Scotland uses to retain the pound. An irrelevance whipped up in hatred into a souffle of contempt. Vote No, because we're better together with lying bastards who drip with disdain. Vote No, because you are nothing.

But the Westminster system is one in which a party can say whatever it likes before an election, and do whatever it likes afterwards. Labour has promised for over 100 years to abolish the House of Lords. In 1997 they promised a Scottish Parliament with tax raising powers and gave us a Parliament whose tax raising powers were so limited and hedged about with caveats that they are unusable. That's a kept promise from Westminster. The promise there will be no currency union is the same. There will be a currency union, they'll just call it something else. It's the great Westminster fudge, the only reliable thing about them.

UK party manifesto promises are not promises, just ask Nick Clegg, David Cameron or Tony Blair, and polls are not predictions. Polls are - in theory - snapshots of public opinion at a given moment in time. But they're not glossy high definition panoramic photies of a Scottish landscape, they're blurry and pixellated images of a tiny cross-section of a landscape as seen by Mr Magoo without his glasses on, standing on a hill and looking down from far away.

The landscape is a Scottish sealoch as the high spring tides approach. On the beach at the head of the loch stands a sandcastle, a paper union flag stuck at a slant into a crumbling tower. The moon is waxing, and soon the spring tide will reach its high water. The beach is strewn with the detritus of 307 years of radioactive militarism, of broken promises, shattered hopes and the footprints of the emigrants who made their way to the ships taking them away from a land whose wealth was sheared off, shot up, sooked up, packed away, and sent off to the lairds and lords in bundled fleeces, the glassy eyes of a stag's head mounted on a baronial wall, and barrels of oil to power the global city far from the land of broken dreams. Scotland the brave, Scotland the beautiful. Scotland the empty and dispossessed.

Mr Magoo sees the grey overcast skies bleach the colour from the grass, the shapes are vague and indistinct. The dark water indistinguishable from the black rocks. He doesn't see the movement in the water, the waters that carried away the emigrants, the waters that are now coming home. He can't make out the women on the shore talking to one another about what might have been, and what can still be. They're talking about dignity, about self-respect, about taking charge of their own lives.

The women are quietly turning cannae into can and have a lesson for their children. A lesson about the day they thought would never come, and how to make it come by building it for yourself. Trust yourself with your own future, they'll tell them. Listen to your own inner voice, not to others who tell you you can't. You are a child of Scotland and you can be anything you want. All you need is your own strength and the love of those who care about you. Trust yourself, trust your loved ones, don't wait for the powerful to grant your wishes, seize the power of your own strength and talents and resources. Define yourself or be defined. They'll teach the children of Scotland how to change the world, one conversation at a time.

Mr Magoo can't hear or see the conversations, high on the hill where the two hundred windbags whistle don't leaves in his ears. He doesn't see the current he sees currency, putting a price on a soul.

The tides of independence lap at the shore, washing away the hurt and the pain, scouring away the shame, cleansing the land. They rise, they fall, they ebb and flow. And with every passing day they reach ever higher as the Moon looks down and smiles.

The waters reach the sandcastle, washing away the foundations. The castle of can't is crumbling. The spring tide is coming. The waters are talking, listen to the current not the currency.

12 August 2014

Shy bunnies

Are you shy and retiring, a wee bit of a wall-flower? When your best pal asks you if her outfit makes her bum look big do you cower in fear like a straight man? When watching Eurovision do you refuse to admit that you're going to vote for the woman in the big frock from Malta because you fear you will be mocked by supporters of the drag queen from Ukraine? According to the No campaign, and the polling company YouGov, Scotland is chock full of quiet and timid sowels who're dead set on a No vote but are just too feart to mention it in case the Yes voting 70 year old granny next door challenges them to a fight behind the Co-op. It's all square goes and square slice. It's too scary to reveal you're a No voter in case some net curtains are twitched at you in a threatening manner.

But this is Scotland, and by this stage in the referendum campaign if you've got a settled view you'll have shared it with someone. And that someone will invariably have mentioned it in passing to another someone, because that someone is right nosey and you know that the first someone has a gob on them like the Clyde Tunnel. And before you know it half the Co-op knows whether you lean towards the Vote No Mind Bleach, or the Tide of Independence washing powder - guaranteed to remove even the most stubborn nuclear missile stains - long before you've got anywhere near the voting products aisle and are still trying to get your trolley around the piles of annoying freeze dried currency threats that are being heavily pushed in a TV and newspaper advertising campaign.

I'm struggling with the notion that there's an ocean of quiet wee naws out there who're too shy to mention it. I know a few folk who're planning to vote no, and they're very vocal about it. Loudly so, and they have no compunction in saying that they believe themselves to be better educated and to have a bigger flat screen TV and a flashier motor. They're usually the same people who mistake cynicism for wisdom. People who are disconnected from their hearts only vote with their heads, or more accurately what the papers and the telly tell them about their bank balances. It's all about the money for some folk, although if those views were taken to their logical conclusion we'd just abolish all this democracy business and just let our neighbours choose our governments for us. Oh wait...

But then I'm quite vocal about yesness, so fair enough. I quite like having my heart and my head in the same place, and it's the heart which motivates you to discover that the information the media has filled your head with isn't accurate information. The No campaign wants us to ignore the wee voice in the heart that says "They're telling you a load of auld pish".

It could well be that there are some tortured sowels for whom nawness is a dirty little secret, like a wee fart to blame on the dug, and they don't want to mention it because fingers might be pointed and scoffs guffawed. But they're only going to feel that way if they believe themselves to be a tiny minority of fartiness amongst people who've refused Alistair Darling's offer of a pile of beans and who take responsiblity for themselves.

The shly elusive timid Naw, like bambis and fluffy bunnies and other easily startled creatures, has very big ears. Shy Naws are just as able as anyone else to listen to what people around them are saying, and if a significant number of them are also No, then the shy ones have no reason to be shy. They're safely amongst bambis and bunnies who've never been known to monster anyone. And there's a media which is almost uniformly telling them of the great advantages and safety in numbers of being a bunny frozen in the headlights, and that bunnies vastly outnumber the wee ginger dugs. In fact the media has pretty much already declared a victory for No. So any perceptible Nawness from those around them will demonstrate to the shy Naw bunny that it's safe to come out of the undergrowth and they're not going to be set upon by any wee ginger dugs that are voting Yes.

The polling company YouGov adjust their figures to take account of shy Naw bunnies hiding in the undergrowth. They do this because of "anecdotal evidence" that No voters are reluctant to say that they're No voters. Possibly this is based on an anecdote told to them by a hauf pished Labour MP in a Commons bar, before he's been physically restrained from starting a fight, but we will never know. YouGov are hiding their corrective formula deep in the undergrowth with the hypothetical No bunnies.

In my experience, I come across a lot more shy Yes voters than shy No voters. They're the ones who say that they're unsure and don't know enough. They say that because their heart is telling them Yes, but they're confronted with an onslaught of media reports telling them that they are selfish, stupid, and shortsighted. They are strongly inclined to vote Yes but don't want to say so because they don't feel they can defend their position from the braying belly laughs of people who have larger flat screen TVs and nicer motors and write for the Daily Record. There is only one side in this campaign which is being accused of racism, of being ill educated anglophobes, and of not thinking clearly or logically, and it's not No voters.

The Radical Independence Campaign have now released the results of their latest mass canvass of Scotland's working class districts. Yes 42%, No 28%, Don't Know 30%. It's that last 30% who are the shy

Yeses. They're the ones who still can't reconcile their hearts with the heads.

But when your heart and your head are divided you are unhappy and confused. That holds for nations as much as it does for individuals. Those of us who are already singing the song of independence have got the tools, we've got the passion, we've got the information, we've got the heart and soul. The shy Yes voters are the ones who are invisible to the polling companies, not the shy No voters, and they're the ones who will tip the balance. It's going to be up to those of us who are not so shy to reassure, persuade, and reconcile the shy ones so that their heads and their hearts sing the same song.

And then together we can create the chorus of Yes, singing a song we write for ourselves. Independence means your heart and your head sing as one.

14 August 2014

The audacity of Yes

I went to church last night but I was among the converted they were preaching to, which was a novel experience for me. Canon Peter McBride of St Thomas church in Riddrie had organised a debate on the referendum, which was originally going to be held in the church hall, but a double booking meant a change of venue to St Bernadette's church hall in Carntyne. Despite the late change of venue, there was still a good turnout - around 100 people attended, so many that the wee church hall wasn't able to hold everyone and the event was moved into the church itself so there would be seats, or rather pews, for everyone.

However the debate turned out not to be a debate because Better Together or whatever they're called didn't manage to provide any speakers, although a number of requests had been made to them. Now there's a surprise, they're normally so keen on public engagement what with them being romping home in the polls and have supporters and donations coming out their ears.

But we must demonstrate some Christian charity, what with this being a church and everything, and assume that it's not a deliberate strategy to keep people disengaged from the referendum debate, but their poor ears were so full of supporters and donations that they were unable to hear the polite request for some speakers for a debate. "What was that? You want streaker's furry deer bait Father? Can priests ask for that? I'm sorry I can't quite make you out, I've got a Tory business donor trying to privatise my cochlea." So the good Father got slung a deafie. He's clearly an SNP front organisation.

So we didn't get a debate, and perhaps it was all the better for that. Free from the need to spend most of their time rebutting people who only want to talk mince about the currency (we're going to keep using the pound, in case you were wondering) the speakers were able to expand upon more profound reasons for independence and what Scotland can achieve by taking her future into her own hands. For once we did not get bogged down in the trivial mechanics of the process of becoming independent.

There were three excellent speakers, the Scottish Government's Health Secretary Alex Neil, Jeane Freeman, former advisor to Jack McConnell and founder member of Women for Independence, and the veteran Jim Sillars. All three spoke with passion and conviction about the kind of country that Scotland could become.

Alex Neil spoke about how we need independence in order to protect the health service from the creeping privatisation taking place south of the border. Even though Scotland's health service is already fully devolved, the overall budget is still set by Westminster. It's only with independence that Scotland can ensure that our health service is kept in public hands.

In an impressive speech, Jeane Freeman spoke about her journey to Yes from her traditional Labour background, and how over the course of her experience in politics she came to realise that devolution is not enough - Scotland requires the full powers of independence in order to develop into a mature and fully developed country. For Jeane, Scottish independence is the only way to fulfil the dreams and aspirations of the founders of the Labour movement, the people who first inspired her to get involved in politics.

But it was Jim Sillars I'd really come to hear. Jim has no need to go to Specsavers, he knows how to do the vision thing. Jim spoke about the oil. He mentioned the rumours of huge new discoveries off the west coast, and also explained how Westminster's obsession with nuclear weapons led the MoD to ban oil exploration and development in the Firth of Clyde and the Atlantic approaches, despite significant oil resources lying under those waters. At the same time that Thatcher was taking an axe to the traditional industries of Scotland, her government actively blocked the development of a resource which could have led to a Clyde oil boom.

But then he pointed out that for decades, politics in Scotland has been reactive. We've devoted our energies and time to defending ourselves from the poll tax, from privatisations, against attempts to introduce fees in Scottish education, the bedroom tax and on and on in a litany of malign policies imposed on this country by governments we didn't vote for or support. It's only independence that can change that, and unleash those energies spent defensively to allow Scots can live in a country where we are no longer constantly fighting to maintain what we already have, but where we can take positive action to improve our lives and change things for the better.

Jim spoke of a Scotland of possibilities, a Scotland where working class people can have the audacity to dream bold dreams and seize the initiative. In passing he said that any independence negotiations must not be held in London, where the Scottish delegation could find its hotel rooms bugged by the intelligence services. We should insist that the negotiations are held in Edinburgh - that would really bug Westminster.

And he mentioned a mad off the wall and audacious idea, one which a friend had advised him not to bring up. The UK Government is currently building two massive aircraft carriers, even though they only expect to bring one into operational service - and that only after they're able to find planes to put on it. The other was meant to be sold off on, but no one wants it. It's a white elephant, a massive liability. Jim suggested that Scotland should do Westminster a favour and take it off their hands for them. It could become the flagship of the new Scottish navy, but not as an aircraft carrier bearing weapons of war and birds of destruction. Let's convert it into a hospital ship, and send it to war zones and troubled regions around the world. With independence Scotland's contribution to the wider world would no longer mean sending off our young men and women to fight and destroy, to kill and blow things up. Instead they would be healing the sick and caring for the wounded. It's a vision of the kind of Scotland we can create.

Jim said the vessel should be named after that great Scottish humanitarian, Robert Burns. But that was the only point at which I disagreed with him. We should call it the Margo MacDonald.

But I'll give the last word to Canon Peter McBride. In his closing words, he thanked the contributors, praised the audience for their polite and respectful reception of the speakers, and said that when considering how to vote in September we must not think solely of ourselves. It's not about whether you personally will be £300 a year better off or worse off, you can do that by changing your electricity supplier, it's about what's best for everyone. Voting Yes, it's the Christian thing to do.

Vote Yes. Dream a bold dream, dream of audacity, dream of taking your future into your own hands. Vote Yes, for compassion, empathy, and for those worse off than yourself.

17 August 2014
Changing the world with a Yes cake in Shettleston

The dug and me, well mainly the dug but I got to tag along too, had a great time on Friday evening meeting the enthusiastic and committed volunteers at Yes Shettleston in the East End of Glasgow. From a wee group of less than ten a few weeks ago, Yes Shettleston's ranks have now swollen to some fifty volunteers, and more keep arriving every day eager to make a contribution.

Earlier that day, Ruth Davidson the Action Krankie took a wee break from being sporty to give an interview to the Guardian. Being an Action Krankie and a big fan of Davie Cameron, Ruth believes sporting metaphors describe her politics perfectly - "Oh look someone got a gold medal for running about a bit" being the closest we've ever got to a positive case of the Union. With Ruthie there's a lot of grunting, striving, tearful promises that she's doing it all for

Great-Auntie Annabel, and then she runs round in ever decreasing circles and ends up worse off than where she started. So exactly like the Unionist parties' promises of extra powers for Scotland then.

But it's a hard and lonely life being the only lesbian Tory Glaswegian in Scotland. I follow Ruth's career with great interest, since part of the reason I came out as gay and made a general nuisance of myself about gay rights all those oh so many years ago was so that future generations of lesbians and gay men could pursue their dreams and still be true to themselves. But it turns out it was so some wee careerist abseiler could decide she wanted to be a Tory MSP and become the glittery lesbian bauble in Davie Cameron's modern Conservative PR plan. I could weep sometimes, I really could.

In her interview Ruth explained what motivates her, and said: "If somebody says I can't do something then it's: 'Right, I'll show you,' and I'll go and do it."

You got that one right Ruthie hen. Yes Shettleston is full of people who share that sentiment in full, and so are other Yes groups up and down the country. We've heard Ruthie and her pals tell us we can't do it, we can't govern ourselves, we need Westminster to do it for us. Aye right. We'll show you. We're going to go and do it ourselves. The message from Shettleston is that we have the confidence in our own talents, skills, experience to know that we can do it. We have the confidence of our own audacity and the strength of our passion to know that you'll not only watch us do it Ruthie, but yer wee jaw will have abseiled down to the floor. Watch - and learn what gallus means. Cannae? Aye, right.

The Yes Shettleston volunteers want Scotland to break out of Ruth's style of politics where a small minority run around energetically in circles getting nowhere while the majority tune out and watch soap operas instead. Like so many of us, they're fed up fighting against the latest austerity threat, the latest Tory cut, the latest Labour betrayal. They want to fight for something positive. They want a plot line with a resolution, a story that develops. They want a Scotland where politics becomes a documentary of the possible and not a melodrama of you cannae.

You don't get the quantity and quality of commitment and energy on display in Yes Shettleston in a campaign which feels like it's losing. And that's because we're not losing, we're winning. The media has been crowing for the past week that it's all over for the Yes campaign, but while they've been stuck in their currency rutting, real people have been talking about fairness and justice.

People have been talking about oil, and rumours, and about politicians who think they have a right to lie to us. People have been talking about Shettleston, about Castlemilk, about Methil, about Niddrie and the Raploch, and about how the only way things will ever change is for those of us who live here to take matters into our own hands and change them ourselves. The words of Shettleston's grannies ring in our ears: If ye want somethin done, dae it yersel.

The No campaign has the media, it has the corporate interests and the right wing foreign politicians trading favours with their Tory pals. The Yes campaign doesn't have any of that. It doesn't have the corporate backing, or the weight of the state, or the massed ranks of the media. The Yes campaign just has people in it. Real people, lots of people. People who give their time and their energy and their talents and skills and experiences. The authentic version of the kind of people that politicians invent so they can find quotes for their leaflets. Yes groups speak for themselves. Yes supporters think independently. We're the people being told we can't, watch us change the world.

Yes Shettleston is full of women and men of every generation, most have never been involved with politics before. They're the Scotland of the friendly welcome, the Scotland of the enquiring mind and the passionate heart. The Scotland you always wanted to live in but were too ground down by the cynicism to believe could ever exist. It exists already. It's here, and it's in a Yes group near you. Come and make it happen everywhere.

There are loads of ways to get involved. From staffing the Yes centre and making tea for footsore canvassers, to chapping on doors, signing up to drive elderly or disabled voters to the polls on the Big Day, stuffing envelopes, or just providing a listening ear. Come and connect with Scotland. This isn't party political. It's people political, it's about our lives, our futures, and about making our voices heard.

The political is personal, and that person is you. And Agnes might bake you a Yes cake.

Meanwhile in other news, the respected historian Tom Devine has announced that he's decided to vote Yes. Tom Devine, now there's a history man for you. Dan Snow, eat your heart out.

18 August 2014
The dug you can trust

It's another great debate next Monday, the totes unbiased and completely neutral Beeb version whoo-hoo. But we can all save ourselves the bother - Alistair is going to bang on about the currency and how there's no plan B but if there was it would be utter rubbish as well, as would plans C through to Z. No doubt while doing the pointy finger thing. And the UK media will write it all up as another glorious victory for the logical clearmindedness of Brittania over the woolly thinking of sheepish separatists. And they'll be doing the pointy finger thing too, only in print.

The only other place you see pointy fingers with such regularity is in religious fundamentalist propaganda videos, or if you're 15 just after your dad has discovered some cans of beer have gone missing from the fridge. I just thought that should be pointed out. In Alistair's eyes Scotland's the naughty wean that's taking the beer out of Westminster's fridge and threatens his subsidised swally in a Commons bar. And it's all the fault of that evil Al-Iqsammin who didn't do the pointy finger thing at all, even though he's got a fundamentalist name. Because that's how evil he is. Leading us astray like that. That's the great achievement of 307 years of union, it's turned one of Europe's most ancient nations into a basket case of recalcitrant children who can't be trusted with the TV remote control. Scotland the infantilised nation, makes you so proud doesn't it. It brings a tear to our eyes as we weep with despair.

Anyway, that will be your Scottish independence killed stone dead again. Just like it was last week and the week before. It's been killed off more often than Christopher Lee in a Hammer Horror fillum. But then along comes a wee round of opinion polls and there's your Yes support clawed its way out of the grave and standing there with a knowing smirk on its face, in its best clothes without a crease or a smudge of dirt on them. I never understood how vampires could do that, the clothes thing, the smirk I've got off pat. We should ask Michael Forsyth, he ought to know.

The theme song for this month is the repeat chorus of George Osborne's sermon on the pound, which earlier this year first leapt into the hit parade of blows to Alicsammin like the annoying Birdie Song in an episode of Top of the Tops. Howzabout that then. It was even accompanied by its own special dance moves, consisting of sticking two fingers up to the people of Scotland and telling us to fuck off or submit to Osborne's abuse. We have nothing, we're owed nothing, we're entitled to nothing. Independence was killed off then too, and the UK media was full of the crows of the Noes. But it didn't work then and it isn't working now.

The only solid track record Westminster possesses is a scratched 45 rpm that sticks on lies. They lied to Scotland in 1979, when they told us that the oil would have run out by the 1980s. They refused to allow the development of the oil fields in the Firth of Clyde and off the west coast of Lewis because it might interfere with their war toys. They lied in 1997 when we were promised a Parliament with full tax raising powers and we got limited powers over income tax that were so hedged about with caveats that they're unusable. They're doing it again now, warning of the volatility of oil and how it's a declining resource while the internet buzzes with rumours of major oil discoveries.

It's bad enough that our elected representatives lie to us, but what sticks in the craw is that they believe they have the right to lie to us. They can only do that because there's nothing we can do to prevent them, nothing we can do to hold them to account. The Tories can lie because they don't need our votes. Labour can lie because they take us for granted. And the Lib Dems just lie because they're fantasists who are easily seduced by the promise of a ministerial Mondeo. And if we do manage to vote one of them out of power, they just go to the Lords while the grasping careerist circus spins merrily on. Vote No, vote to be lied to. Vote No, vote to say you're fine with being treated like a small child.

Alistair Darling's currency threat relies on convincing the electorate of Scotland that Alicsammin is a liar who can't be trusted. And since

Alicsammin is the Marmite of Scottish politics, they're halfway there. Unfortunately for Alistair the electorate of Scotland doesn't trust him and his pals either, and unlike Holyrood elections there is nothing we can do to get rid of Westminster's untrustworthy basterts. We're lumbered with the party that people vote for south of the border, and the political rejects just get rewarded with a seat in the Lords like Michael Forsythula, the Right Count of Stirling.

Cynical Scottish voters are faced with a choice. You can choose untrustworthy basterts that you can't do anything about, the ones who have a track record of lies, deception, disappointment and crushed hopes, the ones who don't have to take your views into account they're only interested in the views of the banks, of big business, of the rich and powerful. That would be Alistair and his pals. Or you can choose untrustworthy basterts who do have to take your views into account or suffer a boot up the arse - that would be the MSPs at Holyrood. If they lie to you, you can get rid of them and they don't get a nice wee seat in the Lords as a booby prize.

In the end it all boils down to trust. The No campaign wants us to surrender our trust and place it in the hands of politicians who are not answerable to us, not accountable to us, and who think they have the right to lie to us. The Yes campaign wants us to trust in ourselves, in our potential, in our talents, resources and skills.

Who do you trust more - a rabid Westminster dug that is out of control, that eats you out of house and home, that steals from your plate, that stops you entering the spare bedroom and pisses radioactive waste in your living room, that regularly attacks the neighbours in the Middle East, and threatens to savage you if you don't surrender, or a wee ginger Holyrood dug that's taken to obedience classes on a short lead and a muzzle. A dug we can teach to do tricks.

Vote for control. Vote for the short lead. Vote yes.

19 August 2014

Proud like a Yes swan

I saw a Better Together referendum broadcast on the BBC last night. It was full of proud and patriotic Scots proudly telling us how proudly proud they were to be proud and patriotic Scots. We've got lovely scenery you know, and they were all dead proud of lots of other stuff that's never going to change because it's already happened, like things achieved by people who are long since dead.

The video featured that lovely wummin that retweeted the oh so funny wee joke that Catholics are like Christmas lights because they'd look better hanging from a tree. So that's just patriotic and Cool Britannia then, in an Orangey grassroots way. And oh so very proud she was. Alicsammin doesn't know what a joke is. Britishness is so inclusive isn't it. And the ordinary mum who just happens to be the chair of her local Labour party was there as well, being proudly and patriotically grassroots too. And some wee manny, being proud in Gaelic, proudly proud of a Union that's killing his language.

They were all proud of a Union that's dead, a partnership that's a takeover, an equality that's subordinate. Proud of a Union that tells us we have no right to anything. They're proud of the ball and chain that restricts their freedom of movement. Proud to surrender their choices to others. We're better together because then we don't need to accept any responsibility. We can remain children. We can remain like the cygnets in the pond in the park and think that the world is bounded by the fence. Ugly ducklings forever.

It was all a bit desperate, over-compensation. The only people you should ever need to tell how proud you are are the people you are people of. But the people the ProudScots are proud of are all dead. They're proud of the dead because they can't be proud of the living. So they stress how proud they are, to cover up the vanishing dignity, the evaporating hope, the death of aspiration.

The essence of Unionism is being proud of the dead and the inanimate. Perhaps it's safer that way. It's a passive pride, a pride that stands on the dignity of others, without a sign that you might dare to imagine that you could make people proud of what you could do yourself. Or that you might be proud enough to dream of what the people of Scotland could do together as a nation, not in the past but here and now. You might dare to think that pride is about an active present not the passive past. But an active Scottish pride is a dangerous pride. The ProudScots keep it safe and quiet, they're proud of the scenery viewed through the window of the coach as it winds its way through a the estate of an absentee landlord in a landscape denuded of humanity. All aboard the ProudScot tour bus.

There was enough chest expanding pridery on display to inflate the egos of a pride of Unionists - that's the official collective noun for them, in case you were wondering. They like to think that they're the British lions. Did you know that lions eat their young and turn on the sick and wounded? True fact that. And most of their food is stolen from hyenas and other far more successful hunters. 'Nother true fact that.

I don't much fancy being a proud British lion, it's just a less successful hyena with better hair. Hyenas have more laughs anyway. But I'm proud too, proud enough to know that things should be better than this, proud enough to dream of a country that doesn't just mouth justice but practises it, proud enough to do something about it. And proud enough to understand the difference between being proudly self-regarding, and the pride others could have in you.

Today the doctor called from the hospital. We spoke about the pride and dignity of a beloved man whose life is slipping away. She needed to know if she should strive officiously to keep my partner alive. Sometimes the ones you love are so broken and worn out that you need to let them go free. She wanted me to know that the time for a decision is approaching. It's not here yet, but it will be soon. He's not coming home again.

So I watched the proud Scots being proud of having no answers, proud of the certainty of lack of faith and ambition, passively proud of the past. They live in a broken dream but are too afraid to let it go, blinded by their own passivity and pride they can't see it can never be fixed, can never be healed. So they distract themselves with currencies, alicsammins and cynicism. They don't want to face the decisions that face us all. The decisions required to take charge of your own life by yourself. It's too hard, too frightening. So they retreat into denial, it's all good, it's all just fine, look at the dead and be proud. No future just a present that looks to a past that's vanished.

But the time to let go is coming. Be brave. Face the fear. Accept it. And life will go on and you'll discover the strength within you. The strength you can't see because you're too busy looking at the past.

I went to the park with my friend Mary and the dug to feed the swans. I had some Yes cakes left over from Friday, and on the basis that you are what you eat, I fed them to the cygnets in Alexandra Park and imagined they will grow up into Yes swans. They'll leave the safety of their wee pond and will fly off to recolonise a loch in a Highland estate long since cleared of human beings. The swans will do what the people can't. They'll fly free.

Swans start out life as ugly ducklings, and then grow into graceful and elegant creatures, who can be right nippy wee buggers if you cross them. They take to the skies and find their own paths and soar above the proud lions, the imagination flies free. And they don't care what anyone thinks of them.

Scotland can fly free and find her own path, in grace and beauty. I want to be proud like a Yes swan.

21 August 2014
Pride and prejudice

Well that's us telt then. According to a new opinion poll, a large majority of voters in England want to dock Scotland's pocket money and send us to bed without any Barnett supper. Over half the respondents wanted Scottish public spending to be cut to the UK average in the event of a No vote. The newspaper reviewers on Sky News discussed the story and all agreed that it was a massive blow for Alicsammin. It's the default position on all Scottish news stories.

I'll summarise the rest for you:

"Naughty Caledonians, naughty. No Great British pudding for you lot, oh no. You'll have had your jam. It's terribly unfair that Scotland gets more money and all those free universities on prescription. Everyone knows you only have to swan into a Scottish university and they're throwing free drugs at you. They'll even look after your granny for free - and give her drugs as well. That's how that wily Alicsammin gets them to support the Scottish Nationalistic Party, because they're all on free drugs. And they hate English people too. That's the only reason they have free education, so they can teach hatred of the English. It's so bad that it's not safe for an English person to walk down a street in

Falkirk without someone leaping out a close and demanding that they say the word 'murderer' then mocking them because they can't say R. That's Scottish people, they even steal consonants out of the mouths of the English. Then they yell cruel hateful things like 'Germany's won on penalties' and fall about laughing. And it's English taxpayers who have to foot the bill you know. It's unfair."

That's the kind of reporting that led to the poll findings which led to yet more of that kind of reporting. It's the consequence of the Great Lie, the lie that told Scotland it was subsidised by the rest of the UK so it wouldn't get ideas above its oil and gas station. It may have started off as a deliberate lie, a political tactic, then it took on a life of its own and became one of those things that's only true because everyone thought everyone else believed it to be true. But when you move in the rarified circles of the UK media commentator what you think everyone else believes to be true becomes pretty rarified too, and then you end up with people who believe that the globe-bestriding mighty British nuclear defended state which punches above its weight and is MI5'ed up to its oxters is being bullied by woman in Clackmannan whose daughter bought her an iPad for her birthday. If a mountain can be dwarfed by a pebble, it can't have been much of a mountain to begin with. Certainly not if it's Ben Fogle. Although if Ben Fogle really was a Scottish mountain it would be Beinn Foghail in Gaelic, which translates as "heap of offensiveness" and is spookily appropriate.

The truth of course is that Scotland more than pays its own way within the UK. Yet there are still people who ask themselves "Where is the money going to come from?" when they think about Scottish independence. The money is already here. It's just collected by a Parliament which isn't here, and which decides how much of it it's going to give us back after first meeting other needs it considers more important, weapons of mass destruction - like Trident or a Better Together strategy meeting - or London commuter rail projects.

Thanks to the Barnett Formula, Scotland is protected to some extent from the gross imbalances in UK regional spending, but the real imbalance is within England. London benefits disproportionately while the English regions suffer. But it's Scotland that gets the blame in the UK media, and the Barnett Formula has the same chance of surviving after a No vote as Danny Alexander has of getting re-elected in 2015. And there's £7 billion wheeched off the Scottish budget, on top of our share of the billions of austerity cuts yet to come. But this is scaremongering and bullying, and it's naughty and divisive to bring it up.

The poll didn't ask respondents whether they also believed that public spending in London should also be cut to the UK average. The Sky News reviewers never thought to ask that either. Funny that.

While promising to slash Scottish funding, at the same time a majority in the poll want Scotland to remain a part of the UK. Which is a bit like expecting a dug to come and greet you enthusiastically when it knows you're going to kick it. Vote No for a kicking, there's a good Scottie.

So after two years of the UK media being full of Better Together press releases and UK politicians telling everyone that Scotland is a basket case which is only saved from tripping over its own feet thanks to the financial zimmer frame of the English tax payer, and spreading the foul lie that the independence campaign is motivated solely by an atavistic hatred of English people, we discover that most voters in England want to punish us and cut us down to an even smaller size and consequence if we vote to stay a part of this greatest partnership of nations in the time space continuum of the multiverse.

Those ProudScots must be oh so very proud of themselves now. Actually they are, because one of the symptoms of ProudScottery is that nothing is ever your fault. It's the defining characteristic of the condition.

It's the logical consequence of ProudScottery, because what they're most proud of is that being Scottish exempts them from blame and responsibility. It's easy being proud when you can always blame someone else for everything that you dislike. England can vote Tory, but the ProudScots can safely blame someone else for the ill effects of Conservative governments on a Scotland that didn't vote for them. It's not our fault, we're ProudScots, we don't vote Tory. And they can safely escape responsibility for a hypocritical hollowed out Labour party desperately chasing the support of Tory leaning voters in England's Labour-Conservative marginals. It's not our fault, we're ProudScots, we despise Tony Blair.

And it's not their fault or the fault of the No campaign for whipping up an atmosphere of bile and contempt against Scotland in the UK media, and cheering enthusiastically whenever Scotland receives a PR generated blow to Alicsammin. It's all the fault of Alicsammin, it always is. Alicsammin's Fault is a geological fixture in the ProudScot political landscape. It's always someone else's fault when you're a ProudScot. They're not ProudScots, they're shameless infants who revel in their lack of responsibility.

Independence? Oh gods no, we're ProudScots, we don't accept responsibility for Scotland. If you have no responsibility, you have no pride.

But that's what independence means. It means that the people of Scotland take charge, take control, and take responsibility. Then if we fail we have no one to blame but ourselves. That's what scares the ProudScots. Real pride comes from responsibility.

25 August 2014
Getting a good feeling

I've been getting a good feeling of late. Admittedly there's a muckle black cloud looming on my personal horizons, but the Yes campaign seems to be going from strength to strength - at least in my small bubble of confirmation bias. Because that's all positive feelings about the progress of the Yes campaign can ever be, according to media commentators too numerous to mention. For much of the media the words "progress" and "Alicsammin" can only be understood in the sense of a suicide's progress off the end of a cliff. They're already getting themselves set up for another knockout blow for Alicsammin, and it's going to be all over for the Yes campaign just like it was last time. And the time before that. And the time before that.

It's all been over for the Yes campaign since before the campaign even started. But here we are. Putting posters in windaes, chapping on doors, talking to friends and neighbours - and feeling pretty damn bouncy. A face to face conversation with a friend is a bombproof shelter against the anti-independence air campaign. You trust your friends and your family more than you trust some distant person with a column in a newspaper that no one in your street reads.

And that's where Yes is winning. A couple of stories I heard this week brought it home to me. A few wee anecdotes don't make data, but this referendum isn't about data. It's about people, and people have stories. When you put all those stories together you can make Scottish history.

When the campaign started all those oh so many long months ago, my mother was the only Yes supporter in her wee group of six friends - all women in their 70s, mostly retired teachers. The others were going to vote No. A couple of them were vehemently No. They're precisely the demographic that's supposed to be least likely to vote Yes - older women who are retired professionals. Yet every single one of them is now going to vote Yes. It was the same story with the mother of another friend, a Labour stalwart in her 70s, she's now a Yes voter too.

They each have their own individual paths to Yes. For one of my mother's friends it was going on holiday to the south of England. She met a lovely older woman from Birmingham, and spent the day with her. Her new companion told her she only ever went on holiday in England, and the previous year had gone to Inverness. My mother's friend pointed out that Inverness is not in England but in Scotland, only to be told: "Oh it's the same thing." It was the wee off the cuff remark that crystalised the entire debate for my mother's friend, that brought into focus decades of Westminster neglect, of a Scotland that cannot control her own destiny. Vote No for Scotland to remain a part of England.

Meanwhile another woman who has been a friend for decades is facing some very tough decisions of her own. She was recently diagnosed with breast cancer and is facing chemotherapy and an operation. She told me that last week as we exchanged our personal woes that she was discussing the chemotherapy with the medical staff and told them that she wanted to start it the week after the referendum. She wants to go and vote Yes to give her grandweans a future. She's not voted since the 1980s but she's voting now. This is a different vote, a vote that is so important that she is prepared to delay her chemotherapy treatment in order to participate and make a difference. With commitment like that - how can the Yes campaign possibly lose?

But with all of them it's not so much that they've been swayed by the promises of Alicsammin. It's more that they've been turned off by the No campaign, and in particular the Labour party. They've stood shoulder to shoulder with the Tories and their wee LibDem hingers on and told us that absolutely every single option that Scotland might exercise as an independent nation is worse than the possibility of Boris Johnson becoming the UK Prime Minister and a Westminster Parliament with Nigel Farage in it. Not just worse but cataclysmically worse. Scotland has absolutely nothing going for it except the kind hearted love of the Westminster Parliament and Dan Snow. And the oil is going to run out at 4.30pm on the first Wednesday after the declaration of independence.

We're too wee and poor for our economic collapse to have any significant impact on the rest of the UK, but we're too big a financial risk for them to enter into a currency union with us. We can't have a currency union because we might raise taxes differently, but if we vote No we are going to be offered all sorts of lovely new tax raising powers. We're being asked to believe all these propositions are true. But they can't all be true. We're coming to realise that none are true.

The No campaign want the currency to be the only question. A matter of a practicality is to determine the principle. It's not allowed to be about Trident, it's not allowed to be about social justice, it's not allowed to be about politicians being held to account, or Scotland determining her own political choices. It's about the price of everything and the value of nothing. This is, apparently, the positive case for the Union. That and the promise that Kate might get pregnant at some point. Ooooh intshe lurvely.

Labour lines up with the LibDems, and George Galloway and Brian Wilson are the welcome guests of the Tories. The Guardian and the Daily Mail look at one another in the pages of the Mirror. The bankers and the businessmen cheer along. And they all look the same.

Faced with a barrage of claim and counter claim, of facts and figures that contradict one another, women like my mum's friends listen to what people around them are saying. And they think for themselves. Then they realise that it's the Yes campaign which is saying exactly what they tell their own weans and the grandweans. Think for yourself. Believe in your own talents and your own abilities. Don't listen to those who tell you you can't do it because you can do anything if you put your mind to it. You'll have your family and your friends to back you up.

They're not trusting Alicsammin. They're trusting themselves. They're trusting their families. They're trusting Scotland.

26 August 2014

Bloodsports for vegans

Well that was fun. Alistair Darling was reduced to a stuttering pointy fingered cabbage, jibbering on about a Plan B despite not having a Plan A of his own, nor indeed any positive vision for Scotland. But Alistair's already decided that it doesn't matter if there's a Plan B, or Plans C, D through to Z and then starting on the Greek alphabet. They're all rubbish. Scotland is the only country on the planet which is unable to implement any currency at all. Not even Yapese stone money. It would wreak havoc on the Scotland curling team.

The currency scare died on Monday night, when Alistair was forced to admit that "Of course Scotland can use the pound" - words that will haunt him until his dying day. In uttering them he spelled out the end for the carefully constructed strategy of fear and threat upon which he was pinning all his hopes, only to see his clever plan booed by an audience that wanted to talk about more important things. Of course Scotland can use the pound, and now that's settled we can get on to discussing those more important things, like the vision for the future that Alistair's not got.

What is it with insulting Panama? It's the only country other than England and Ireland that Scotland has ever invaded, with that Darien business and everything, and they've had the immense good grace not to hold it against us. But now Alistair Darling has given us a new certainty from the No campaign by guaranting that the people of Panama will refuse him entry to their country after he spent much of the debate slagging them off. That's him screwed his chances of a round the world cruise to escape the humiliation of a Yes vote then.

So on behalf of the people of Scotland, I'd like to say, *Lo siento mucho Panamá. Discúlpanos - no somos todos gilipollas como Alistair*. And we love the hats, we really do. Even if they do come from Ecuador. Games of bools just aren't the same without them.

The debate was terribly shouty in parts. Alistair kept on asking for an answer to the question about the currency he'd already answered himself when he'd admitted Scotland would keep using the pound. Perhaps he thought that if he talked over the answer then it didn't exist and he could pretend it hadn't happened. Unfortunately that doesn't work when you've just uttered the words yourself. It was fun to watch, a bloodsport even a vegan could enjoy. And indeed, many did.

Glenn Campbell didn't intervene during the rammyness. His mind was was too busy wondering what he'll do with himself after independence when he won't be able to jet off to America to find people who are scandalised by the very idea that Scotland might get rid of nuclear missiles or release Libyans with prostate cancer from jail. Meanwhile Alistair's finger was in overdrive, trying to ram home a message that no one's listening to any more, dementedly pressing the PIN number on the imaginary ATM that he thought would spit out sterling debating points. But a currency, as we've all learned by now, only has value because people put their faith in it. Precious few of us put our faith in anything that comes out of Alistair's gob, however much he jabs that finger.

Alistair was determined to make it all about Alicsammin, and so his jabbing finger was always hitting the wrong target. It's about self-determination, it's about trusting the people of Scotland. Alicsammin's a big fat liar you say Alistair? Aye and does it not take one to know one? We're voting yes so we can keep the lot of them on a short leash. It's about changing our entire way of doing politics. Alicsammin gets that. Alistair doesn't.

Alicsammin gave better than he got, and without the pointy finger for the most part. He was enjoying himself. His final words were suitably rousing and inspirational. This is our time, our moment, let's seize it.

Darling's last words were supposed to sum up the entire case for No. If ever there was a time to give us that long promised positive case for the Union, this was it. Instead it was about all the things we can't have and we can't do, all about Alicsammin and how we can't trust him. A personal attack instead of a positive case.

Vote No for tribal politics - and for a political class that thinks we're gullible and which atomises us into isolated fragments of fear. Vote No because there's absolutely nothing that an independent Scotland could do better. Vote Yes for change, for accountability and collaboration. Vote Yes for Scotland to have the power to shape her own destiny. Vote Yes to build a society that's worth living in.

But the twin highlights of the evening were provided courtesy of two women in the audience who cut through all the jargon. There was the woman who put Alistair on the spot over his backroom meetings with private health companies. Go Glesca grannie. I am now officially in love with her. Honey, I'm a gay man. But I'd turn for you. And there was the woman who summed up the entire story of this debate - the Yes campaign are fighting to save Scotland, the No campaign are fighting to save their careers.

So flush from the yessuccess, and reports that the post rammy polls were saying Yes had won by 71% to 29%, I watched the press review on Sky News for a laff. I really need to stop watching the press review on Sky News, but it's become my favourite comedy show. Tonight's featured two press persons, one from the Mirror and the other from the Mail, who were doing a very good impression of the cantankerous auld gits in the Muppets. They started off by declaring that the Scotsman newspaper had always been neutral in its coverage of the referendum and then wandered off deeper into the tangled jungle of the Brigadoon with Buckie that passes for commentary on Scotland on Sky News.

Mirror man and Mail man were quite sure that Alicsammin will have played very poorly with women, undecideds, Labour voters, SNP voters, the last remaining Lib Dem supporter, English people, pandas, Mirror journalists called Kevin Maguire, hamsters with tooth decay, people born on a Thursday, and combine harvester operatives. The audience was clearly biased, and a tiny number of over emotional Yes supporters were making a lot of noise which was going to put off undecided voters and make quite a few Yes voters jolly well change their minds after seeing the company they keep. And wasn't Alicsammin terribly rude.

So it was another blow for Alicsammin then, although it was cunningly disguised as mauling for the No campaign. But they were of the view that it wouldn't make much difference anyway, unlike the last debate which the media decided Alistair won and was of course another blow for Alicsammin and a gamechanger which meant it was all over for the Yes campaign.

The UK media will no doubt be full of damage limitation exercises today. A whole lot of words which essentially boil down to: "Our team got its arse kicked, and we didn't like it."

The tide is rising. The momentum is building. Yes is coming.

27 August 2014

Snap, crackle, pop

And lo it was prophesied. On Tuesday St Dougie the Diminutive manifested his wee Holy Wulliness in the pages of the Guardian to preach the gospel of damage limitation. We still don't know what currency we're going to use, he bleateth. It's the pound Dougie son, were you not listening to your pal Alistair last night?

But the Pharisees of Labour weren't listening either, and told St Dougie in a vision that repeating Plan B ad nauseam was the only plan they'd got. So get out there and preach to the people that absolutely anything an independent Scotland might choose will be even shitier than having Boris Johnson as Prime Minister, share the revelation just in case anyone might think differently. Those weren't boos from the audience when Plan B was called for, oh no, they were appreciative moans of love. Up is down and black is white and the Labour red isn't Tory blue.

The debate came as a bit of a shock to them after the last time, when even people outside Sky Press reviews said Alistair had won and

Be'Yesbezub had been sent back to the dark pit of perdition, which is just outside Paisley. Depite this, Yessatan obstinately refused to be exorcised, and before you knew it people in Arbroath were chanting verses from the wee blue book of the prophet Stu and Yes Shettleston was sacrificing chickens for a barbecue. Well OK, they were frozen drumsticks from Aldi - but that's still evil and satanic. Anyway, in a flash of miraculous inspiration, like Johann Lamont constructing a grammatical sentence, it all became clear to the Divine Dougie. Debates don't make any difference at all. So that's alright then.

Go unto the Guardian and preach the word, the Archangels Ed and Ed told him. It's all based on emotion, not at all like Project Fear. Tell them that you're pure affrontit that some people on Twitter called you a Quisling and a Judas, and how that proves the evil divisiveness of the separatists. You're even more oleaginous than Jim Murphy, so you're perfect for the gig. Show them that you're really a wee creeping Jesus and spread the numbing balm of the true word of Gord like vaseline on the bleeding haemorrhoids of the Labour party. It's the only redistribution that Labour practises, and it can be claimed on expenses.

So Dougie tells the tiny readership of the Guardian that Scotland is in need of family therapy counselling and it's all the fault of the nasty nationalists. After a No vote he is willing to offer his services as an emollient between the tender cheeks of a well skelpt Scottish arse and the hard and shiny lavvy paper of Westminster.

The social division is so bad that the Patronising BT Lady from the advert last night is already receiving trauma counselling from people who aren't related to former Labour Lord Provosts of Glasgow. She doesn't do politics because she's a girly. No voting women only think about little things in the kitchen, little things like pencils and Paul's leadless pencil. The No campaign wants it to stay that way. Patronising BT Lady can't stay long though, she has to touch up the lippy and get back home to make Paul's tea. He's just so clueless you know, men what are they like girls - before he infects the kids with the virus of nationalism and gets rice crispies caught in his beard. Explaining independence at the same time as having his breakfast - everyone knows men can't multi-task and weans are too stupid to think for themselves. Now everyone stop thinking. Eat your cereal.

Don't think that the Tories believe that they can teach the poor to stand on their own two feet by cutting their legs off. And don't think that when Labour gets into power it acts exactly the same, because the only way it can get into power is by persuading Tory leaning voters to vote for it. These are your only choices, don't think there can be others.

Don't think that with its limited powers, the Scottish Parliament is the clinic which is left with the victims, but all they've got are some bandages and plasters. Dougie wants us to complain that the doctor's still got a packet of plasters that she's not used, and not to do anything about the bastards with the axe. Stop thinking. St Dougie and the Patronising BT Lady want us to eat our cereal.

There are other choices. We could choose cornflakes, or Weetabix. We could choose to have a Labour party that can only get elected if it attracts the votes of SNP supporters, or Socialists or Greens, or even the last Lib Dem. A different Labour party from the one that Dougie offers. One that when it promised to help create opportunities for the poor to get out of poverty actually did that when in power. Or suffer the consequences of a Scottish electorate. Snap, crackle, pop.

We can choose an end to the tribal politics that Dougie offers. Westminster rules make that gemme a bogey. We can have a new game, a more consensual game, a fairer game. Dougie doesn't want that. He doesn't want reconciliation, he wants obedience to the old rules that constrict our choices. Some people say they want peace when what they mean is that they want victory.

It's crunchy. There's fruity bits. More jam than you'll ever get from a Labour government. Eating cereal and thinking. Thinking it's about power. It always is. We get spoken down to and told what we can't do because we have no power. Holyrood is the regional branch of a subcontracted Westminster sovereignty. It gets told what to do. Dougie and Patronising BT Lady think that will still be the case if Scotland votes Yes. That's why Dougie has no vision of the future, only fear and calls for Plan B. Dougie's Scotland is at the mercy of Westminster's elements and always will be.

But that will change with a Yes vote. With a Yes vote there are suddenly two sovereign bodies in the UK. The Westminster Parliament and the people of Scotland. We will have taken back the power of decision making. The power of control. The power of self-determination. Westminster tells us that means we'd become foreign. Oh right - so like an equal sovereign state that Westminster has to treat with mutual respect? Now there's a big strawberry in the muesli.

If Scotland votes Yes, the balance of power radically shifts towards the people of Scotland. There will be independence negotiations, and Westminster is woefully unprepared for them. Who'll be patronising who then.

Patronising BT Lady nods in agreement as she makes the tea. We're eating our cereal and thinking.

The mental chains go snap, crackle, pop.

28 August 2014
The message and the messenger

Scotland's breakfast tables are still reeling from the gobsmacking arsery of Tuesday's patronising Eat Your Cereal broadcast for Better Together and the hysterical Twitterfest of pisstakes that followed. Cornflakes are being crunched accusingly. But at least it stopped people talking about just how badly Alistair Darling bombed in Monday's debate.

It's being reported that the advert was so dire that it's convinced some No voters to vote Yes, which is very good news, but that's not quite how these things work. It wasn't the advert exactly. What the advert did was to crystalise a decision that was already brewing. The crapulosity of the advert and its channelling of 1950s social attitudes becomes a symbol for the utterly dreary doom-laden backward looking negativity of the case for a No vote over the past two years. The advert is the proverbial dried grass stalk and the dromedary with the spinal injury. Watching it, a wee light comes on like those weans in the Reddybrek advert that glowed in the dark. The entire No campaign distilled into three crunchy phrases like the wee plastic toys that are a choking hazard in a cornflakes packet: Shut up. Eat your cereal. Know your place.

The wee rebellious voice within says - Mother of Parliaments? Aye right. You're no ma maw. And another voter serves Westminster a bowl of Cheerios and decides to vote Yes.

It's been a difficult week for heavily burdened members of the genus camelus. For some the last straw was the inability of Alistair Darling to save the union without jabbing his finger, or it's the Patronising BT Lady and her empty cup, for others it's the wee No thanks badge on Tory Home Secretary Theresa May's dress as she's interviewed about the latest failure of British institutions to protect the vulnerable and hold the powerful to account, or it's Gordon Brown being heckled by a Labour activist as he addresses another closed meeting of supporters and friendly media.

After informing the women of Scotland that thinking is really hard, it's Airchie Macpherson to the rescue. Because trotting out a 1970s TV sports presenter is exactly how to appeal to undecided voters who're concerned you might be just a teeny bit out of date and out of touch. Still, BBC 1970s presenters had much more socially advanced attitudes to women than 1950s public information films.

However Airchie's rousing defence of not wanting to become a foreigner is going to be a gamechanger and will stop the rapidly accelerating camel snapping. We've had a lot of gamechangers already, like every time Gordon Brown intervened in the debate for the first time. There was supposed to be another one on Wednesday, when Gordie intervened for the first time again, only this time with Alistair - having agreed temporarily to bury the hatchet after getting Wee Dougie to remove it from his sister's back. But that one got upstaged by the heckler and Superairchie.

God I hate fitba. I blame Airchie Macpherson and the BBC. I never paid any attention to what Airchie had to say during those interminable wet Saturday afternoons in the 70s when my dad hogged the telly, and I'll be buggered if I'm starting now. It's thon symbol thing again. One person's beloved former sports presenter is another person's symbolic representation of a long gone and unlamented introspective and parochial Scotland. Airchie is fitba, the wee wummin in the kitchen making a bowl of cereal, letting those clever chaps in London deal with the difficult stuff, and sweaters for goalposts isn't it.

Your horizons can stretch no further than you can kick a baw. Don't dream, don't think, eat your cereal and go play fitba. The camels are squashed like roadkill on Airchie's Unionist moral high road. Follow, follow, because you can never lead yourselves.

Today the great evader comes to town, back from his holidays. The man who Airchie is really defending. Davie Cameron is speaking in Glasgow at a dinner organised by the CBI, who're not being political at all. Davie will speak to the business people, he'll speak to closed press conferences, he'll only answer questions from those who've been approved. He won't speak to the little people. He won't speak to you or me, because he doesn't speak for us.

The Guardian publishes the story of Davie telling the CBI to tell us to stay, and in patronising editorials it pushes the case for compliance and passivity. On the same page of the paper is an article called *The Top of British Society is a Racket for the Privileged*. Just read the fitba pages, says Airchie.

Trust Davie, says Airchie, trust Gordie and Alistair, don't trust Scotland, don't trust yourself. Davie, Gordie and Alistair say they'll only trust us with answers when we've voted for them, only after we've signed the warrant to surrender our trust to them forever. The death warrant of hope. Airchie says the fitba is on.

The No campaign struggles with both its message and its messengers. The message is - you can't, don't dare, don't get ideas above your station, leave it to the big boys in the grey suits. Stay where you are until you are attended to. Trust is something demanded of you, not given to you. The messengers are discredited politicians with a history of lies, vacuous celebrities without a clue, voices from a past that was brass not golden, and the squeaky clean young faces in the astroturf video. Now eat your cereal and watch the fitba.

But Yes keeps winning, Yes keeps gaining strength, because the message of Yes is its messengers. The enthusiastic volunteers, the faces with hope, the faces with smiles. They're chapping doors, they're campaigning, they're changing the face of Scotland. The energy and commitment of the grassroots campaign is the message. This is Scotland in movement, a Scotland that can achieve, a Scotland that will not be daunted. The messengers of the Yes campaign are the answers to the questions. Scotland is doing it for itself. We don't need to wait for answers from the distant men in grey suits. We eat our cereal and go to work for our own future.

The message is the medium, and the medium are the people. Yes is a force of nature like the wind on the high mountains that spins the turbines, the tidal flow in the sea lochs that power a green future. Yes does it for itself, Scotland can do it for herself.

Vote yes, trust the message that's the messenger. You are Scotland and the message is you.

28 August 2014

In the limbo inbetween

This is one of those personal posts. Andy's postal ballot arrived in the post on Thursday, and I took it to the hospital for him to fill in. He's very poorly now, with constant infections. The consultant has said that they suspect he has an infected cyst in his lower abdomen. Usually they'd treat it surgically, but he's too weak and frail. Even if he could cope with the procedure, it would only get him back to the condition he was in when he was admitted to hospital after his latest stroke, and then he'd only come down with yet another infection.

So no more poking and prodding, we need to allow him to go. He's getting close to the end now - at the very best it's only a couple of weeks away and perhaps not even that. And that estimate is based on nothing more than my wishful thinking. The important thing is that he's comfortable, he's not in pain or distress. The staff at Lightburn hospital have been fantastic with him.

It wasn't a difficult decision to tell the consultant to stop active treatment, to put him on the do not resuscitate list and to allow him to slip away. When he had cancer some 15 years ago, we knew he was going to recover from it, but we discussed end of life care and funeral plans. He said then he wanted to be cremated, and he wanted a druid to officiate at his funeral. This was in Spain, where the funeral is usually the day after death. "How am I going to find a druid in Spain at 24 hours notice?" I asked. "In the Yellow Pages?" he replied. But he also told me that he wanted to be allowed to go in peace, without being attached to tubes and pinging machines that wouldn't get him any better.

So it was easy now. I didn't have to make a decision. I just had to tell the consultant when she asked me to make a decision. It helped so much that I knew what to tell her, and that I only had to relay his choice to her. And I've even found a druid for him.

He was determined to vote, but his grasp is weak and he struggled with the pen. It took great effort to produce an illegible scrawl that I can only hope the returning officer will accept as his signature. And then he put his X in the box marked YES, dropped the pen and lay back, exhausted with the effort.

As he signed it struck me that this is probably the last thing he'll ever sign. The last time he'll ever put his name to anything. Going from this world in the knowledge that his final act was to deliver an almighty kick in the nuts to the British establishment. He'll like that. He was a proud working class London lad and socialist to his core. He put his name to a vote for an independent Scotland. It's his legacy to me, to my family, to our friends, to all the people who showed him love and support and welcomed him into the Scotland that became his home.

I posted his vote on the way home. He's not ever coming home, but he's not gone. I'm in the limbo inbetween.

30 August 2014

Egg fling flan

I think I've finally got a handle on the No campaign. A No vote is all that stands between Scotland and a descent into grocery-based anarchy. Jim Murphy went out to give us the message, with the assistance of a loudhailer, a bus and a wee clique of party hingers on. He didn't go to get the messages in. You're not supposed to give the messages to Jim Murphy, and certainly not in the form of an egg on his shirt. Listen reverently and eat your cereal instead. Jim has things to shout at you through a megaphone.

I'm certainly not defending ovoid acts of terror. Eggs are evil, you could have someone's eye out with that ballistic potential chicken.

Eggs are razor sharp ophthamological instruments of intimidation. You can't debate with an egg, although to be fair you'd probably get a more coherent argument from a broken egg than you would from a Labour politician explaining the party's plans for more devolution.

But it's full confession time. I'm not greatly moved by Jim's travails with a flung fowl foetus. Readers, I too am a grocery based terrorist, although I retired a long time ago. Honest, your free range Yes eggs are safe.

Back in 1980 I threw a bag of flour at Michael Heseltine when he came to Glasgow University to make a speech and tell us how fabby Maggie and nuclear missiles were. It was not an organised terror attack. I organised it myself with some self-raising McDougal's from my maw's kitchen cupboard. It was disorganised and uncoordinated, a bit like my flinging skills really. He was only 15 feet away, and I missed. I throw like a wee girly. The shame of my crime against grocery-flinging haunts me to this very day. I wondered - if only I had hit Michael Hesiltine with that bag of flour perhaps he'd have had an epiphany and thought "You know, Thatcherism is really bad and I'm going to devote my life and wealth to campaigning for peace and alleviating poverty." But then I grew up. So. Naaa. Throwing groceries at them just gives them an excuse to harrumph and attempt to claim some moral high ground.

Same goes with Jim Murphy. Standing on a soapbox didn't work for him, so he stood on an egg instead. Flinging an egg at him is not an attempt to silence him. He's hardly shut up about it since. It was an attempt to fling an egg at him, in the long and hoary tradition of immature people flinging foodstuffs at politicians that get on their tits, and the politicians dining out on it.

The UK media has naturally reacted with outrage to the foul heartless assault on Jim's laundry and cooked up an egg fling flan. Yes Scotland has hatched a plot to organise a campaign of egg flinging, Alicsammin must condemn it immediately and call off the eggstremists. Did those caring sharing people in Better Together not warn us that the referendum would create discord and division - and now look what's happened. Jim Murphy's got to wash his shirt. Or rather, give it to

Patronising BT Lady to wash it for him. Where will it all end? Will no one think of the children? Now eat your cereal. Naw, ye cannae have a fried egg. Your cybernat da took them to fling at Jim Murphy. Men eh, what are they like?

It was only a fecking egg. Grow up for God's sake. Sometimes I find myself possessed of an irrational urge to herd Westminster politicians and their media hangers on into a room and force them to watch Humpty Dumpty cartoons until they learn to conduct themselves with more maturity than a week old chick and stop with the collective clucking like battery hens. An egg flinging is not symbolic of an intolerant oppressiveness lurking beneath the shiny happy faces of Yes supporters. It's symbolic of an immature eejit that flung an egg and a No campaign that's making a meal of it because their substantive arguments, such as they are, have long since been scrambled, scotched, and fried, consumed, crapped out, and flushed.

The hunt for the egg-flinger is boiling. Or rather, Yes campaigners are keen to identify the individual. Jim Murphy doesn't appear too fussed, because an unidentified egg-flinger could be anyone at all, Alicsammin in a mask, and that means he can continue to claim there's a coordinated plot to prevent him preaching nawness to a handful of passers-by in Fife. It's all a big egg-based conspiracy right up until the time that it turns out that the egg-flinger was some random drunk guy who'd just been to Aldi. Patronising BT Lady had sent him out to get some cornflakes, but men eh, can't get anything right.

Meanwhile there are those in the Yes campaign who are equally keen to prove it's all a dastardly plot by Jim Murphy himself, mainly on the basis that three quarters of the population would probably agree to the proposition that Jim Murphy seems like the kind of person who'd break a few eggs to make a political omelette.

But the truth is it doesn't really matter. It's only an egg. But let us imagine that we are in some dystopian alternate universe - one that's even more dystopian than the one we inhabit so some alcoholic refreshments may be necessary before you can liberate your imagination sufficiently. It's a universe where Scotland is having a typical independence campaign. In typical independence campaigns there are disappearances, shootings, bombings, internment camps, civil unrest, and states of emergency. In that universe someone going to work on Jim Murphy with an egg would pass unnoticed. Jim's wails of oppression would be laughed at, if anyone except Patroning BT Lady paid them any attention at all, and she's only wondering what powder to use to get the stain out.

Back in the real Scotland, this one we actually live in, not the one on the news, the only reason the media is able to whip up an egging into a souffle of accusations is because Scotland's independence campaign is peaceful, democratic, good natured, and inclusive. There has been no violence to compare, not even remotely, to the Troubles in Northern Ireland or the violence that has disfigured the Basque Country. This is Scotland, we don't do terrorism, we don't do civil unrest, we don't do riots. We have the occasional nutter who flings an egg.

You only notice a plook on an otherwise unblemished face. Jim Murphy is that plook and the UK media delight in squeezing it.

Vote Yes - it's a plook cream for Scotland.

September 2014

2 September 2014

Bigger than fear

I've been at the hospital most of the day. Andy's having another crisis. They're getting more frequent. He seems to have stabilised somewhat, but he's on oxygen now and his swallowing difficulties are much worse. He's hardly eating at all. His breathing is laboured, shallow, gurgling. It's 3.30 am and I've just got back home as he's sleeping, the hospital will phone if there is any change in his condition. But we're reaching the end of the road now.

I am afraid. Afraid that he might suffer. Afraid of my grief. Afraid of being alone. The fear nests inside in the depths of the soul, but it is mine, a part of me. I own it and acknowledge it. And when you do that you realise that you are bigger than your fear. Fear is small but the soul is infinite.

I stopped my claim for Carers Allowance yesterday. I still care but am no longer a carer. I feel like I've started to inch over the dark valley between our life together and life alone. The other side is in sight. Getting there is the difficult bit. The short term is painful and full of grief, but in the distance, hazy beyond a veil of tears, there are bright lights ahead that speak of a new future, a new life. There is hope despite everything. As I look down into the chasm it's hope that keeps me afloat, hope that keeps me going. Cling onto hope, trust in your own inner strength, in your family and friends, and all will be well.

Getting home, news of a new poll brightened my mood somewhat. Comfort must be taken where you can find it, and YouGov's latest poll is very comforting indeed. 47% Yes, 53% No - a 3% swing is all that is required to put Yes ahead. It's within margin of error. This poll is highly significant, both for its large swing to Yes, but more importantly because YouGov has always been the polling company which returns the worst result for Yes. YouGov applies the infamous 'Kellner correction' which reduces the Yes result to account for the 'shy No' factor. We are on our way, we are inching over the chasm and the bright lights are ahead. Only this time there are no tears.

Scotland has looked into its soul and found the fear placed there by nay-sayers and doubters, by careerists and opportunists. We've looked at it, examined it. And we've come to realise our fear is as small as their horizons are limited. We are bigger than our fears, we are a people of infinite potential. And we will flourish.

3 September 2014
Sugar coated fluff puffs and leaps of faith

It's coming, you can feel it in the air and hear it in the conversations around you. Today at the hospital as I walked onto the ward four nurses were having an animated conversation about independence, three of them voting Yes, trying to persuade the fourth. In bus depots, factories, offices and schools, staff are talking, discussing, debating. And it's overwhelmingly amicable and good natured. We political amateurs know how to disagree without being disagreeable, unlike the Jim Murphys who say they speak for us.

As the conversations continue, more decide to vote Yes. Positivity and hope are novel experiences in Scottish politics, and they're infectious. It's the virus of hope, not the virus of nationalism. It's propagating itself in the rising tide of positivity, and sprouting from the pages of a wee blue book. It's growing in the laughter of derision that greets each new No campaign poster or broadcast.

The latest in the multimillion pound campaign, the professional campaign designed and implemented by the clever-clever clones in ill fitting suits who determine our lives, is a series of posters with messages more vacuuous that any that has come before. "I love my family so I'm saying No Thanks." "I love my kids so I'm saying No Thanks." People were paid a lot of money to come up with these posters. Politicians previewed them, focus groups discussed them, advertising agencies designed them. And the product of our professionalised political class is inconsequential nothingness, airheaded fluff that even Simon Cowell would reject as too low-brow for his programmes. This is, allegedly, the positive case for the Union, a crass attempt to make us identify our love for our children and families with Jim Murphy and Alistair Darling's careers.

Do you love the party leaders in Westminster? Do you love the House of Lords like you love your own children? David Cameron, Ed Miliband, Nick Clegg and Nigel Farage are not our family. They're not our kids. They're sure as hell not our country. The No campaign hopes you can't tell the difference, it's the only hope they have to offer you.

I don't know the difference between my kids and the Westminster Parliament, so I won't listen to the man off the telly. Heard it all before. Whateeeevahhh. Vote No and revel in ignorance, it's the no knowledge economy with the zero hours contract. Celebrate your passivity, show how proud you are of your dependency. Love being stupid. Do what you're told. Thinking for yourself is so hard. Eat your cereal. Save up the coupons from the packet and enter the Westminster devolution draw. Win a lifetime's supply of sugar-coated fluff puffs, devoid of nutrients but they'll still rot your teeth and your brain.

The Scottish electorate is wise enough to know the difference. That's not granting the Scottish electorate a great amount of political literacy either, a pet poodle knows the difference. The only people those posters will appeal to are those with less insight than a poodle. That's what the No campaign thinks of us. We're intellectually challenged poodles. Sit up and beg for your cereal from the Westminster sugarpuffs daddy. There's a good girl, there's a good boy.

For Westminster, Scotland - just like the rest of the UK - is a province to be raided for resources, labour and capital. The people are just an inconvenience to be humoured, pat on the head, and given a bowl of cereal. They think nothing of us, and think we are capable of nothing without them. We're just the batteries for the vibrator, they're the ones who get the thrill as we are drained.

You don't even have to scratch below the surface of the glossy publicity pics to find the condescension lurking beneath. It's waved in your face like a trophy. Wee Dougie Alexander waved his Holy Wullie in the STV debate on Tuesday night. Two audience members asked what currency he'd advocate for an independent Scotland. Dougie didn't answer, instead he ruled out every option except Scotland remaining a part of the UK. Everything Scotland could possibly do for herself would be a disaster. Scotland can't manage any sort of currency at all. So vote No, vote for the Holy Wullie without a prayer, in a land with no hope and no chance.

The scare stories continue ramping up, the constant background to the referendum campaign. But they fade from the consciousness just as after a while you no longer notice the ticking of a clock in a quiet room. The clock is ticking on Westminster's rule in Scotland. The scare stories no longer work, the positive case for the Union never existed. They have nothing left but more of the same. They're pulling the same old strings, but we're no longer their puppets.

People are talking, debating, changing minds. There's an enthusiasm and interest which has never occurred before. The queues stretched out into the streets as people registered to vote before the deadline, queueing to make history, queueing to be part of a country where we can choose between our hopes not choose between our fears. The dusty and distant world of the politicians has been dragged kicking and screaming into the streets and the bars, the living rooms and bedrooms. That's the carnage the No campaign fears, the carnage that occurs to their reputations as Scotland examines them clinically. We're out of their control, and we scare them. Project Fear has eaten itself.

The clock is ticking. Take a deep breath. Tense your muscles. A cautious country is about to take a leap of faith in itself. And when we land our feet will be planted firmly on a path we choose for ourselves.

5 September 2014

A leaf falls

I wanted to say a few words to thank everyone for the kind messages of condolences, support and love. Thank you, you've helped to make the unbearable a bit less unbearable. I'd also like to thank all the staff in Lightburn Hospital for their genuine care and concern which went over and above the highly professional treatment they gave Andy. They made me feel that he was safe, and they made me feel that he was looked after. They treated him with respect, and they ensured that he preserved his dignity. I will always be grateful to them.

Andy's passing was peaceful. He died without regrets, without bitterness, and knowing he was loved. It was a good death, as good as a death can be. The hospital phoned just after seven on Wednesday morning to say that he was deteriorating fast, and they didn't think there was long to go. I got to the hospital before eight. He was no longer able to speak, and his breathing was shallow and laboured, but he knew I was there. I opened the curtains so he could see the sky and sat with him holding his hand. I talked to him about the good times we'd had together. I told him that I loved him and always would carry him in my heart - but that I wanted him to let go and not to worry about me and the dug.

Then I said that all those years ago when we first met, I was living in Easterhouse, just up the road from Lightburn Hospital. We met, we fell in love, and he took me away on a great adventure. And then he brought me back home again. Everything comes full circle. At that he breathed his last and slipped away, his eyes on the morning sky above Glasgow, his hand in mine.

The world dissolved in tears.

While the hospital prepared some paperwork I went outside to smoke a ciggy, frazzled, tearful, standing under a tree outside the hospital on Carntyne Road. An early autumn leaf gently fell from the tree as I stood there, and landed on my shoulder. It was his last wee gift to me, a reminder of the cycle of life. All things must pass, so new life can grow.

I picked up the leaf and carefully put it in my wallet. When I got home I pressed it between the pages of the White Paper on Independence, a talisman for the future, a token of hope, golden with potential like Andy.

I will bury his ashes in a special place, and plant a rowan tree. In Celtic myth the rowan tree was the protector against evil spirits, the guardian and protector. Andy the London polisman will grow into a rowan tree, and will guard and protect us all.

When he told me, many years ago, that's what he wanted, I laughed and said - "Once a polis always a polis then eh." And he smiled that wee smile. The smile I'm always going to miss.

The funeral will be held at Daldowie Crematorium on Saturday 13 September at midday. It will be a pagan ceremony and Andy doesn't want people to dress in mourning black. He wanted this to be a celebration of life. It was only on reading all the wonderful comments, messages, and tweets of love and support, that I realised just how much Andy's story has touched people and connected with them. If you felt a connection with him, you will be welcome.

Please don't send flowers, instead make a donation to Maryhill Foodbank. Cut flowers wilt and die, but a gift to the foodbank is a gift of nourishment and strength. Andy would have preferred that.

10 September 2014

The breakfast revolution

It's all got terribly exciting of late, but I've not really been following any of it too closely, what with organising a funeral, and when not occupied with that have been fully engaged with full-on Schadenfreude. I have to hand it to my late partner, he certainly picked a time to go which provides a vast amount of amusement at the self-inflicted discomfort of the British establishment.

And we've got a baby. We can't leave Westminster because Kate's pregnant and we're needed to pay the child maintenance - which in this wean's case involves a large shooting estate in the Highlands. If we vote Yes, we won't get the BBC and won't be able to participate in all the bunting and joyful Nicholas Witchelling. Don't say you've not been warned.

Fraser Nelson was on Newsnight the other night. The actual Newsnight, not the wee pretendy one that used to get aired just after the actual Newsnight. You know that Scotland has changed forever when you find yourself getting nostalgic for Gordon Brewer. Scotland is never off the telly these days and has even pushed Willinkatebabe off the top of the news. Nicholas Witchell is receiving grief counselling.

The reason for all the attention is because of a couple of opinion polls showing Yes has closed the gap and is showing momentum have sent the Westminster establishment into a blind panic and the No campaign into a confused and contradictory meltdown - although to be fair they've been confused and contradictory since the start and it's not always easy to tell the difference. Thankfully Fraser is a licenced North Briton who is able to translate the strange Caledonian ogams and portents for an audience who have only just realised that Scotland is serious about this independence lark and that it's far more significant than the small brown blob at the top of the BBC weather map might suggest.

I'm not entirely sure what Fraser was saying as he elocuted at Emily 'Will Scotland Stay Loyal' Maitlis, because I can never get past that, ahem, *idiosyncratic* accent of his. It's not that he's hard to understand, it's just I'm transfixed by his irritable vowel syndrome and miss what he's actually saying. He speaks like a Scottish person as imagined by Inspector Clouseau. Neuou thehnks Freiyzihrh. A phonetic ballet like that only happens when you're so far up yourself that you come out the other orifice and as a lifelong student of language it would only be rude not to sit back and appreciate the performance.

Whenever Fraser's on the telly I keep expecting him to introduce his new range of pasta sauces, the ones with oahreganouuh and touamaahtouhs in them. He's the Lloyd Grossman of Scottish politics, he takes us through the Westminster keyhole to discover that there's a wee floater in the lavvy pan. That'll be what's left of Davie Cameron after the rest of the Tory party have flushed him.

They don't speak like that in Paisley you know, except for a weird guy in a cowboy hat I met in a pub once - he loves line dancing and went on holiday to Miami for a fortnight in the late 80s and acquired a mid-Atlantic accent as a result of a psychotic episode on cocaine that made him realise he was the incarnation of General Custer. We discovered this week that the entire leadership of the UK political parties are also the incarnations of Custer, only they not mounting a last stand so much as a beg-a-thon in the hope of saving their careers and reputations. It has the whiff of desperation about it, in the same way that five thousand litres of raw sewage have a hint of unpleasantness.

And then we had a history bit, and Tom Devine and Niall Fergusson got stuck into one another after Niall said we'd be voting to become like Belarus only with worse weather. Drawing on his great academic stature, his deep understanding of Scottish history, his immense erudition, and an intellect which is galactic in the spacey sense and not the chocolate bar sense - Tam telt Neillie boay tae shut his geggie, stop with the pettit lip and whit would you know anyway ya wee fuckwit self-publicising apologist for colonialists, war mongerers and casino capitalists that's only ever had the one idea in his entire life. Your cringe is showing. Now fuck off and get back to us when you want to be a grown up ya hysterical puffed up balloon. Or words to that effect. Or it might be that's what I wanted to tell Neillie and I imagined it all.

However the main news, apart from the news that the No campaign has melted, is that the Unionist parties are making a last stand on an offer of more devolution which doesn't smack of desperation at all, oh no. Scotland can have all sorts of extra special powers, tax powers, spending powers, and JK Rowling said that she'd had a wee word with Dumbledore and is willing to throw in the power of invisibility too. Mind you, Scotland has had that power for decades, which is how we've made it through the past 50 years with Westminster scarcely noticing us at all.

Well they say more devolution, but they're not able to tell us exactly what it might consist of, except that it will be a very very special prezzie, much better than that naff sweater that your auntie knitted you for Christmas. There will be jam, there will be more jam, and chocolate, and eclairs, and cream cakes, and you can eat your cereal. The shock of

Yes pulling ahead in the polls has electrified the No campaign, which explains why the Westminster parties look like they've been tasered.

Although they can't tell us exactly what extra powers will be coming to Scotland, Gordon Brown insists that there's a definite timetable for delivering the powers that we don't know what they are. Only someone forgot to tell Ed Balls. Someone also forgot to tell Gordon that he's not actually the prime minister any more and doesn't have any power to do anything at all whatever promises and commitments he makes. However David Cameron is also hoping that everyone has forgotten that Gordon isn't prime minister in case anyone asks him to speak to some Scottish people who are not in possession of press passes or Tory party membership cards. Gordie's just a very convenient human shield. You've got to be pretty desperate when your shield is Gordie Broon addressing carefully selected audiences of supporters.

An attempt at love bombing ended in ignominy on Tuesday. Davie Cameron had ordered the Scottish saltire to be flown from Number 10 for the duration of the campaign. It's the very definition of gesture politics, but in the face of a two fingered gesture from Scotland it's pretty much all they've got left. But Number 10 couldn't even manage to fly a Scottish flag. It fell off the pole as staff attempted to raise it. So it's a Sign then, not a flag. Meanwhile a call from Ed Miliband for Labour controlled local authorities in the rest of the UK to fly the Scottish flag met with a resounding meh from the good burghers of England. The only people who care if Scotland leaves the Union are those politicians whose jobs and careers depend on us staying. That ought to tell us all we need to know.

Phase two of the love bombing starts on Wednesday. All four UK party leaders are honouring us with their presence this week, Davie, Ed, Nick and even Nige. They're all going to promise lots of different unspecific things, which they will definitely do as soon as possible. Right away. And have some jam with your cereal. Lots of jam. We can talk about the flavour later. No uncertainty there, oh no not at all. You can trust us. We have the answer, and the answer is jam and cereal. Independence, it's so uncertain, there's not enough information, trust us to make the changes we think are best for you.

The best way to decide when there is not enough information is to become your own teacher. The best way to confront uncertainty is for you to be the agent of change. The best way to predict the future is to make it happen. And the only trust you need is the trust you place in yourself. Be the future. Make your own cereal, make your own jam. This is the breakfast revolution, and we're at the beginning of a new day.

11 September 2014
Fat-cats and hangdog looks

We've been blowed again, because of an opinion poll showing that the gap between Yes and No is within the margin of error, just like the last one that showed the gap between Yes and No was within the margin of error with Yes 1% ahead. Funny thing indypolling error, it only ever errs on the one side. That would be the side of a blow for alicsammin. Rarely have so many been so blown since a Roman emperor last held an orgy.

We got blowed again on the very day that Davie Cameron came to Scotland to do his impression of an abandoned puppy telling us that independence is for life not just for Christmas. Poor Davie with the hangdog eyes told us he was going to be heartbroken and tried to make us feel guilty. Meanwhile Boris Johnson and half the Tory back bench are standing by a canal with a sack, a stack of bricks, and looking impatient. Perhaps they could tempt him over with a bowl of cereal.

It's not about kicking out the effin Tories, pleaded Davie desperately with a tear in his eye as he thought about his place in the history books. Oh yes it effin is Davie. As he keeps reminding us every time he gets involved, he doesn't have a vote and so can't get involved, and I think that means it's us who get to tell him what this vote is about, and not him tell us. The Tories are going to eff Davie if there's a Yes. There's a lovely wee bonus prize.

Ed Miliband was in Glasgow, where he felt it was important that voters in the referendum understood that during WW2 his dad was stationed in Scotland for a few months. Eh, no, I'm not really sure of the relevance either. He mentioned solidarity a lot. And Keir Hardie. The Jarrow March. Fighting the Nazis. And the miners' strike. Oh. No, not the miners' strike. Labour opposed that ... eh ... NHS! Welfare state! Cuddly Toy! And solidarity, lots of that, power to the people as long as they have a politics, philosophy and economics degree from Oxford. Keep that solidarity conveyor belt moving, and try to forget that Labour is a conveyor belt for turning your aspirations into their seats in the Lords. Eat your cereal.

Ed was also keen to tell us that independence is forever. Long time that is. Foreverevereverever. That's much longer than it will take the Sun to use up all its hydrogen and then expand in a big red firey ball and consume the Earth. It's much longer than it will take the fabric of the universe to stretch out so far that the very bonds that hold atoms together will dissolve and the universe will die with a whimper in a thin soup of lifeless particles. Forever is even longer than it takes the Labour party to deliver on the abolition of the House of Lords, although not by much. So if you're waiting on the arrival of a big red firey thing to burn away the disfiguring privilege and self-rewarding patronage of the Westminster system, you'd be better off with the death of the sun than the Labour party. The sun will expand and consume the Earth in about three and a half billion years and is unlikely to be deterred by a Westminster sub-committee and a series of written objections from Baron Warmonger of Safeseatshire. Labour will take some while longer, although to be fair it has already turned into a thin whimpering soup of lifeless particles. Just keep that solidarity subsidy rolling in like a blank cheque.

Nick Clegg was lost in the Borders someplace. He was probably warning that independence is forever too, but no one has listened to Nick since 2010. He's the one hit wonder who hangs about in the hope that he'll develop into a minor cult. He's succeeded richly in this, if you overlook the fact that he's out by one letter. Nick understands forever. It's the period of time that will elapse before anyone will ever again believe a word he says.

I'm not entirely clear why the No campaign has suddenly decided to tell us that independence is forever, perhaps they're trying to appeal to that segment of the electorate which is confused between "national sovereignty and self-determination" and a trial subscription to Woollens Monthly. That'll be PatronisingBTLady then. Look out for October's special edition featuring macramé mug cosies, hand knitted currency unions, a sexy tweed thong for Paul, and comfort blankets for distraught MPs.

Most Scottish people have by now grasped the concept that independence is not like a fortnight's holiday, and for those who have already decided to vote Yes, the foreveriness part of it is one of the major attractions. No more nuclear missiles, forever. No more Etonian Tory Prime Ministers, forever. No more Scottish Labour policies being determined by the need to chase after UKIP voters in Essex, forever. No more governments we didn't vote for, forever - or at least until the arrival of our alien lizard overlords from Alpha Centauri in the 23rd century. It is true to say that Scotland will not be as prepared for this event as the rest of the UK, which will already have had centuries practising for life under alien lizard overlords, and will scarcely notice the difference. This may be the only positive case for the Union which has any credibility left. After two years of Project Fear, the mass emoting of the Westminster leaders was more than a little creepy, like a bouquet from a stalker.

Project Fear is of course continuing unabated, only more so as Westminster politicians frantically begged for favours from future members of the Lords. There was another blow again after all the banks announced that they are going to leave if we vote Yes because Scotland is the only country on the planet that can't have any currency at all. And they'll take all the cash machines, and your credit card, and those wee plastic bags for loose change and all the artificial plants. No one will ever get a mortgage ever again, and you'll have to stay with your parents and you and your significant other will have to have sex really really quietly. But the annoying recorded message phone calls that tell you you might have a claim for PPI compensation will still disturb you when you're trying to have very very quiet sex on a Saturday morning when your dad's a bit hung over and your maw has popped out for the messages - only they'll call twice as often. But that will only be a problem until your parents' phone gets cut off because they can't pay the bill because money won't exist. And your maw won't get any messages because there won't be any money. Then we'll all starve to death. And Davie's heart will be broken, because that's what happens when bankers fear they might have to operate in a country where they could be regulated.

Oh, and the oil companies are all leaving too. Even that wee petrol station on the way to Oban. There's no oil left and Oban is far too volatile, and no one will want to buy any of the Scottish oil that there isn't any left of anyway, on account of Scotland not being allowed to have any money at all. So that's us telt then. It's all so uncertain and there aren't any answers to ridiculous questions. Yes, I am so treating you like a grown up. Just eat your cereal and vote No.

The No campaign will be ratcheting up the pressure over the next week, although if the pitch of hysteria gets any higher there won't be an unshattered windae in the country. Politicians will be calling in favours and making promises to business people and journalists as they attempt to find new ways to scare and intimidate. Don't be scared by the scaredy fat-cats.

They hope that we're going to bottle it, and then they can breathe a collective sigh of relief and get back to business as usual - the usual business of ignoring and sidelining us. Keep firm, keep steady, keep your eye on the prize and in a few short days we can neuter the fat-cats and put the politicians on a short leash. They're already squealing. They're afraid of what we might do to them. Keep your nerve and let's keep them squealing.

****

I won't be writing anything over the next few days as it's Andy's funeral on Saturday. It's going to be an emotional day. I plan to post a wee eulogy for him on the day, but apart from that for the next few days I'll post some guest posts. I know Andy would want me to keep posting over the last few days of the campaign, so I will be back with you on Monday. I'm doing this for Andy.

12 September 2014

Arresting Ronnie Kray

I wasn't going to post anything today, but for the past couple of days Scotland has been subject to the most intense napalming of fear and scares since the referendum campaign began. We are warned of meltdown on the markets, a plunging pound, share prices wiped out overnight. Prices in our supermarkets will double, all businesses will leave the country, and since we won't have any currency we won't even be able to club together to buy a cairry oot for the party we'll have when Michelle McMoan moves south. And all this because a country which is too poor and insignificant to notice, which has oil reserves due to run out at 10.01 pm on Thursday, and has nothing to offer except a ticket on the Megabus to London, might decide to start governing itself. Something doesn't add up.

Let us suppose that Scotland is indeed the high risk basket case of No campaign myth and legend. This country in a geo-politically stable part of the world, with a strong democratic tradition, a country with a highly educated population and an embarrassment of resources. Taking that raw material and turning it into a poverty stricken charity case requires governmental incompetence of a quite spectacular degree. And yet our poverty and dismal future is the very reason we must continue to put our faith in the system of government which produced the poverty and failure. Something doesn't add up.

I was trying to write a few words for Andy's funeral service this evening, trying to reduce a beloved man's life into a few paragraphs and failing, so I stopped for a bit and watched the news instead. It was wall to wall with unexamined threats, claims of ruination taken at face value by a BBC which has abandoned all pretence of neutrality as all hands rush to the pumps to rescue the sinking British ship of state. I remembered something Andy told me, many years ago.

In the 1960s when Andy was a police officer in the East End of London, he arrested one of the Kray twins. There was no big and thrilling police chase, it was nothing like the telly or the movies. He arrested Ronnie Kray for traffic offences. He knew exactly who it was he was going to arrest, he knew all about the Krays twins' reputation. And Andy went by himself, into a crowded café in the East End of London, armed with nothing more than a truncheon which now lives in a drawer in the bedroom, and said "You're nicked" to one of the city's most intimidating gangsters. Andy was tall, and powerfully built, confident in himself and capable of a gaze that could pierce right through you. Ronnie Kray had no chance.

He huckled Ronnie Kray along the street, into the police van. On arriving at the station he dragged an unwilling and protesting Ronnie out of the van. Two nuns were passing along the street at the time. Ronnie screamed at them: "Look at my face! It's unmarked!" He was convinced he was going to be beaten up. It was only when the prisoner was signed in that Andy noticed the smell, and discovered that Ronnie Kray had crapped himself. Literally, not figuratively.

Ronnie Kray called his lawyer to pay the traffic fines, and was home within a few hours. Face unmarked but in desperate need of fresh underwear.

This episode didn't make it into the movie with those guys from Spandau Ballet.

I asked Andy if he had been scared. He shook his head, and smiled. He said that Ronnie Kray was just a bully. He was very brave when he had his mates, but what really scared people was his reputation. When you looked past the reputation, all that was really there was a nasty and selfish little man who was too used to getting his own way and who crapped his trousers when someone stood up to him. Bullies, said Andy, are always afraid of people who are more confident than they are.

Westminster is too used to getting its own way, and it's trying to frighten us with its reputation. It's calling on everyone in the gang to help it do its dirty work, calling on those who have a vested interest in its reputation. But there is nothing behind the reputation except selfishness. They held us in contempt because we were afraid of them, and now they're trying to scare us into allowing them to continue to hold us in contempt.

But we have confidence in ourselves. Hold a steely gaze. Pierce through the rhetoric. Do not be intimidated. We're challenging their reputation and they're keeching in their pants.

13 September 2014

In memory of Andy

Andy Kavanagh-Mosson was born in 1936 into a different world, the son of an unmarried Irish mother who fled to London to ensure that she could keep her child. She was a strong and determined woman, whose strength and determination were inherited by her son. In order to make a living she fostered homeless children, and was one of the few in that racist era who willingly fostered children from African or Asian backgrounds.

Andy grew up surrounded by strong women who struggled and survived in poverty, who faced up to racism and discrimination, and developed a burning sense of fairness and justice that he carried with him all his life. It was a life that took him far.

Andy was a Royal Marine who saw active service in Suez and Cyprus. He was a Metropolitan policeman who once arrested one of the Kray twins - for traffic offences. He went alone to arrest one of London's most feared gangsters, Andy was afraid of no one. He stood up to bullies, he was unbowed by threats. He would not be told that he couldn't do something. He knew the difference between right and wrong.

But Andy was not defined by the Marines or the Met. He was a man with a rich life, with a love of nature, a deep knowledge of plants and wildlife, and a sensitive and expressive artistic ability. He found love, and he returned love.

Andy was complete within himself, but he was no island. Andy was connected and saw the connections that link every living being. His greatest gift was the ability to help others see those connections too.

Andy's great achievement was his inner calm and tranquility. He was a man who was at peace with himself. He had a strength deep in his soul, a strength that he shared with those he loved, a strength and determination that was his gift to those who knew him.

His happiest days were spent in Spain, sitting in the warm evenings on the balcony, a glass of wine in hand, his dog Lottie by his side, watching the sun go down over the mountains to the west, a smile of contentment on his face.

But it was Scotland that became his home. It was in Scotland and amongst Scottish people that he found his family. His last years were spent in Scotland, where he was accepted, and valued, where he felt safe and where he knew he would be cared for and loved. His last conscious act was to cast his postal vote in the referendum, a few days before he passed away. He voted for a Scotland that will stand up to bullies and will be unbowed by threats, a Scotland that will not be told it can't, a Scotland that is complete within itself and at peace with itself, that knows the difference between right and wrong, a Scotland that knows how to love and how to care.

Faced with summing up a deep and beautiful and beloved man in a few short words, I have only silence and grief. No vision through the tears, no music amongst the sobs. There is no justice which can be done to him in a few paragraphs, no fine words can be enough. All there is is the aching loss, the absence of a part of myself. But I've learned the lessons he taught me, I have shared in his inner strength, I have learned to be complete within myself. These are the things that Andy gave me, and I will treasure them like I treasure the precious bundle of memories of our time together.

His body has gone, he will be missed, he will be mourned. His smile will only be seen again in photographs, his warm embrace felt only in the privacy of the mind. But his spirit lives amongst and within.

Andy will always be with us, in a raindrop that falls in Carntyne, in the falling of a leaf, and in the branches of the rowan tree.

15 September 2014
The shlock of naw

A few random thoughts at the start of a new week and a new life. Queen Betty has spoken, she wants people to "think very carefully" before exercising their vote on Thursday. The No campaign has, predictably, taken this as an endorsement of their position, although thinking carefully is the exact opposite of shutting up and eating your cereal, refusing to send speakers to public debates and events, and claiming that Scotland is on hold. It's probably a safe bet that Betty is a Unionist, this is news of the milk makes your cornflakes soggy variety. But the Nawnentities are now desperately clutching at any fresh rice crispies that are going.

There's not much else a world power that punches above its weight can do when it's put on the run by two guys with a rickshaw, the theme tune to the Empire Strikes Back, and a sense of humour. The British establishment is intimidated by a tune. Mighty Britannia stands before the people of Scotland intent on cowing us with shock and awe and we laugh and point out she's got nae knickers and nae vision, only managementwankspeak, unfocussed focus groups and glaikit glares. The shlock of naw scares no-one except those who were already cowering.

So this week we're going to bring about a new global depression if we vote Yes, as opposed to last week when a Yes vote was going to turn us into an unnoticed non-entity. There was me quite resigned to a future where where Scotland would be so insignificant that Belarus would seem like a giant striding the world stage, and now I need to get my heid around being personally responsible for a global cataclysm that will see New York bankers leaping out of windaes in Wall Street and landing on Buster Keaton. See that damp patch in an Armani suit, that's Scotland's fault that is.

Can these people not make up their minds? Scotland, incapable of tying its own shoelaces or wiping its own arse, but an evil genius of catastrophe creation which can paralyse the entire planet and bring about the downfall of capitalism. Ach feckit, I can live with the guilt. People already tell me I look like Lenin. I was going for a Beatles' look and it all went tragically wrong, but I've learned my lesson and am now immune to the pernicious influence of style-icons. So David Beckham's letter begging Scotland not to leave has come a bit late. It was supposed to have been published a couple of weeks ago, but it took a while to decipher the crayon.

Mind you the free thinking Viviane Westwood has said that she's all for a Yes vote and thinks it would be "absolutely great". Scotland could become an inspiration to the world once it's got out of Westminster's bondage trousers.

The No campaign's message for this week is "we're not panicking" and an entreaty to people who don't know to vote no. There we go with that just don't think thing again. Being told by John Reid not to think and to put our trust in him and his pals is precisely what got us into 13 years of Labour's wasted opportunities and the Iraq war. You can trust John, you can trust him to push for ID cards, rendition, cosying up to defence contractors, and a Labour party made in his own image.

Meanwhile in order to prove that it really is a mass movement, no honest, the No campaign published a photie a No logo formed out of ordinary people. Or as they were described in the Irish Times Posh Edinburgh cricket types.

We're also getting a dose of love-bombing. The No campaign is closely following the Canadian Federal Government's Quebec referendum playbook, which likewise involved making a big deal of currency threats. But having overdone the negativity, the U-KOK campaign is struggling badly with the happy clappy cuddly stuff. The Canadian government subsidised thousands of plane, train and bus tickets so Canadians from the rest of the country could go to Quebec to say je t'aime to a Quebecois. There was a mass rally in Montreal a few days before the vote, with tens of thousands of Anglophone Canadians swearing blind that nous adorons toutes les choses francophones and had even realised that French speakers do not in fact finish every utterance with beep beep like they did on the audio in French classes at school.

However in the UK Naw version, the lovebombing rally is being held in London, which would be a bit like the Canadians holding their rally for Quebec in Vancouver or Calgary. This decision was taken in the knowledge that the only critical mass in Scotland is the mass of critics that greets every hauf-airsed intervention by a clueless celeb. However it's also because they really love us even more than the Canadians love Quebec, as holding the event in London means it's really REALLY important. If it wasn't important it wouldn't be held in

London. Besides, the UK Government is both too cheap to subsidise trips to Scotland, and knows that damn few would take them up on the offer. Most people in England don't give a toss - and this is part of the problem.

Over the next few days the combination of scare stories, threats, and patronising condensension will continue unabated. We will have no let up, no respite. We're going to get a lot more of the same stuff that drove many undecideds to turn Yes in the first place - just today the CBI and other business people made yet another entirely predictable warning that doom and gloom can be the only outcome for an independent Scotland. They think that the system in the UK isn't broken, but they're amongst those broke it.

Our job is to persuade, to reassure, and to include. Time is running short now, so focus your efforts where it can make a difference. Stay calm, stay positive, stay happy. Don't get frustrated with people who don't seem to be receptive, move on. Not everyone is going to be convinced by you - but that doesn't mean that they can't be convinced, it may just require a different approach so let someone else do it.

We can do this, we are doing this. Scotland stands before the first days of a new future, or we are looking at a return to the hopelessness, powerlessness, cynicism, and apathy that disfigured this country for decades. Moving on is hard, it's difficult, it can be frightening. At this particular juncture in my own life I know that better than anyone. But I will not be bowed, I will not cower, I will draw on my inner strength. I choose hope, choose power, choose self-belief.

We stand hand in hand, we can do anything.

16 September 2014

Making a vow

There was a vow on the front page of the Record yesterday. Britain isn't just great, it's superduper and comes with fruit preserves. Davie, Ed and Nick have promised Scotland jam, and marmalade, and curd if the uppity Caledonians get back into their tartan decorated shortbread tin. There will be massed choirs singing our praises when Scottish visitors get off the train at Euston where they will be bedecked with garlands of flowers and winning lottery tickets. Everyone is going to get devo-max, even Berwick. The BBC weather map is going to be redrawn so that north is at the bottom, and newspaper reporters will remember that Stirling doesn't have an e in it. It's going to be just lovely back in the shortbread tin, although you still can't get the TV remote control. It's a vow, a solemn pledge, a shiny pledge buffed with jam flavoured candy floss.

Vow is an interesting word. Like almost most words starting with v, vow is not natively inherited in the English language. Vow came into English in the Middle Ages, borrowed from the French vœu. Well I say borrowed, it's not like we plan to give it back anytime. It's not a borrowed word in French. French is a daughter language of Latin, and the Latin word from which vœu descends is votum - the same word which English borrowed directly as vote. So Davie and Ed and Nick are really telling us that if Scotland votes No, then Davie Ed and Nick will vote on our future for us. They'll decide, not us. So they were telling the truth, just not the truth that they wanted us to hear.

The Delware Indians on Manhattan at least got some shiny beads, some blankets and mirrors, in return for the surrender of their sovereignty. Scotland gets a shiny vow made by shiny politicians promising nothing of substance.

That's what you get if you vote No. No shiny beads, only a mirror in which to reflect on misery. You vow your vote to Davie, Ed, and Nick. You give a blank cheque to Westminster the home of the wizards of weasel words. You grant consent to thoughtlessness, you concede to powerlessness, you surrender responsibility and place yourself at the mercy of those who tell us Scotland is too helpless and hopeless to manage its own affairs.

Too wee too poor too stupid. Those words have never passed the lips of a No campaigner, they've never been uttered by a Unionist politician except to deny that a Unionist politician has ever uttered them. But that's what all their arguments boil down to. Many in Scotland believe them - those who ask "Where is the money going to come from?" They can't believe that the money is already here and has been here all along. It just gets siphoned away by a distant Parliament before anyone gets to see it. Our wealth is drained away with our confidence.

We're told we're too poor by the very same people who have created this Scotland that's supposedly too too poor. If you vote No you place yourself at the mercy of those who created a Scotland which is too helpless and hopeless to manage its own affairs and who are intent on keeping it that way.

Vote No, think about the X-Factor, think about Royal Babies, think about cereal. Remember your place in the shortbread tin. Don't dream that things can be better. Dreams are for romantics, hopes are for idealists. Vow No, and revel in apathetic cynicism.

Now they beg you that if you don't know you must vote no. Don't think. Thinking is dangerous, self-belief is heresy. You can sup your regrets as you eat your cereal. Ignore your heart, ignore your longings, forget that you can reason. Pretend that your head is supposed to tell your heart how to love and live. Live with regret and remorse in return for a vow with no heart or head. Going nowhere in the head cart before the heart horse. Shhhh. Don't think. You might imagine a better Scotland.

Here we are. Poised on the brink. Breath bated. Nerves stretched. We got this far. You, me, the wummin alang the street, the guy with his wee boy in Rutherglen, the doctor in Skye, the grumpy auld git in Dumfries, the carer in Easterhouse, the mother with the autistic son, the student, the granny, the joiner, the polisman - we've turned into druids and bards, we've turned into voices that sing and laugh our way into a future that we write ourselves. We've turned into the power of a people in movement. We've taken on the British state. We scoff at the combined weight of almost the entire UK media. We challenge the privilege of the rich. We defy the corporate interests. We pull the plug on the warmongers. We change the world. We paint a picture of a future where other paths are possible. We're doing that. Ourselves. With nothing more than our passion and our belief. Just think what we can do with a country. We are Scotland.

Our dreams will not be chained. Our aspirations will fly. Our hearts will tell our heads what we want to do and we'll use logic and reason to get there. We can read and we can write and we have a guid Scots tongue in our heids. A tongue which will not be silenced. We look to the past and the struggles to defend and preserve what our grandparents fought to build. We dream of building. We aspire to creation.

I'm making my own vow. My heart and head sing as one. I am doing this. I will be the master of my own destiny.

I'm voting YES.

17 September 2014
Scotland be brave

I look to my past. Afraid and scared. Pushing gingerly at the closet door, fearful of doom and rejection. Fearful of myself. But I came out into the light, and discovered I already had the tools to allow me to face any challenge. And I learned that self-determination starts with the self, and I grew and I flourished and I learned the meaning of fulfilment. And now many years later, Scotland is on the same journey. Learning the meaning of self-determination, learning how to flourish. Scotland, the country that came out of the closet.

The time is here. The road has been long. We've laughed and loved and lost along the way, and on our journey we found ourselves. We've looked into our souls and found an ocean of strength, a Scottish rainforest of potential. We learned how to hope, we learned how to make dreams come real. We learned that the people can be the power in this land, we learned that we scare the establishment. We learned that Scottishness is a state of mind, a state of justice, a state of looking forwards, a state of inclusion, a state of self-belief.

We march arm in arm, the born Scots, the become Scots, we are all Scottish and we are diverse and beautiful. We've learned that Scotland can be what we make her be, and she can be good, and she can be witty and wise, and she can graceful and joyous. These are lessons we will never unlearn.

These are potentials that always lived within us, and now we know how to make them sing. This is the start of a new sang. Our voices will not be silent in the new Scotland.

The No campaign tells you to vote No if you love Scotland. They ask if you love Scotland then to surrender her care to those who do not love her. That is not how you treat the ones you love. I vote out of love. I surrender the care of Scotland to those who love her, the people of Scotland. Vote to give Scotland to the ones you love. The time of choosing is here. Choose love, choose faith in yourself.

I never thought the day would ever come. We've arrived at the doorway. It stands half open. Beyond lie the open fields, the streets of the city, the mountains and glens, the islands and the shining sea, the pathways that connect us to the world on our own terms. It beckons. Define yourself or be defined. It's time.

Do not be afraid of your own potential. Do not fear your strength. Focus on the singing voice within. You're as good as anyone. You can dream, you can hope. You can change the world. You can make a difference, create a legacy. This is our time. The time of loss and regret is over. It's time to build a future.

Take a deep breath. Hold your nerve. Take history by the balls and shape your destiny. Grasp the thistle.

Scotland be brave. Step into the light, and breathe.

18 September 2014
Jangling nerves and bitten nails

Oh God. I wasn't going to post anything, but watch the results come in instead. Only I'm so nervous I can't watch the results. I've decided Twitter is evil. I already knew Facebook was evil. But Twitter is eviller. It's more evil than the Star Trek dark universe version of Iain Duncan Smith. You can't get much more evil than that. Every half hour I go from the heady heights of optimism to the deepest gloom and back again. So I've turned down the sound on the telly, I've switched off the Twitter feed, and I'm listening to some nice calming music instead.

I keep repeating the mantra "It's only a vote not the end of the world." But somehow I'm not convincing myself. The end of the world would be less nerve wracking. There's yer alien invasion, we're wiped out by the death rays, and it's all over before Bruce Willis can do anything heroic. You don't have to sit through hours of Glenn Campbell first. So, definitely preferable to the BBC referendum coverage. Unless it was an alien invasion fleet of smug Jim Murphys complaining about their dry cleaning bills. Then it would be pretty much the same as the referendum.

The turn out has been incredibly high. So much for no one being interested in the referendum. And whatever happens, we know that the No campaign's initial claims of a 70% plus vote for the Union have been proven spectacularly wrong. The desire for Scottish self-determination hasn't been put back into it's wee shortbread tin - we've moved into the living room and are building an extension to the house. Scotland now has an entire nation of politically engaged and educated people who know how to self-organise. Things are never going to be the same again. So whatever happens (and be still my jangling nerves), we can take great comfort in that.

Ohgodohgodohgodohgod. We've reach the top of the indyref campaign rollercoaster, too late to do anything about it now. Let's hold on for the ride.

19 September 2014
The tide goes out

We stand on the shore of the sea loch, and watch the tide go out. Now is the time to shelter the flame of hope from the howling gale. No has won through fear and threats of loss. But the dream is not dead, the dream still lives within the hearts and minds of hundreds of thousands who refused to be bowed by fear, who refused to succumb to the one sided stories of the self-interested. It is not a dream that will be forgotten. The flame of hope still burns within.

I've already lost this year. I've already had to grieve. But I will not grieve for Scotland, because Scotland still lives and hope still lives within me. I do not feel ashamed for the shame of others. Now is a time for building, for defending what we have built, for ensuring that the politicians keep their worthless words. We achieved so much with so little, we learned how to organise ourselves, and we must use those skills to maintain the pressure for change. I didn't come this far only to give up now. It is only if you slink away that they will have won. We cannot go back into the shortbread tin. We have outgrown it.

It was always a big ask, to break through generations of apathy at the first attempt, to leap the prison walls of cynicism in a single bound.

In the end we could not overcome the weight of a media almost uniformly opposed to change, and because of that a million minds remained closed and out of reach. We have a media overwhelmingly owned and controlled outside Scotland. A media that speaks for the established interests and is beamed into the shortbread tin, where it turns a debate on national self-determination into a warning about the price of car insurance. They ensured the debate revolved around money, and ignored morality.

For all Westminster's talk of home rule, they're keeping their paws firmly on the TV remote control. Now we all know why. It allows them to set the agenda. So we must build a new media, one that truly represents the diversity of this land and gives a space to Scotland's voices, and take it beyond the internet, onto the TV screens, into the press, into every street, into every home. It must be owned and controlled within Scotland. We have work to do.

The Labour party must be held to account. No more can they claim to stand shoulder to shoulder with the poor and the excluded. No more can they claim to represent the working classes. No more will they leech moral authority from our struggles, sucking the life blood from change, managing the expectations of working class people. Labour is a creature of the bosses and the banks. It is the problem, not the solution. Labour cannot claim to defend us from the Tories after they and the Tories stood side by side. I will never vote for them again. Labour for Indy must consider their future. Perhaps it's time for a new party of the left in Scotland. Independence cannot be the preserve of just one large party. It must be a broad based national movement, and be seen to be such. We have work to do.

I will scoff at the pride of those who are proud to be small, proud to be bullied. Proud not to think, proud to eat their cereal. And I will have the pride that comes from knowing that I stood with my sisters and brothers and dared to hope and dream of something better. The hoping and dreaming doesn't end here. It has only just begun. A set back is not a death, a defeat is not annihilation. This is not the path over the mountain, but we have learned how to climb. We must climb to another path. We have work to do.

I have work to do. I must build a new life for myself. I must learn to be me after decades of we. But hope still burns within me. My life with Andy has left me strong enough to face the challenges that lie ahead, it gives me the resolve to build a new future. These past few months and years have given Scotland the strength and resolve to face the challenges that lie ahead. We will survive. We will flourish. We will strengthen our roots and grow.

No struggle for civil rights or reaching for self-determination achieves its goal easily. There are losses along the way. Take time to mourn and cry. Take time to grieve and weep. But guard the flame of hope within you, it is the cure for your wounds. It will see you through the dark nights. It will give you the resolve to go on. The future still waits for you, and it still burns bright with hope.

The tide goes out. The tide will return. Stand on the shore undaunted and unafraid, building for the future, and waiting the tide's return. The high tide will come again. But we have work to do.